WE ARE INTERNATIONALISTS

WE ARE INTERNATIONALISTS

Prexy Nesbitt and the Fight for African Liberation

MARTHA BIONDI

UNIVERSITY OF CALIFORNIA PRESS

University of California Press
Oakland, California

Cataloging-in-Publication data is on file at the Library of Congress.

ISBN 978-0-520-41771-7 (cloth : alk. paper)
ISBN 978-0-520-41772-4 (ebook)

Manufactured in the United States of America

GPSR Authorized Representative: Easy Access System Europe, Mustamäe tee 50, 10621 Tallinn, Estonia, gpsr.requests@easproject.com

34   33   32   31   30   29   28   27   26   25
10   9   8   7   6   5   4   3   2   1

In Memory of James Thindwa

Contents

Abbreviations

AASC	African American Solidarity Committee
ACOA	American Committee on Africa
AFSC	American Friends Service Committee
AIS	Africa Information Service
ALSC	African Liberation Support Committee
ANC	African National Congress
CBTU	Coalition of Black Trade Unionists
CCISSA	Chicago Committee in Solidarity with Southern Africa
CCLAMG	Chicago Coalition for the Liberation of Angola, Mozambique and Guinea-Bissau
CIDSA	Coalition for Illinois Divestment from South Africa
COBALSA	Campaign to Oppose Bank Loans to South Africa
CONCP	Conference of Nationalist Organizations of the Portuguese Colonies

COSATU	Congress of South African Trade Unions
FNLA	National Liberation Front of Angola
Frelimo	Front for the Liberation of Mozambique
IFP	Inkatha Freedom Party
ILNAA	Illinois Labor Network Against Apartheid
MNR	Mozambican National Resistance
MPLA	Popular Movement for the Liberation of Angola
MSN	Mozambique Solidarity Network
MSO	Mozambique Solidarity Office
NAIMSAL	National Anti-Imperialist Movement in Solidarity with African Liberation
PAC	Pan-Africanist Congress
PAIGC	African Party for the Independence of Guinea and Cape Verde
PIDE	International and State Defense Police (Portugal)
Renamo	Mozambican National Resistance (Portuguese acronym)
SWAPO	South West African People's Organization
UAW	United Auto Workers
UCC	United Church of Christ
UDF	United Democratic Front
Unita	National Union for the Total Independence of Angola
WCC	World Council of Churches
ZANU	Zimbabwean African National Union
ZAPU	Zimbabwean African People's Union

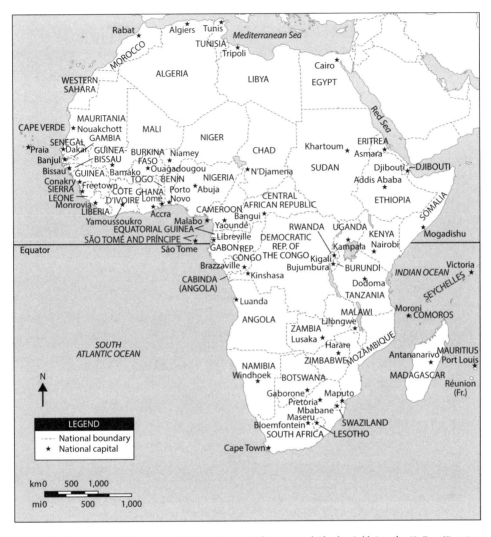

Map 1. The Continent of Africa. From William Minter, Gail Hovey, and Charles Cobb Jr., eds., *No Easy Victories: African Liberation and American Activists Over a Half Century, 1950–2000* (Africa World Press, 2008).

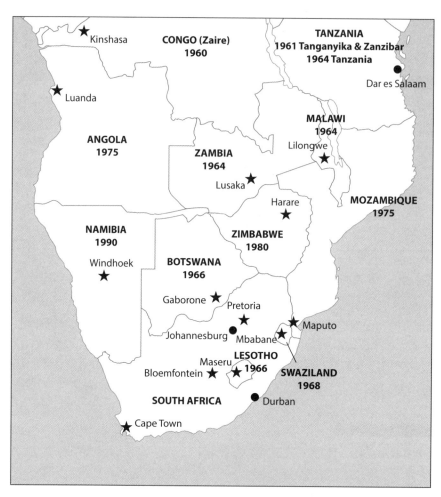

Map 2. Southern Africa, with dates of independence. From William Minter, Gail Hovey, and Charles Cobb Jr., eds., *No Easy Victories: African Liberation and American Activists Over a Half Century, 1950–2000* (Africa World Press, 2008).

INTRODUCTION

THIS IS A POLITICAL BIOGRAPHY of Black Chicagoan Rozell (Prexy) Nesbitt Jr., who organized support for freedom struggles in southern African from the 1960s to the 1990s and beyond. Raised and nurtured in the context of the Black freedom struggle, Prexy immersed himself, like few other Americans, in the fight against colonialism and white supremacy in southern Africa. I use Nesbitt's activist arc to tell a broader story of a remarkable social movement that powerfully shaped developments in southern Africa and the United States. We know the Black freedom struggle transformed many conditions of life in the United States, but we don't typically imagine that US social movements influenced foreign policy or intervened in national liberation struggles in the global South. This book upends that notion.

This era of internationalist engagement reshaped Black and American social justice organizing and influenced the role of the US in the world. This study is a movement biography more than a personal one—enabled by the fact that Nesbitt's activist journey traversed the critical developments of the 1960s to the 1990s, from the crucible of Black Power to the end of apartheid—and concludes with a look at how solidarity activists have processed post-nationalist developments and disappointments.

In a jarring juxtaposition, as the Black freedom struggle toppled legal segregation in the 1960s, the segregation, political exclusion, land dispossession, and economic exploitation of Black people in South Africa—a system known as apartheid—was thriving. And deeply disturbing to many, it was enabled and subsidized by American government and corporate support. Moreover, in violation of United Nations mandates, South Africa illegally occupied neighboring South West Africa, now known as Namibia. Rhodesia was another settler-colonial society in southern Africa forcibly maintaining white rule and Black subjugation. And shoring up this extraordinary landscape of injustice and white hubris was Portugal's insistence on its right to rule over the peoples of Mozambique, Angola, and Guinea-Bissau. Portugal was the last remaining European colonial power in Africa. The United States justified its diplomatic, economic, and military support for the apartheid and colonial regimes by claiming that they acted as bulwarks against the potential spread of Soviet influence or communism. The Cold War looms large in this story, as does the effort of grassroots organizers to push it off stage in favor of recognizing the legitimate claims for self-determination of still-colonized peoples.

The debacle in Vietnam—the American military defeat and the revelations of government lies and slaughter of civilians—pushed many Americans in the late 1960s and 1970s to reject seeing global liberation struggles through a Cold War lens. The many lies in the conduct of that ruinous war revived the notion that it was perfectly appropriate, and indeed just, for Americans to critically engage the foreign policy of their government. Congress too, was inspired to assert its authority in shaping foreign policy and reining in the executive branch, a development that created opportunities for activists. Small but influential groups of activists, including veterans of the domestic Black freedom struggle, began to shift their activist energies toward southern Africa—finding new and creative ways to advance the struggles against Portuguese colonialism and white minority rule. Rather than seeking to export a US-centric conception of Black Nationalism, Nesbitt and his cohort were instead deeply influenced by their encounters with African anticolonial thinkers and leaders, especially those from the African Party for the Independence of Guinea and Cape Verde (PAIGC); the Popular Movement for the Liberation of Angola (MPLA); the African National Congress (ANC); and the Front for the Liberation of Mozambique (Frelimo). Eduardo Mondlane, an exiled Mozambican student in the US who became the first president of Frelimo, met Prexy Nesbitt's family while he was a doctoral student at Northwestern University. Even in the urban North, Mondlane encountered great difficulty in finding a church that would marry him and his white fiancée. They ended up getting married at the Nesbitt family's church on Chicago's West Side, the same one that would host Martin Luther King Jr.'s organizing a decade later.

Born in 1944 to highly educated, politically progressive parents—children of the Great Migration, epic labor struggles, and the Marcus Garvey movement—Nesbitt's internationalist outlook took root in his youth. He spent a high school summer in Sweden and his junior year of college living and studying among revolutionaries in Dar es Salaam, Tanzania. Prexy was in college during the height of the southern civil rights movement and in graduate school during the height of Black power. His time in Tanzania seeded a powerful bond with Africans and African liberation struggles that would shape his entire life. Prexy spent his adult years consumed with social justice organizing—through employment with the American Committee on Africa, the United Auto Workers, the mayoral administration of Harold Washington, the World Council of Churches, the government of Mozambique, and the MacArthur Foundation. As an activist, Nesbitt founded several pivotal organizations, including the Mozambique Solidarity Network, the Chicago Committee for the Liberation of Angola, Mozambique and Guinea-Bissau, the Chicago Coalition for Illinois Divestment from South Africa, and the Chicago Committee in Solidarity with Southern Africa. This just scratches the surface of an extraordinary internationalist network.

One secret to Prexy's success and longevity as an organizer was his fusing of local and global concerns, especially in constantly seeking to interrelate domestic antiblackness with colonialism, apartheid, and racial capitalism. In a lucid and accessible manner, he connected injustices in southern Africa with ongoing Black American concerns and experiences with structural racism. A deep grounding in Chicago's Black communities, unions, churches, and politics helped Prexy build local, regional, and national support and reciprocity for faraway overseas struggles. Moreover, he exemplifies the power of "people-to-people" diplomacy. He has traveled to Africa more times than he can count, likely close to a hundred; has brought scores of groups and delegations on political and educational trips and has hosted over sixty visiting southern Africans at his home in Chicago. Nesbitt has sustained lifelong ties with global leaders, but especially with leaders of Frelimo, South West African People's Organization (SWAPO), and the ANC. Adept at public speaking and coalition building, Prexy Nesbitt led scores of efforts to organize material aid projects, influence US foreign policy, gain state and local legislation, impact corporate practices, and shape public opinion. Apart from the anti-apartheid movement, the thriving solidarity movements of this era have been virtually forgotten.

US Pan-Africanists and internationalists were deeply engaged in affairs in Africa well before the rise of the anti-apartheid movement. Travel and organizing for freedom across the African Diaspora has roots as deep as the diaspora itself, but personal connections, contacts, and travel between Africans and Black Americans greatly accelerated in the post–World War II era. The Council on African Affairs, the leading African advocacy organization of the mid-twentieth century made major strides in raising awareness about African struggles, lobbying the United Nations, and organizing material aid, but it fell victim to government repression during the McCarthy era.[1] The Pan-Africanism that arose during the civil rights era of the 1950s and 1960s deeply influenced the arc of the internationalism that accelerated in the 1970s. African Americans cheered the successes of anticolonial struggles, which buoyed their own struggles for equal rights. In 1957 Coretta Scott King and Martin Luther King Jr. attended independence celebrations in Ghana, whose first president Kwame Nkrumah, embraced Pan-Africanism, both as a state strategy of unification to empower postcolonial societies and as a diasporic strategy, which included welcoming Black Americans to assist in nation-building efforts. Tragically, wars and coups in Algeria, Kenya, Ghana, and Congo signaled the intense commitment of imperial powers to thwart decolonial aspirations toward autonomy and self-determination. Portugal in particular invested enormous sums to wage war in a vain attempt to preserve its far-flung empire. Internationalists and Pan-Africanists who later became leaders in the anti-apartheid movement cut their teeth in solidarity organizing for the freedom of Angola, Mozambique, Cape Verde, and Guinea-Bissau.

After the ouster of Nkrumah in a coup d'etat in 1966 and the pronouncement of the 1967 Arusha Declaration, which boldly laid claim to a vision of African self-reliance and socialism, Tanzania began to attract African American visitors and expatriates. President Julius Nyerere embraced Pan-Africanism, which he saw as a state project of comradery to end white minority and colonial rule on the continent, and bravely offered space and support to the national liberation movements challenging apartheid and colonialism in southern Africa. His solidarity would impact southern Africa and its internationalist orbit for decades. The Pan-Africanism of the frontline states—those independent nations bordering the colonial and settler-colonial regimes in the south—meant providing humanitarian assistance and logistical support for armed struggles and would be crucial to the fall of minority rule.[2]

Prexy Nesbitt's work is a rare example of a deeply intertwined local and transnational activist story. He helped make Chicago a center of internationalist organizing, which began in the 1970s and flowered in the 1980s and early 1990s. He ensured that the key tactics of the nationwide solidarity movement, including demonstrations, divestment, boycotts, political education and civil disobedience, took root in Chicago. He made Chicago a destination for scores of visiting South Africans, Namibians, Zimbabweans, Mozambicans, and others, just as he organized travel to the continent for likely thousands of Americans. Prexy helped to make Harold Washington's mayoral administration supportive and connected to southern African liberation organizations, including the ANC, which was on the Reagan administration's list of terrorist organizations. He also worked to ensure that unions in Chicago and nationally were responsive to the needs of workers and unions in South Africa and southern African more generally.

While I tell the story of solidarity activists, another inescapable dimension of this study is the catastrophic consequences, for people and the planet, of the many wars waged to defend apartheid and colonialism. Millions lost their lives and economies and infrastructures were devastated. Portugal, Rhodesia, and South Africa, and the groups they trained and funded were the major aggressors in the region, but the United States bears great responsibility for funding regional insurgents, especially in Angola, and for extending the life of the apartheid regime, thereby enabling Pretoria's violence both domestically and in the region. Anticolonial leaders in southern Africa sought to gain self-determination and freedom from colonial domination through peaceful means but were pushed into armed struggle as Portugal and Pretoria proved unrelenting and resistant to change. Likewise, the internationalist community in the United States was constantly pressing Washington to forego arms shipments and war-making in favor of, variously, negotiations, sanctions, humanitarian aid, and social investments.

Chapter one explores Prexy's childhood and adolescence during the era of the Northern civil rights movement and explains how a child born in racially segregated Chicago would come to spend a year amidst anticolonial freedom fighters in Dar es Salaam, Tanzania. Prexy's formative years were spent among an extraordinary extended family who co-owned a building on the West Side, forming an unusual communal living arrangement that stressed mutual care and reciprocity. Prexy's college-educated parents learned early that they would need to be ready and willing to fight against Northern Jim Crow in order to realize the fruits of their education and class prospects. Their fierce opposition to white supremacy and demand for full equality in American life—side by side with a celebration of Black American culture and history—profoundly shaped Prexy's aspirations and outlook. Prexy's year in Tanzania, and an earlier educational experience in Sweden, were life-changing, instilling in him an abiding solidarity with like-minded comrades of varied racial and national backgrounds around the world. Prexy had experience integrating white educational institutions slightly ahead of the historical curve—timing that likely shielded him from the more aggressive backlash of later years. And importantly, both his Chicago high school and Ohio college were politically progressive institutions that facilitated friendships with individuals who would become influential and connected and who helped support and nurture his lifelong activist work.

The second chapter examines the dynamic and evolving ideological character of the US Africa-solidarity movement in the 1970s, highlighting differences between a Black nationalist–inflected Pan-Africanism, which emphasized shared identity and culture even as it moved to the left, and a rising left-leaning anti-imperialism, or what many termed "internationalism." Certainly, the national liberation struggle of the Vietnamese and the mass mobilization against the US war in Vietnam had created a new climate in the United States for critiques of US imperialism and spawned a variety of new mobilizations to push back against US militarism. For many Black American activists, Africa was a particular focus of concern. Various expressions of Pan-Africanism had found deep traction in Black American communities since the early twentieth century, including the Pan-Africanist Congresses convened by W. E. B. Du Bois and the immense popularity of the Marcus Garvey movement in the United States and Caribbean. While many of these early initiatives bolstered resistance efforts and institution building in the Diaspora, after World War II, when struggles against European colonialism began to succeed, African Americans shifted their focus toward building Pan-Africanist ideals on the African continent itself. After gaining independence in 1957, Ghana became an important destination for African Americans. A consciousness of shared histories of racialization and displacement resulting from the international slave trade and European colonialism inspired the Pan-African quest for the political unity of Black peoples in Africa and the diaspora.

However, military coups and imperial machinations soon dashed hopes that decolonization would deliver the genuine autonomy from Western interference that was needed to reorient economies away from foreign extraction toward local needs and development. As a result, state and national liberation leaders began to look more intentionally to models of development outside of the capitalist West. The 1970s saw a surge of interest in socialist experimentation across the global South, including in Africa. This shift, which identified neocolonialism and Western imperialism as critical challenges, both propelled the rise of left internationalism and reshaped Pan-Africanism, imbuing the latter with a sharper critique of political economy, even though, in contrast to internationalists, many US Pan-Africanists kept a major focus on questions of culture and racial identity. The Black Panther Party's explicit embrace of socialism alongside what they termed "revolutionary Black nationalism" illustrates the rise of an internationalist orientation among Black American radicals.

The second chapter traces the left internationalist network and its global influences and connections. I examine the critically important role of Amilcar Cabral, the Cape Verdean leader of the PAIGC, and Walter Rodney, the Guyanese scholar who spent years in Tanzania and Jamaica, in influencing African American outlooks; I also examine the pivotal struggle around Angola, where Black Nationalists and internationalists clashed over which liberation group to support. The US solidarity movement was marked by internal schisms and debates, especially around race and ideology and, to lesser extent, gender. Prexy was part of a Black Left that reasserted itself in the 1970s, clashing with both Black Nationalists and white liberals in determining which groups to support in the liberation struggles across southern African. Fissures and contentious debates were the order of the day. Prexy developed new relationships with ANC leaders in London, strengthened relationships with Frelimo leaders in Tanzania, and created new solidarity organizations in the US—including the African American Solidarity Committee, the US Out of Angola Committee, and the Africa Information Service.

The meaning of Pan-Africanism changed in a decolonizing world. Pan-Africanism on the continent began to assert itself as a geopolitical strategy, spearheaded by leaders of nation states, while self-identified Pan-Africanists in the US were individuals or organizations, typically motivated by racial affinity, who worked to strengthen ties with African culture and history or who aimed to assist African liberation or find refuge and belonging beyond the shores of majority white societies. The differing approaches to Pan-Africanism across the Black world would come to a fractious head at the Sixth Pan-African Congress in Tanzania in 1974. I argue that the clashes within US solidarity organizing, particularly around Angola, amplified the stature of left-internationalism and ultimately laid the groundwork for a robust US anti-apartheid movement in the 1980s.

Chapter three is one of two chapters that use Prexy's engagements to tell a different story about the US anti-apartheid movement. In contrast to accounts that focus on the leading role of TransAfrica, the Washington-based African American foreign policy lobbying group that catalyzed a year-long campaign of civil disobedience at the South African embassy in Washington and at South African consulates nationwide, Prexy's organizing orbit shows the importance of a much wider group of activists from diverse organizations who were in regular dialogue with international activists and African liberation leaders. Beginning in the 1970s, Nesbitt became a leading global anti-apartheid activist, and by the 1980s and 1990s he helped make Chicago a key center of solidarity for Southern Africa. Prexy developed a reputation among southern Africans as a reliable and steadfast American ally with extensive knowledge of the region. New York, Chicago, and Geneva were key bases of organizing but regular travel to Africa and connections with African exiles in the US proved key to Prexy's effectiveness. The UN Centre Against Apartheid helped to nurture and extend his international relationships and strategic thinking.

Mass protests in Soweto, South Africa, in June 1976, and the government's murderous response, ushered in a dramatic new stage of international mobilization. Over the next decade and a half, activists in the United States intensified their effort to show the full extent of American complicity with apartheid via research, picket lines, legislative campaigns, and ultimately mass protest and civil disobedience. Protests at the South African consulate in Chicago were a major site of the national Free South Africa movement. Prexy organized and ran COBALSA, the Campaign to End Bank Loans to South Africa, and founded CIDSA, the Chicago Coalition for Illinois Divestment from South Africa. He strove to invent names with acronyms that in his view "sounded African." The World Council of Churches tapped Prexy to run their Programme to Combat Racism, through which he was able to direct funds to African liberation groups.

After years of organizing and struggle, the movement won important victories nationwide in pressuring universities, cities, states, pension funds, and unions to divest from entities doing business in South Africa. Prexy was key to many of these campaigns. The movement also reshaped public consciousness with its brilliant media and organizing strategies, which helped set the stage for the passage of American sanctions, over President Ronald Reagan's veto, in 1986. As part of a broader international push to isolate South Africa, this act of Congress was pivotal to the fall of apartheid.[3]

The fourth chapter explores the forgotten story of how the international Left, including Americans, flocked to newly independent Mozambique to build a socialist society in postcolonial Africa. In April 1974, exhausted from the long colonial wars, colonels in the Portuguese army ousted the dictatorship in Lisbon, setting Mozambique on a path to independence. Frelimo ambitiously set out to transform an underdeveloped and largely illiterate society into an educated and egalitarian Mozambique. Just as Cuba became a beacon and destination for many progressives who wanted to help build socialism, so too did Mozambique. But Frelimo faced immense challenges. Portugal had done nothing to prepare the country for independence. The managers, doctors, merchants, technicians, administrators, and other trained personnel were for the most part Portuguese or Asian, and the vast majority left at independence.

Frelimo's vision for Mozambique included universal access to education and health care; women's equality; popular engagement in governance; the reorganization of agriculture toward cooperative and collectivist experiments; and a strong emphasis on forging national unity—moving beyond tribal, regional, linguistic, racial, and religious identities in favor of building a new Mozambican identity and culture. In need of skilled talent, Frelimo recruited professionals, known as "cooperantes," to come and stay for two years or so. They hailed from everywhere, notably Eastern Europe, Cuba, Scandinavia, Chile, Canada, Italy, and many came from the United States as well. American activists contributed to the vibrant internationalism of Mozambique with tours and delegations, material aid and technical assistance, and long-term visits by cooperantes.

Rhodesia and South Africa saw this socialist internationalist neighbor as a threat to their regimes of minority rule, and each took their turn in organizing and training a rebel group, known as Renamo, to rollback development and destabilize the government. War ravaged Mozambique in the 1980s and early 1990s reversing many of the nation's early gains in health and education infrastructure and taking a devastating toll on human life and social well-being. A harrowing history, barely reported and mostly forgotten in the United States, the Renamo insurgency shows how South Africa's apartheid regime—albeit with willing local partners—brought death and destruction to the whole region.[4]

To guard against the kind of American aid that was going to the Unita rebel group in Angola, Mozambique pressed its friends in the United States to organize support among ordinary Americans and to influence policymakers. This led to the creation of the Mozambique Support Network. Members of the network were involved in medical and agricultural support drives, fundraisers, legislative initiatives, and research efforts for Mozambique. But their biggest effort was to use the media, speaking tours, and other tools to educate Americans about what was happening in Mozambique. They wanted to put to rest the notion that this was some kind of tribal conflict and to reveal the covert but well-documented role of South Africa in financing and training the Renamo soldiers.

To counter Renamo lobbying in Washington, Mozambique hired Prexy Nesbitt to run an advocacy campaign in the United States. By the time a ceasefire was reached in 1992, hundreds of thousands of people had died, many more were displaced, and the economy lay in ruins.

The fall of the socialist bloc and advent of neoliberalism created a crisis for the solidarity community; Prexy played a key role in continuing to foster support for the beleaguered nation even as war and international aid forced the unravelling of its socialist aspirations.

The fifth chapter follows an intense period of change as Namibia won independence, Nelson Mandela won his freedom, and the first democratic elections were held in South Africa. An escalation of violence inside South Africa and across the region and immediate maneuvering by global capital and Western governments to constrain the egalitarian vision of the ANC coincided with the genuine celebration and hope sparked by the fall of apartheid. Prexy and the solidarity movement developed new ways to support the ongoing township revolts and explosion of Black worker protest and union organizing. To continue organizing in the aftermath of divestment, Prexy launched the Chicago Committee in Solidarity with Southern Africa (CCISSA). Chicago's trade unions rose to the frontlines of the region's anti-apartheid movement in this era and joined forces as the Illinois Labor Network Against Apartheid. CCISSA, ILNAA, and activists in the Trinity United Church of Christ organized annual Soweto Day walkathons to commemorate the 1976 brutal massacre of protesting Black South African students and to raise money for material aid projects.

After his historic release from prison in February 1990, Nelson Mandela traveled extensively to thank the international anti-apartheid movement and to strategize and push for the end of apartheid and free elections. Allies in the United States kept the pressure on Washington to continue to punish and isolate Pretoria. Over the next four years, the South African government fomented an extraordinary wave of violence in Black townships to sow disunity, fear, and havoc in the runup to elections. The government's efforts fed into and exacerbated already existing ethnic and political rivalries among different African groups competing for power. The apartheid state and US government both sent millions of dollars to the Inkatha Freedom Party (IFP) which was launching lethal attacks on the United Democratic Front (UDF), the major anti-apartheid formation inside South Africa. The IFP attacked residents of the beleaguered Alexandra Township, which had become a "sister community" to Chicago.

This chapter also describes an emerging tension between solidarity activists and ANC leaders as they pivoted toward becoming state leaders. In 1993 Mandela called for the end of sanctions and the return of international investors to South Africa, yet many longtime internationalist allies, echoing many voices in South Africa, voiced concerns over the failure to win pledges of economic redistribution as part of the settlement toward majority rule. The first democratic elections in South Africa were a global affair. Prexy was among the five hundred Americans and thousands from around the world who went there as observers and joined South Africans in celebrating the ANC's resounding victory. But the many compromises that the ANC had made in the settlement to end apartheid haunted the moment.

The final chapter offers reflections and analyses of post-apartheid southern Africa and examines the legacies of the movement for many of the key activists in this narrative. The concerns that solidarity activists raised in the early 1990s in South Africa, Mozambique, and elsewhere turned out to be prescient and powerful. Behind the scenes, the International Monetary Fund, global corporate elites, and South African business leaders were demanding austerity and privatization as the price for a new South Africa. The ANC, focused on the political goal of securing a multiracial democracy and feeling perhaps vulnerable and short of options in the post-communist world, made the fateful decision to agree. The neoliberal triumph elicited a range of reactions in the solidarity community, including feelings of betrayal and disappointment, and it sparked among many, a new posture of critique. The long years of solidarity with national liberation groups in the insurgent Third World, better known now as the global South, generated significant debate over how internationalists should imagine and negotiate their relationships with groups they had supported but didn't agree with in every instance, especially as those groups assumed state power.

Prexy added his own voice to these critiques, and yet, in response to a rising tide of criticism directed toward the policies of African nations in the 1990s and early aughts, Prexy reminded the internationalist community to be attentive to contexts and conditions that were narrowing the options of the new governments. In addition, he urged American solidarity activists to redouble their efforts to reshape the US role in the world. He noted that the instruction given to Americans from Amilcar Cabral was to undermine imperialism from within. "And I think it's truer now than it's ever been before. The United States sets the pace, and shapes the framework, for so much of world affairs that it's only going to be when there is real change in the United States that there will be possibilities for change in other parts of the world."[5]

On the question of how race shaped the movement, Prexy argues paradoxically that racial tensions and divisions in grassroots organizing undercut efforts to mobilize even greater support for southern Africa but also that the anti-apartheid movement ultimately did provide new opportunities for multiracial organizing in the aftermath of the Black Power era. Inspired by, and often taking direction from his southern African allies, Prexy strongly advocated for engaging in multiracial organizing, for both philosophical and tactical reasons.

Prexy Nesbitt's organizing arc, and the broader trajectory of US solidarity with southern African freedom struggles, raise important questions about the role of ordinary people who seek to intervene in and influence international conflicts. A major point is that ordinary people can organize, through a variety of means and methods, to influence their government's foreign policy. A counterpoint is that their hopes for the aftermath may well be undercut by either the mistakes or betrayals of allies or the machinations of the regrouped arrangements of power. Internationalist solidarity can be challenging in that grassroots actors and organizations typically forge alliances and build trust with national liberation organizations or nation states—entities that are inexorably enmeshed in national and global power dynamics and hierarchies. Aspiring to hold one's own government to account may be the more important lesson of this study. Prexy's cohort looked outward to participate in anti-colonial and anti-imperialist struggle, but they learned that being politically engaged domestically was vital to advancing justice on a global stage.

1

FROM THE WEST SIDE TO DAR ES SALAAM

The Roots and Routes of Prexy Nesbitt's
Internationalism

HOW AND WHY DID a child born in 1944 in racially segregated
Chicago seek to join the armed struggle against Portuguese
colonialism in Mozambique rather than enlist in the US military to fight in Vietnam? This chapter explores Rozell (Prexy)
Nesbitt's formative years among an extraordinary extended
family who consistently strove to interrelate global and local
concerns and were deeply mindful of their working-class origins, yet robustly cosmopolitan and high achieving. Prexy's
parents were born to the Southern migrant working class
and became middle class and highly educated, raising their
expectations and fueling their deep commitment to social
justice. Their lives encompassed epochal labor struggles, the
global fight against fascism and colonialism, and domestic
struggles for civil rights. They learned early that they would
need to be fighters: ready and willing to act against Northern
Jim Crow to realize the fruits of their education and class
prospects. Their fierce opposition to white supremacy and

demand for full equality in American life—side by side with a pride and celebration of Black American culture and history—profoundly shaped Prexy's aspirations and outlook.

In narrating Prexy's formation, I emphasize three themes that describe his family, and likely a wider arc of Black life amid the burgeoning mid-twentieth-century Northern civil rights struggle.[1] The first theme is a pride in Black identity and a willingness to stand up to injustice. In Prexy's family, race was understood to be a fiction—socially constructed and a source of continuous critical dissection—and yet, as culture, consciousness, and power, it was real, global, and every day. His elders sharply diagnosed and assailed the mechanics and dangers of white supremacy and nurtured a strong pride in Black identity and African American culture. Prexy's family members resisted and challenged antiblack practices and policies through a variety of means—including the law, community and labor organizing, and personal confrontation. As Prexy witnessed more than once in his childhood, the Nesbitt men expressed their love of self and family through armed self-defense. At the same time, Prexy's family also taught and modeled a principled commitment to interracial living and a belief in a shared humanity. A strong ethical foundation infused his family's outlook and aspirations.

A second theme that was instrumental in shaping Prexy's outlook was a family emphasis—especially from his mother—on acquiring a rigorous, yet innovative, education. This propelled his move out of a struggling public school to a progressive private school and, later, his choice of a small experimental college over a football career at a large university. The third theme was a pro-union, egalitarian orientation and consciousness that included a reflexive distrust of the anticommunist orthodoxy that pervaded the nation during these years. In contrast to many accounts of the Black middle class that contrast its ethos and politics to those of the working class, the Nesbitts exemplify the prolabor, social democratic outlook that shaped many in the Black middle class in the era of the Great Depression and New Deal. Prexy inherited a strong identification and solidarity with the multiple struggles that surrounded him locally, nationally, and globally. Cutting across and infusing these three themes was a respect for women's leadership, instilled in him, and modelled for him, by his mother, aunts, and other women from his childhood.

Prexy's family on both sides were part of the Great Migration. Strivers and travelers, they modeled resilience, reciprocity, and love of family. One of five sons, Prexy's father, Rozell Sr., was born in Champaign-Urbana, Illinois, where his parents Lucian and Christine Nesbitt had migrated from Tennessee. Prexy's grandparents were service workers in that university town: his grandmother cooked for the fraternity house and his grandfather cleaned yards and washed windows. Undoubtedly, living and working in the shadow of the University of Illinois shaped his grandmother's insistence that all her boys would attend college: "It was Christine who pushed to educate her children," Prexy noted. "She wanted not just college but professional schools as well." In contrast, Prexy recalls that his grandfather "had no desire for his sons to do anything but what he did." The mother's dream prevailed and "in the middle of the Depression years, all five of them went to college," and beyond; her encouragement produced "two doctors, one lawyer, one physicist, and my father, who was an engineer." The Nesbitt brothers took a while to complete their degrees because they held down jobs to pay for their own education and for each other's. "All the brothers worked at different odd jobs," Prexy recalls. "They cleaned houses; they raked yards; they washed windows; they weeded gardens; they painted; and they delivered the *Chicago Defender*."[2]

Indeed, the Nesbitt brothers' coming of age illustrates the extraordinary importance of the Black press in shaping a socially engaged, globally conscious Black citizenry. According to Prexy's uncle George, the Nesbitt brothers devoured every issue of the *Defender*, learning about "Negro educational institutions, doctors and lawyers" as well as Nat

Turner, Denmark Vesey, Frederick Douglass and Harriet Tubman. Prexy's father and his uncles also read of "white brutalization—the beatings, the floggings, the shootings of southern Negroes" and "long sickening accounts of the Southern peonage system." As George Nesbitt, who became a lawyer, put it, "The *Defender* at any time would have deeply affected an eight-year-old reader. But I was eight in 1919. This was the time of return for the Negro soldiers of World War I, looking at home for the democracy for which they had helped Mr. Wilson make the world safe, but all too often only to be greeted by lynch mobs."[3]

After graduating from the University of Illinois School of Law, Prexy's uncle George took on local antidiscrimination cases. He defended a group of Black and white students who had tried to integrate a cafeteria and store—places that were routinely segregated in the 1940s. "They did some sit-ins and they got arrested. And my uncle defended them," Prexy said. After moving to Chicago, George moved in Popular Front circles and became close to legendary Black Communist Ishmael Floury: "I don't know how deep my uncle's ties to the party were, but he clearly was very close to them." George Nesbitt built a career fighting housing discrimination and expanding housing opportunities for African Americans and would gain a top position in the federal government in the 1960s.[4]

Rampant racial discrimination in the North meant that Prexy's father Rozell, who graduated with an electrical engineering degree in 1938, was never able to work as an engineer. He followed his brother, George, to Chicago where they became very involved in organizing Black baggage porters—or red caps—at the central train and bus stations into a union. The employment barriers Rozell faced meant that he worked all manner of jobs, even after he became a public school teacher. His pro-union outlook and respect for laborers made a lasting imprint on his son Prexy, who himself would work as a baggage handler one summer and over Christmas vacations during college. And

Prexy would also work as a union organizer, establishing a base in the local working class and labor movement that would be very helpful when he expanded his work to international solidarity organizing.[5]

While the era's union organizing and Communist agitation influenced the Nesbitt brothers, their uncles' support for Marcus Garvey also shaped them. Two brothers of Prexy's paternal grandmother were followers of Marcus Garvey and imbibed his message of race pride and entrepreneurial initiative. They lived on Chicago's South Side but owned a blueberry farm in Michigan where they often hosted Prexy's father and uncles, especially during summers. They sometimes did target practice there. "My dad had several guns," Prexy recalls. The Nesbitts grew up hunting. "Up there on the farm they had weapons too." Rozell taught his son how to shoot when he was young. "We had this big garage. We'd empty it and he'd set up the range. He showed me how to use a .22; he showed me how to use a .45 pistol. He showed me how to use shot guns very, very early."[6]

Prexy's mother Sadie Crain was born in 1913 in Ensley, Alabama, the youngest of eight children, to Nellie Reid and William Crain, a minister in the Colored Methodist Episcopal Church (now Christian Methodist Episcopal Church.) His hardscrabble ministry brought him across the Midwest, so Prexy's mother grew up in thirteen different cities including Chicago, Detroit, St. Louis, and Champaign-Urbana where she met Prexy's father. In contrast to the Nesbitt brothers, Sadie Crain was the only one in her family to attend college. She majored in education at the University of Illinois and was in a dance company taught by the legendary Katherine Dunham, one of many cultural giants that Sadie would befriend in her lifetime.[7]

Rozell and Sadie married in 1940. Despite the wartime labor demand, defense contractors still resisted hiring Black professionals. Sperry-Gyroscope hired Rozell to instruct army technicians on the use of airplane radios after he scored high on a test, but when Rozell showed up for the job in New Jersey and they discovered he was Black, he was fired on the spot. A civil rights struggle was brewing in New York, and a brief mobilization arose around his firing. New York congressman Adam Clayton Powell and First Lady Eleanor Roosevelt added their voices to the protest but to no avail. Perhaps unsurprisingly, given how little his country had done for him, Prexy's father refused to serve in the US armed forces during the war. Instead, he worked at various army bases as a civilian instructor teaching pilots how to use electronic equipment. While Rozell Sr. was stationed at a military base in Ohio, his son Rozell Jr. was born at Provident Hospital in Chicago on February 23, 1944. After a family friend predicted he'd be the first Black president of the US, the nickname stuck. Prexy's sister Roanne came two years later.[8]

Prexy's coming of age in the segregated, and segregating, Chicago of the 1950s and 1960s was unusual for its racial and ethnic exchange. Committed to the strong family ties and communal ethos of their childhood, the Nesbitt brothers and their wives raised their families in a jointly purchased building on Chicago's West Side. Their building of ten apartments at 1514 S. Albany Avenue became legendary for its eclectic and diverse mix of residents—family and family friends—who shared meals and nurtured and supported each other. "It was not just a home," Prexy recalls. "It was an institution." Dozens of visitors from southern Africa would stay there in the ensuing decades. The Nesbitt brothers lived there with their families and sought out like-minded people as tenant-neighbors. "It was a very multiracial house," Prexy recalls. "At different times there were Puerto Rican families, white families, Black families, there was a Congolese family, and there was a family from Scotland." The international world of 1514 S. Albany "completely prepared" Prexy for the cosmopolitan ethos of the liberation groups he would later encounter across southern Africa. He grew up amongst an experimental multiracialism, so when he encountered Frelimo, SWAPO, and the African National Congress, "it fit in with how I had been raised." Tommy Danish, a left-wing Jewish resident who became like an aunt to Nesbitt, lived there for about ten years before moving to New York to marry Herbert Tabb, a veteran of the Abraham Lincoln Brigade, a group of American leftists who fought against fascism in Spain. Prexy remained very close to the couple, whose son Bill wrote *The Political Economy of the Black Ghetto*. When Prexy was a child, Danish, who worked with the Amalgamated Clothing and Textile Workers Union, took him to hear Paul Robeson speak at a union hall. Lifelong bonds between the next generation of Nesbitts were also solidified at 1514 S. Albany: "The interaction between the brothers was always very strong . . . so my thirteen cousins, we all view each other more as brothers and sisters."[9]

Sadie Nesbitt was a dynamo—a consummate organizer who brought people together and built connections for family and communal advancement. An educator and catalyst for a wide array of projects and endeavors, she was at the center of a range of like-minded social circles that knit together the civic fabric of Black Chicago. "She was known as a gentle mover and shaker," Prexy recalls. A teacher and later assistant principal, Sadie taught at Johnson Elementary School in the Lawndale neighborhood for close to thirty years and worked as a social worker at the Maxwell Street YWCA as well. She became a leading advocate of progressive education and traveled easily in circles of prominent artists, writers, and civic leaders. "My mother was very ahead of her time," Prexy notes, pointing to her friendship with Maria Piers, a white woman and one of the founders of the Erikson Institute for Early Childhood Education in Chicago. "She and my mother introduced to the Board of Education that people could take early childhood education credits and get accreditation for it in the Chicago Public School system."[10]

Arts and culture were close to his mother's heart. She was part of what scholars would later dub the Chicago Black Renaissance. Coming a decade or so after Harlem's, this cultural flourishing owed more to public rather than elite subsidy and shaped Black working and middle class experiences in the city. A former dancer, Sadie Nesbitt was steeped in the world of Black expressive culture and close to artistic icons and innovators—women like Katherine Dunham, the modern dancer Pearl Primus, and Etta Moten Barnett, a "powerhouse on the South Side of Chicago in terms of arts and culture." Sadie was very close to the poet Robert Hayden—later a US poet laureate—whom Prexy knew as Uncle Bob. A gifted pianist, Sadie loved music and took her children to scores of concerts. Prexy grew up seeing performances by Paul Robeson, Pete Seeger, and Big Bill Broonzy among many others. Mahalia Jackson was a great friend of Sadie's. "I can remember taking recipes back and forth when I first learned to drive between my mother and Mahalia," Prexy fondly recalled.[11]

Prexy's family straddled the worlds of Southern Jim Crow and budding Northern interracialism. He savors memories of summer visits to the large home in Nashville, Tennessee, of Theodore "Uncle Teddy" Acklen, the brother-in-law of his godmother and dear family friend Bunny Brunson. Acklen started out in the numbers business and then launched the Club Del Morocco, a legendary jazz and blues club that attracted nationally known musicians and performers for decades. The club became a gathering place for Fisk, Tennessee State, and Meharry students. Acklen also owned a baseball team the Morocco Stars, and since Prexy was the oldest child, and tall and athletic, Uncle Teddy took him to many ball games. Prexy met Willie Mays at Uncle Teddy's house. Years later, when apartheid South Africa played a Davis cup tournament in Nashville, Prexy helped Uncle Teddy organize a protest by the Black community. Prexy also noted the irony that the white-looking Acklen lived as a Black man in Jim Crow Nashville.[12]

Prexy's parents aimed to expose their children to a wide array of cultures and communities. They spearheaded initiatives that cut against the grain of the powerful forces segregating mid-century metropolitan America. Especially important to Prexy and his cousins was the creation of the Fox Lake Friendship House. In 1946 six African American couples, including Prexy's parents and relatives, bought a farmhouse near the small town of Fox Lake, Wisconsin. The families enjoyed it for decades. The parents wanted their kids to experience a free, rural life; for Prexy and the other children, it expanded the meaning of family and created lifelong ties. But it took time to forge community with their largely German and Swiss American neighbors. Prexy recalled one day when some white children yelled racial slurs and threw stones at some of his younger cousins. Following the example of his elders to actively confront racism, Prexy organized the older cousins into action: they "bloodied several noses" and put an end to the conflict. Over time, neighborliness prevailed and connections grew, as the Nesbitt children helped in their neighbors' harvests and dairy operations. Years later when Sadie Nesbitt was hospitalized with cancer, carloads of these white neighbors drove to Chicago to bid their farewells as she lay dying.[13] The Bowen Country Club, in Waukegan, Illinois, was another interracial opportunity Prexy's parents and uncles embraced for their children. A youth camp spawned by the famed Chicago settlement house leader Jane Addams, the "BCC" immersed Prexy, his cousins, and other African Americans in folk dancing and square dancing with Italian, Polish, and Mexican Americans. As Prexy recalls, this experience contrasted sharply with the news of Emmett Till's murder and the violent white mobs blocking the integration of the Trumbull Park housing project on Chicago's South Side.[14] Another summer, Prexy's parents sent him to the predominantly Black working class Pleasant Valley Farm camp, where unfortunately he was beaten up by fellow campers who, as he put it, "didn't like the way I spoke." His mother visited midway through his stay and noticed that Prexy had a stress-induced twitch in his eye. She wanted to take him home, but his father's view that Prexy needed to learn how to maneuver this challenge prevailed.[15]

In another "bold move," Prexy's parents integrated the Warren Avenue Congregational Church in Lawndale, which unbeknownst to them, paved the way for the church's selection by the Southern Christian Leadership Conference (SCLC) as the home base for Martin Luther King's 1966 Chicago desegregation campaign. Prexy recalls attending Sunday school there with a broken leg. "I remember being rolled into the church and being aware that I was different. And I remember being told that I was chocolate, that I was a chocolate boy." This antiblack experience at the church, however, thankfully ended with his childhood, as Warren Avenue became a progressive force in the neighborhood and introduced Prexy to people who would change his life. As fate would have it, the pastor, Reverend Edward A. Hawley, had become close friends with fellow Oberlin student and Mozambican exile Eduardo Chivambo Mondlane, who would later lead the Mozambique Liberation Front (Frelimo). While doing graduate work at Northwestern University, Mondlane became engaged to Janet Rae Johnson, a white woman from a Chicago suburb, but the couple couldn't find a church that would marry them. In stepped Ed Hawley, who married the couple in 1955 at Warren Avenue. The Mondlanes visited the Nesbitt household, a connection that would be important to Prexy in later years. Moreover, a church posting in Tanzania a few years later for Rev. Hawley, enabled him to pave the way for Prexy to attend the University of Dar es Salaam during Prexy's junior year in college.

Since organizing support for Mozambique would anchor decades of Prexy's life, we need to get to know the extraordinary Mondlane and the story of Portuguese colonialism in Mozambique. Even though Portugal liked to claim that it had ruled its African colonies for 450 years, this claim to dominance is wildly inflated. The Portuguese only moved from coastal ports to the interior after the Berlin Conference of 1886 drew Mozambique's borders and designated it a Portuguese colony. And the Portuguese only quelled resistance—for a short time—in the early twentieth century. Mondlane, the son of a Tsonga chief in the southern province of Gaza, whose grandparents and great-grandparents had fought in wars of resistance against the colonial invaders, herded sheep and cattle until he was twelve. Then his mother pushed him to attend a Swiss-Presbyterian mission school. "She insisted that I go," he later said, "in order to understand the witchcraft of the white man, thus gaining the ability to fight against him."[16]

Mondlane later defied restrictions against seeking higher education by sneaking into South Africa to attend university, but his campus organizing attracted notice—and eventually led to his expulsion. Perhaps hoping to discipline him into colonial acquiescence, the Portuguese sent him to study in Lisbon. But in a wonderful happenstance, Mondlane met and bonded there with fellow Lusophone African intellectuals and activists, Amilcar Cabral of Guinea-Bissau, Agostinho Neto of Angola, and Marcelino dos Santos of Mozambique—all future statesmen who would give their lives to creating a postcolonial world free of exploitation and racial animus. But subject to continuing Portuguese harassment, Mondlane—with the support of missionary friends—fled to the United States in 1951. He spent the next twelve years in the US, studying at Oberlin and earning a PhD in anthropology from Northwestern, becoming the first Mozambican doctorate.[17]

While living in the United States Mondlane worked "tirelessly to change the image of Africa in the minds of Americans," writes historian Carla Stephens, "in order to mobilize support for Mozambican independence." Mondlane became very well known in circles of influential liberal-minded activists. As the scholar-advocate Bill Minter has noted, Mondlane traveled in "sectors with particular connections with Africa and with issues of global justice: the mainline Protestant churches, Oberlin College, Northwestern University and the emerging network of African studies scholars, and, finally, the cosmopolitan milieu of United Nations staff and internationally minded professionals in New York City."[18]

Mondlane forcefully rebuked Portuguese propaganda that their colonial system was somehow enlightened. Stephens contends that "by his mere existence in the United States as an educated and cultured

Mozambican who denied being Portuguese, Mondlane defied the Portuguese myth of cultural superiority." As a result, beginning in the early 1950s, there were two Mozambiques—one "that Portugal claimed to be an overseas province and the emerging Mozambique that, for much of the world over the next two decades, was Eduardo Mondlane."[19]

Like Mondlane's time in Chicago, his stay in New York was serendipitous. Strikingly, "his neighbors in Parkway Village, Queens," notes Bill Minter, "included Peter and Cora Weiss and Dan and Carol Bernstein, who were already prominent activists and funders of progressive causes, including African liberation." These relationships turned out to be crucial for the ensuing decades of struggle. In a trip to Mozambique in 1961 for the United Nations, Mondlane was met with a hero's welcome, igniting in him a passionate desire to serve his people and fight for Mozambican freedom. In 1962, at age 42, while an assistant professor of anthropology at Syracuse University, Mondlane was elected the first president of Frelimo, the Mozambique Liberation Front. Mondlane's life trajectory was exceptional because the Portuguese almost entirely blocked the possibility for educational attainment for Africans under their control. Illiteracy rates were staggering until independence.[20]

The core of Portuguese colonial infraction in Mozambique was a highly exploitative constellation of labor arrangements from forced labor on foreign-owned plantations to compulsory cash-crop farming to pay taxes to extremely low-paid contract labor to South African mining—which garnered a tidy commission for Portugal. Ostensible reform in the 1960s seemed to ban forced labor, but it continued in practice. "As a result, by the 1960s and the renewal of African armed resistance against Portuguese colonialism, at least one-third of the labor force in the South African mines was Mozambican," and "an estimated two-thirds of able-bodied Southern Mozambican men were working in foreign territories." For young Mozambicans in the south, "there was a sense of fatalism, resignation, and powerlessness regarding their futures"—the majority would spend most of their lives as miners or as laborers on white owned-plantations. Under colonial laws, "those men not lost to mining and farming in South Africa and Southern Rhodesia were otherwise required to work on cotton concessions, public works, or plantations."[21]

Alongside labor extraction were colonial laws that granted rights around mobility, citizenship, and education to the "non-indigenous" and deprived these rights to the "indigenous." Incredibly enough, but to some international effect, the Portuguese cloaked their colonialism in a banner of supposed nonracial upward mobility, offering Africans access to the category of *assimilado* by achievement of various metrics, including educational attainment. As Mondlane asked, "What then of the assimilados? I am an assimilado. I am one of the half of one percent of the population of Mozambique who have been able to overcome the many obstacles to the educational advancement which is a necessary precondition to obtaining that status." And critical to understanding the long life of Portuguese dominion in Africa is the fact that Portugal was led by a fascist dictatorship for much of the twentieth century and did not extend political rights or access to education to its own population, never mind to the peoples in its so-called overseas provinces.[22]

Three different groups came together to form Frelimo in Dar es Salaam in 1962: they aimed to unify the colony's various ethnicities, linguistic groups, religions, and regions to form a new nation and uproot the colonial pretense that Mozambicans were Portuguese. Portugal's refusal to entertain any gradual moves toward self-determination precipitated Frelimo's first military campaign in 1964; over the next decade they succeeded in liberating more and more territory in Mozambique, mostly in the north. But even with many advantages, Frelimo's progress was slowed by the vastly greater power of the Portuguese military forces and their NATO support. The non-aligned nations—Algeria, Egypt, Zambia, Tanzania—provided Frelimo its first arms and training. As conflict intensified, China and the USSR provided the bulk of financial and military support. NATO gave Portugal massive assistance. PAIGC leader Amilcar Cabral stressed that "Portugal would never be able to launch three colonial wars in Africa without the help of NATO, the weapons of NATO, the planes of NATO, the bombs of NATO—it would be impossible for them."[23] This arrangement of support radicalized Frelimo, as it starkly illustrated that it was the Third World and socialist countries fighting against racism, colonialism, and oppression. Mondlane was constantly asked about Cold War divisions: "I tend to be asked by Western audiences whether Frelimo is pro-East or pro-West, pro-Communist or pro-capitalist. My answer is that Frelimo is quite simply pro-Mozambican." And yet, to his dismay, he stressed that Frelimo could not be unaware that Western nations—through economic, military, and political investments and transfers via NATO and the UN—were clearly siding with Portugal.[24]

For many readers, mid-century racial integrationists are likely remembered as moderates, or at least as more moderate than late-1960s Black Power activists. But this perspective is perhaps presentist. We have internalized the many defeats of the integrationist project and have developed a view of it as a passive, overly legal, working-within-the-system kind of thing. But for the Nesbitts, challenging white supremacy was urgent, risky, and daring. One of the risks was violence—meted out by police or ordinary whites. When the Nesbitts moved to Lawndale, the area was predominantly Jewish. "I think we were amongst the first Black families, west of Western Avenue," Prexy recalls. There was antiblack feeling for sure, but he doesn't recall it coming from the neighbors, a few of whom became treasured friends. But he vividly recalls police aggression toward his family.

"There were many, many encounters with the police," especially with the men of the family. The collective response by his family to threatening situations made a big impression on Prexy. The Nesbitts created an alert system; if someone was under threat, they'd honk their horn and people would respond. Most of the Nesbitt brothers and many of the men who resided at 1514 owned guns. For many Black migrants to Chicago, gun ownership was rooted both in the rural practice of hunting and also in a long-standing culture of self-defense against racial violence. One time when two plainclothes white police officers followed him home, Prexy's father honked as he approached the alley in the rear. Prexy snuck out and watched his father challenge the cops, saw his mild-mannered obstetrician uncle Lendor warn them not to touch his brother, while another resident, a large man from Alabama, held a shotgun as he stood nearby. They diffused the situation. Alongside racial animus, Prexy recalled, there was another motive for police harassment: "They used to shake down Black people they found in Lawndale; it was a systematic thing."[25] Prexy's father trained him in the use of firearms precisely because of police racism. "My father was a gun man. My mother wasn't, and she used to just overlook that," Prexy remembers. His dad taught him to fire guns "because we were being harassed so much by the police in that neighborhood."[26]

Prexy had his own harrowing encounter with the police but was rescued by his family's reputation for resistance. In 1963, a police car pulled Prexy over, and a white officer—gun drawn—threw him against the car. They locked him up at the infamous Fillmore Street Station, but in the meantime, two cousins who had been with Prexy went to 1514 and alerted the family. His father and uncle Lendor quickly arrived and demanded to see Prexy. As Prexy faced a white police officer in the interrogation room, the desk officer who had recognized the Nesbitts burst in to say that higher-ups decided "it wasn't worth another fight" and to let Prexy go.[27]

The Nesbitts' commitment to multiracial living in Lawndale was challenged and eventually undercut by the fierce and predatory nature of the racialized housing market. His neighborhood underwent the classic cycle of postwar racial change—sometimes with overt violence and threats, but more typically with covert racist banking and real estate mechanisms. Whites were offered financial incentives to move to shiny new suburbs, while African Americans were met with severely constrained options. "We watched between '48 and '58, essentially a ten-year period, that neighborhood go from 98 percent Jewish to 98 percent Black, and largely working class and poor Blacks," Prexy recalls. "When my family moved in, it was more middle-class Black families, but by the end of the fifties it had become home to many, many poor people." Prexy's family stayed on the West Side, far from the rising enclaves of Black professionals on the city's South Side.[28]

Prexy credits the Francis Parker School in the city's North Side Lincoln Park neighborhood for powerfully affecting the course of his life. And yet, it was a chance event that brought him there. One day his father happened to visit his fifth-grade class at the Nathaniel Pope Elementary School and found his son teaching! Prexy explained to his stunned father that "the teacher always goes to get coffee, and I teach the reading class." One can imagine the subsequent scene in the principal's office. Both of Prexy's parents were educators. Sadie had been urging Rozell to think about sending their children to Parker, a private school known for its progressive philosophy and gifted faculty. Well, Prexy's father "went home that night and said to my mother, what's the name of that school that costs all that money on the North Side? Put him in it." Prexy suspects that the exorbitant cost of private high schools today would likely keep him out, but with the financial help of his mother's sisters, who had no children of their own, "we scraped up the money for my sister and I to go."[29]

Prexy transferred to Parker in the fifth grade. On the first day, "a student, who would later become a great defender of mine, called me a nigger, so I hit him and bloodied his nose." Prexy's father had taught him "not to take any nonsense." But most students and faculty were welcoming. His mother "always did things in cohorts, so she very quickly organized for my cousins" and other Black families to attend as well. "She essentially created a posse to go to Francis Parker. It was quite prophetic."[30] Sadie admired Parker for its emphasis on arts and culture and for the fact that it was both educationally and politically progressive. This was the McCarthy era and Prexy thinks many of its teachers wouldn't have been hired anywhere else. Jack Ellison, a founder of the leftist Monthly Review Press, was a teacher at Parker and, shortly after Prexy left, became principal. When Prexy graduated Ellison gifted him a collection of *Monthly Review* magazines. As Prexy got older he revised his youthful view that it was his father who was the "politically savvy one." He came to appreciate "more and more that my mother was very, very political" through her work in arts and culture. Prexy integrated a predominantly white private school in Chicago before white resistance to public school desegregation escalated. Many of the friendships and connections he forged at Parker lasted for the rest of his life. His positive experience there would encourage his later advocacy of multiracial organizing and propel a lifelong practice of reaching out to people across lines of difference.[31]

Prexy began his love for global engagement in the summer before his senior year in high school when he did an Experiment in International Living program—he was the only Chicago teen in the program that summer. Going to Sweden on his own shows Prexy's openness to the world and taste for adventure, and surely, his parents' as well. "My parents were big advocates of international exposure," Prexy recalls. Indeed, his sister went to Japan the following year with the same program, a desire likely inspired by her close friendships with Japanese American students at Parker. Prexy grew very close to his Swedish family the Holmgrens, and many of them and their friends later visited the Nesbitts and vice versa. "We're like one family with this family in Stockholm, Sweden." Prexy's parents and an aunt and uncle had a great time visiting the Holmgrens who, at Sadie Nesbitt's request, arranged for a trip to Oslo to visit the place where Dr. King had received the Nobel Prize.[32]

Prexy likely first learned about apartheid in a course at Parker where he had to write a paper on South African novelist Alan Paton's *Cry, the*

Beloved Country. According to Prexy's longtime comrade Bill Minter, *Cry, the Beloved Country*, a bestselling novel first published in 1948, was "one of the most important influences solidifying critical American views of the South African racial system." Minter notes that the "message of the novel was liberal rather than radical . . . but its impact in shaping the world-wide image of South African racism was enormous."[33] Apartheid was the name for a comprehensive system of laws in South Africa that deprived the Black majority of political rights and free mobility and assigned the majority of land, all the wealth from the gold and diamond mines, and political power to the white minority. "Apartheid was perfect racism," according to South African performing artist Trevor Noah. It was a police state, "a system of surveillance, and laws designed to keep Black people under total control." In Noah's view, the general thrust of it should be easy for any American to understand. "In America, you had the forced removal of the Native onto reservations coupled with slavery, followed by segregation. Imagine all three of those things happening to the same group of people at the same time. That was apartheid."[34]

In Prexy's senior year, Sadie Nesbitt mobilized to secure her son's collegiate future. Prexy played football at Parker and served as student government president but had a mixed academic record. "I did well in some subjects, but I did horribly in chemistry," he recalls. He was advised to apply to a few local colleges not of high stature or reputation. "I came home and told my mother, and she said 'No, no that is not what you're doing. You're applying to Yale, you're applying to Oberlin, you're applying to Michigan.'" He did, and "got into all of them." But Prexy's father wanted his son to visit Antioch College in Yellow Springs, Ohio, which had an experimental work-study curriculum and a reputation for innovation. Rozell also knew that Yellow Springs was a town in southern Ohio considered more receptive to Black people. As luck would have it, during their campus visit, the Nesbitts saw a folk-dance performance that mesmerized the young Nesbitt. He chose Antioch.

Prexy notes the irony of being a football player who "fell in love with folk dancing" and how this brought him to the college that eventually took him to Africa.[35]

Prexy was in college during the height of the Southern civil rights movement—and he'd be in graduate school during the height of the Black power movement. It was an extraordinary time, and he engaged with it deeply. He was part of what scholars have dubbed the "Till generation," the cohort of Black baby boomers whose life paths were profoundly shaped by Chicagoan Emmett Till's widely publicized lynching in Mississippi. And certainly, as we've seen, Prexy's own family had been active in the earlier and ongoing Northern civil rights struggle. So Prexy was no stranger to fighting racism. In 1964 he wanted to go to Mississippi to participate in Freedom Summer. But his mother was fearful and against it. He battled her, but she was unrelenting. "I will pay for you to go anywhere in the world," she said, seeding an idea to pursue study abroad, but "I will not let you go South." This initially propelled Prexy into local activism with the Antioch Racial Equity Committee. "And we got involved in the fight against the barbershop in Yellow Springs that wouldn't cut black hair," Prexy said. Antioch may have been liberal-minded, but it wasn't racially diverse—few colleges were in Jim Crow America. Like many other Black students who integrated white college campuses, Prexy encountered discrimination both on campus and off.[36]

Prexy took a leading role in the protest at the barbershop: "I was the guy who got into the chair." Lewis Gegner draped his barber's apron over Prexy's head, and Prexy snatched it off. He accepted the discipline of the nonviolent movement but recalls wanting to hit the guy. In the meantime, "all hell had broken out on the streets of Yellow Springs." Two sets of forces were marching toward each other: civil rights activists and Antioch students, on the one hand, "and these right-wing racist crackers from Xenia and Fairborn and Wright-Patterson Air Force Base," on the other. Standing between them was the state highway

Figure 1. Prexy Nesbitt protesting racial discrimination at Lewis Gegner's barbershop, Yellow Springs, Ohio, 1964. Courtesy of Prexy Nesbitt.

patrol. Suddenly, a man who was a well-known pacifist sat down on the ground in between the two groups and pleaded against violence. "It was this incredible moment," Prexy recalled. "He does this Gandhian kind of thing in Yellow Springs." And Yellow Springs was the comparatively "liberal" part of southern Ohio—the town manager and police chief were both Black, which was highly unusual. "So here I am sitting in the chair. All shit is about to break loose out on the street," and the police chief and town manager enter the barbershop. The chief "walks right over to me and supposedly puts me under arrest." They put Prexy in the back of the police car and with lights flashing drove to city hall. There the town manager invited Prexy into his office where the two Black officials urged him to calm things down and call off the protest.[37]

Another case of local white hostility to integration happened as Prexy drove a white girl to a baseball field where he coached kids for extra money during college. "These peckerwoods" hit her forehead with a pellet from a BB gun as she was riding in the basket of his bike. There were other incidents when people from surrounding areas "shot into the dorms at Antioch because they hated us so much." Antioch had the reputation of being a "Commie" school and a "free love" school. This violence became so serious that a group of older white Korean War vets who were at Antioch on the G.I. Bill, approached Prexy. "I'll never forget this. They said we don't want to see anybody get hurt here. We're trained. And we want to station people in each of the dormitories," to be look-outs, "because these attacks are getting very serious." They wanted Prexy's support "because I was a very much an activist figure on the campus by then."[38]

Prexy drove from Ohio to attend the 1963 March on Washington, but missed the major speeches, including Martin Luther King's famed address. He and others at Antioch had organized about ten buses to go to Washington. It was a great success. But as the buses were pulling away, Prexy thought to himself, why didn't I go? He decided to drive. "I had an old Chevy stick shift," and five others piled in "and we tore out for Washington." As he got tired and sought a backup driver, he learned that none of the others could drive a stick shift. "And so, I had to drive all the way to Washington, and when King was speaking, I was asleep on the grass. I never heard a single word and then had to drive all the way back to take an exam. That was the kind of crazy stuff you did in those days."

Prexy's decision to study abroad during his junior year at Antioch would profoundly shape the rest of his life. In that crucial year, he developed a love for Africa and a deep and abiding respect for the ongoing struggles to wrest freedom from colonial domination and control in southern Africa. These inclinations were deeply rooted, but they flowered at the University of Dar es Salaam, Tanzania, in 1965. Key to his parents' acceptance of this venture was the happenstance that their former pastor Reverend Ed Hawley was in Tanzania and would be there to pick up and shepherd their son. Prexy traveled by ship to England—he was constantly nauseous—and then flew to Nairobi, where Ed Hawley and his family met him and drove him to Tanzania. "It took us at least three nights," he recalls, "so we stopped in different places and stayed overnight, me and this white family."[39]

When they arrived in Dar, a "group of South African refugees met me. They knew this African American guy was coming to be a student." Literally upon his arrival they brought Prexy to listen to a record of Nelson Mandela's "Why I'm Prepared to Die" speech, which he had given at the Rivonia Trial; the speech ended with his and other ANC leaders' incarceration. "We would listen to this again and again and again, there in this hot, humid heat of Dar es Salaam." That was actually the first time Prexy recalls ever hearing of Nelson Mandela.[40] "I had a roommate from South Africa. I arrived with two bags and two trunks full of clothes for a year's stay. He arrived with maybe a shopping bag's worth of clothes." That was all he had because he had walked to Tanzania from South Africa, a journey of several months. "That blew my mind right away."[41]

Dar es Salaam, capital of the newly independent Tanzania, had a population of 250,000 in a nation of twelve million. Its first president, Julius Nyerere, had pledged to transform the ex-colony by pursuing a form of African socialism that he called "Ujamaa," which means familyhood in Swahili. Like Kwame Nkrumah in Ghana, Tom Mboya in Kenya, and many other anticolonial leaders for whom the highly exploitive economic practices of European colonizers were part and parcel of capitalism, Nyerere aimed to chart a new path. For him, Ujamaa meant trying to revive or be inspired by a precolonial, egalitarian past. Change came slowly but his outlook attracted attention and support by many in the African Diaspora. Nyerere also signaled his solidarity with those places still under colonial or settler-colonial rule

Figure 2. African Liberation leaders: Eduardo Mondlane, president of the Mozambique Liberation Front, second from left; Cora Weiss, American Committee on Africa, middle; and Amilcar Cabral, president of the African Party for the Independence of Guinea and Cape Verde, fourth from left. Dar es Salaam, Tanzania, 1965. Courtesy of Cora Weiss.

by offering Dar as a refuge for a range of nationalist movements and organizations in exile. Leaders of the Conference of Nationalist Organizations of the Portuguese Colonies, or CONCP, convened in Dar in 1965, an event that likely made an impression on the young Nesbitt. Founded in Morocco in 1961 by leaders of the major liberation movements, CONCP promoted a dynamic of collaboration and mutual support across lusophone Africa. Tanzania also began to attract people on the Left who imagined a new way to build socialism: a British socialist scholar recalled that "socialists from all over the world came because of solidarity, because of a belief that maybe the Third World would mount the drive for world socialism and overtake the developed countries."[42]

As a student at the University of Dar es Salaam, Prexy crossed paths with luminaries who helped make the university a hub of radical anticolonial intellectuals. Scholars came from all over the world, including, among others, Giovanni Arrighi, John Saul, Lionel Cliffe, Ann Seidman, and the legendary scholar activist Walter Rodney, who arrived right after Prexy left. Many of the foreign teachers were young and Prexy formed lifelong relationships with a few he met that year, including John Saul and his wife Pat. Saul became a key consultant for the Frelimo leadership in the 1970s and 1980s, and upon returning to his native Canada after seven years in Tanzania, he helped organize various solidarity initiatives. He later wrote that "it was clear that President Julius Nyerere, whatever the strengths and weaknesses of his various presuppositions and practices, was, on a continental and world scale, a figure of enormous importance and consequence."[43]

Irene Brown, a political scientist and Prexy's tutor, "was just fantastic." Prexy recalls her as "one of the great influences on [him]." Her husband was the attorney general of Tanzania, and her good friend happened to be the secretary to President Nyerere—connections which likely came in handy when Prexy found himself in hot water after participating in a protest against Rhodesia. Oftentimes foreign students avoid getting involved in political demonstrations that might lead to arrest. But not Prexy. During a protest against white-settler control of the nation that would become Zimbabwe, Prexy and another guy "jumped on top of a British Rolls Royce and were stomping on the roof," the police arrested everybody. Back at the university President Nyerere reprimanded the students and looked right at Prexy, who feared expulsion. "'You're the African American, aren't you?' he asked. And then on his way out "he leaned over, and he winked." Irene Brown also came to Prexy's aid in a more commonplace way—but one a young person far away from home would long remember. One day in Brown's class, Prexy kept getting up to go to the bathroom—back and forth. After class, the professor called him over and offered a bottle of pills. Prexy remembers that she was caring and discreet, and the pills worked.[44]

Colonial powers typically cultivated a small elite class to fortify the imperial project. In a legacy of this strategy, many college students at Dar expected to assume elite positions in society upon graduation. Upward mobility rather than postcolonial socialist transformation was the guiding spirit for many Tanzanian college students. Indeed, in many postcolonial nations, critics would argue that decolonization was thin veneer, as power had been handed over from a foreign elite to a local elite without inaugurating much change for the rest of the population. President Nyerere sought to interrupt this pattern and redirect student energies toward his Ujamaa vision. The year after Prexy left, the ruling party imposed mandatory national service in the countryside for college students, and many students rebelled.[45]

Even though he had little knowledge at the time of these larger processes, Prexy noticed the conservatism of the Tanzanian students. For example, he introduced a resolution to the student government to condemn the US war in Vietnam, but they wouldn't pass it. "They didn't want to offend a foreign government" and felt that they shouldn't be involved in foreign matters. The students, in his view, were very invested in "proper" presentation and comportment. "They all wore shirts and ties for instance, long sleeve shirts, and the South African refugees and I we used to laugh, and they would laugh at us because we went around in shorts and T-shirts. They knew they were an elite, and they were preparing themselves already for that role."[46]

In another vivid memory, Prexy was on a bus with other students to the city center, and "we passed an accident where a truck full of flour had smashed into another truck." The driver was pinned inside, and people were trying to pull apart the two vehicles with their hands. Prexy said he "and the South Africans got out to help. But many of the students on our bus wouldn't help, because they didn't want to get dirty. They didn't want to get their hands dirty." Another example of how Prexy felt politically closer to the South Africans was his openness to interracial dating. "One thing that surprised me and the South

Africans was the racial and ethnic exclusiveness of the Tanzanians." Prexy noticed some tension between the Africans and East Indians in Tanzania, some of which may have "derived from economic relationships because so many of the East Indians were shopkeepers." But on campus, Prexy felt "the Africans were really disdainful of the East Indian students." Prexy felt this keenly because he had begun to date a Muslim Indian woman. "She defied her community to spend time with me, and the African students didn't like seeing us together. It was too radical. The South Africans always had my back, but the Tanzania students, the Ugandans . . . they were very conservative in those years."[47]

An American in Dar es Salaam who became an important contact and local family figure for Prexy was Bill Sutherland, an African American Quaker working for the American Friends Service Committee. He welcomed Prexy to stay in his air-conditioned home and use his car when he was away. "Bill and I were very close friends. He had great parties." They had political disagreements though, as Sutherland's formation in the United States was in liberal anticommunist circles. "That carried over in his relationships with the liberation movement people—with MPLA, with Frelimo, with the ANC people. He didn't let it come out directly, but when he and I would be talking about things, he would always, for instance, try to dissuade me from becoming too close to MPLA or too close to Frelimo because of this virulent anticommunism."[48]

During that extraordinary school year, Prexy also got to meet and know people from the various African liberation movements who had offices in Dar. Prexy babysat for the three Mondlane children, and "Eduardo and I would have a ball" watching videotapes of American football games at a hotel in Dar. Interestingly, though, Prexy was initially drawn to the more free-spirited ways of the African National Congress members. The South Africans there were closer to Prexy's age, while the Frelimo people were older "and a bit daunting because they were so disciplined and so committed. And I wasn't as disciplined at that point." Similarly, he remembers the MPLA members as "very aloof." Prexy loved to dance and party—many of these gatherings took place at Bill Sutherland's—with the ANC youth and Namibians too. But Dar "was full of parties. There were always parties."

Prexy also spent time at the African American Institute's School for Refugees, located in a suburb of Dar es Salaam, which housed refugees from southern Africa and student-teachers from Harvard. Because he was coming to understand the harrowing journeys of the student refugees in Dar and their intense commitment to education, Prexy "felt extremely honored" when the refugee students invited him to "brief them about Malcolm X" who had been assassinated earlier that year. Interestingly, in Prexy's recollection, "the southern African students knew far more than I did. Many of them knew that Malcolm had visited Dar es Salaam during the year before his killing" and that his time there had "greatly impacted his thinking and strategizing." Despite the gaps in his knowledge, Prexy made a strong impression and, years later, "prominent members of Namibia's major political party, SWAPO," who had become government ministers, "vividly recalled my speaking to them when they were students in Dar es Salaam."[49]

Prexy's time in Dar es Salaam was foundational to his political, intellectual, and professional development. It pushed him to consider graduate school in African politics and history, and it schooled him on the complexities and dynamics of race, class, gender, ethnicity, and nationality in a newly decolonized African nation. That year abroad made solidarity for African liberation struggles—in Mozambique, Namibia, Guinea-Bissau, Angola, South Africa, and Zimbabwe—central to the rest of life. But as Prexy understood it at the time: "I was a junior in college and just beginning to sort all this stuff out." Most of all, that time in Dar initiated a love of Africa and a love for Africans and their struggles for freedom and independence.

After returning home in late spring 1966, Prexy discovered that the Black freedom struggle had literally moved into his own backyard.

After passage of the Civil Rights and Voting Rights Acts, Martin Luther King and the Southern Christian Leadership Conference (SCLC) decided to bring the nonviolent movement northward. They chose to confront structural racism in one of the North's most segregated cites: Chicago. Their challenge to housing segregation—the single largest driver of the racial wealth gap in the country—produced fierce white resistance. "Before the summer was over," one observer wrote, "movement activists held marches and prayer vigils across the city in all-white neighborhoods from Chicago Lawn and Gage Park on the Southwest Side to Belmont-Cragin on the Northwest Side and several places in between. Almost everywhere the non-violent marchers went they were met by whites armed with rocks and rage."[50]

SCLC's decision to base their Northern campaign in Chicago unsettled the city's Black elected officials and clergy who were in various ways tethered to the political machine of Mayor Richard Daley. The SCLC was taking on Northern Democrats rather than Dixiecrats—and this rocked the coalition that Democrats in Washington had used to win congressional legislation. As was becoming apparent, Democratic Party leaders in the North supported civil rights initiatives—as long as they stayed south of the Mason Dixon line. As a result, SCLC needed an independent and courageous church to be their base and weather the storm they were sure to bring. The interracial Warren Avenue Congregational Church stepped up—and its readiness was due in no small part to the longtime efforts of the Nesbitt family to infuse the church with an antiracist consciousness. "When Chicago's black Baptist churches would not host the Rev. Martin Luther King because of fearing Mayor Richard Daley," Prexy wrote, "tiny Warren Avenue said, 'we welcome you and agree with what you are doing.'" SCLC made it their home and Sadie Nesbitt's great admiration for Dr. King only increased during their stay. "I came back from Africa," Prexy said, and my mother told me to go down to the church and use my time before going back to Antioch to help Rev. King. "So that's what I did."[51]

Antioch students engaged in experiential learning off campus for course credit. This built-in community engagement enabled students, including Prexy, to be student-activists. In the summer of 1966, Prexy got credit from Antioch for working with the Union to End Slums, part of the SCLC's campaign. Prexy had already learned organizing from his father, and his own involvement in labor and civil rights campaigns. But he learned a lot from the SCLC's Reverend James Orange, whose organizing skills were legendary. "It was classic organizing," he recalled. "You had to do a lot of work just helping people with their issues, their problems—fixing screen doors, painting, giving people rides to the grocery store, forming relationships with families on the West Side and getting them into the organization." Orange was "a master craftsman as an organizer. He had such a wonderful way with people." He put himself on the level of people he was organizing, and he listened to them. For Prexy this was the greatest gift. "I brought that kind of lesson to all the organizing I did on southern Africa, which started immediately that fall when I went back to the campus."[52]

The SCLC ministers took to the young Nesbitt whose knowledge of the neighborhood proved very helpful. Moreover, "King wanted to talk to me about Africa because he really was intent on doing his nonviolent organizing work in Rhodesia." Prexy doesn't recall precisely what he told King, but he remembers talking with him for a long time about Africa in a meeting room in the church. Prexy worked on interracial teams of real-estate testers: "A Black person would walk into a real estate office in a white neighborhood and apply for an apartment. Almost always they were told there was nothing available. Minutes later, a white team member would go into the same office and be shown a long list of apartments." A contingent of a few hundred Open Housing marchers were headed to a real estate office that fateful day when King was knocked down by a hurling rock. Prexy served on the security detail for that march in Marquette Park and feels badly that he failed to intercept the rock that someone threw at King's head. "Prexy,

I thought you were this great football player," King later teased him.[53] But it was scary. "Nobody had any idea of the depth of hate until that summer," Prexy told a reporter years later. "In Marquette Park I was really scared. We were surrounded. The women were the scariest. I had never seen such vitriolic hatred in women before. We knew there was going to be a reaction. The vehemence of the reaction is what surprised us."[54]

Prexy returned in the fall for his last year at Antioch. In what would be the first of numerous such committees that he would create, Prexy and fellow student Marty Houser launched the Antioch Committee on Southern Africa. In a striking coincidence, but also revealing of who went to Antioch, Marty was the daughter of George Houser, the founder of the American Committee on Africa (ACOA), the leading US organization that worked on African issues. Prexy would later work for the ACOA. The Antioch students' activism on southern Africa was rare in these years, and they were one of the first to use direct action tactics to pressure universities to cut ties with corporations that did business with apartheid South Africa. Theirs was a multiracial organization as "there were only seven of us in my class," Prexy recalled. "That was what it was like in that period." But as it happened, a few Black students from nearby Central State and Wilberforce Universities also got involved in the Antioch effort.

The students deployed what would become the leading tactics of the campus divestment struggle: researching their college's investments; hosting South African speakers; educating the campus about apartheid; and finally direct-action tactics. In the fall, Prexy and Houser started a committee to study Antioch's investments, and they hosted Dennis Brutus, a poet and "Coloured" South African activist who had recently fled South Africa after years of protest and jailings. Brutus saw sports as a means of shaming and pressuring South Africa on an international stage—and helped win a ban on South African participation in the Olympics.[55]

In the spring, after Prexy's group tried to get on the agenda of a meeting of the Antioch trustees but were denied, they organized a takeover, "protesting the fact that they would not listen to us and wouldn't put us on the agenda to talk about taking the school's money out of South Africa." On the day of the meeting, the students "ended up chasing them all across the campus," because the trustees kept switching the meeting location. Fortunately, Prexy had contacts among the maintenance staff who kept the students informed of the new locations. So, the students kept arriving at the same time as the trustees. Finally, the trustees suspended the meeting, but "then they out maneuvered us," Prexy remembered. They took the meeting off campus to somewhere in Massachusetts. It took ten more years to get Antioch to divest, and at that juncture, students invited Prexy back and saluted his work launching the struggle.[56]

1968 was a year of rebellion and insurgency around the world. In the United States, young people fought for Black liberation under the banner of Black Power and clamored to stop the US war on Vietnam.[57] That spring, Prexy participated in the extraordinary student takeover of multiple campus buildings at Columbia University in New York. Prexy had entered Columbia in the fall of 1967 with a fellowship to study public law and government, but he ended up working with the Africanist historian Marcia Wright, whom he came to greatly admire, as well as with Immanuel Wallerstein, a leading scholar of African liberation movements.[58] Prexy joined with fellow Black students in the occupation of Hamilton Hall. Wallerstein's office was in Hamilton, and evidently some of the students were interested in his books and materials on Africa. "I made them stop," Prexy recalled. "I said, I know this man I've worked with him, he gets it. He needs these books. And they listened to me." Another "run in" between Prexy and the bulk of the occupiers concerned their demands. Prexy urged "demanding an end to the war in Vietnam and not just Columbia out of Harlem." But "nobody would go with me on it. I stood by myself. A bunch of people came up to me afterwards and said, well, I really agreed with you, but I wasn't going to argue with the group." Indeed, most members of the Student Afro-American Society opposed the US war in Vietnam, but they viewed the campus antiwar movement as white and desired to define their protest around a specifically Black agenda. Prexy was drawn to the militancy, pride, and fierce commitment summoned by the phrase Black Power, but the southern African liberation leaders he had met in Dar es Salaam had profoundly influenced him to resist separatist outlooks and to fully embrace solidarity with national liberation struggles.[59]

Undoubtedly, the parents of protesting students experienced a range of emotions. Prexy's were supportive, but naturally worried. Prexy's father flew out to New York to check on his son. While serving on watch duty, Prexy spotted his father in the crowd of onlookers. Evidently a white man next to him said something like, "They ought to put all of them in jail." His father took offense. Prexy saw Rozell Sr. take off his jacket as if readying for a fight. "My son is up there now," he asked the man, "do you want to say anything more?"[60]

Columbia administrators negotiated a settlement with the Black students in Hamilton Hall to avoid a police raid, but the students still faced arrest. Representing Prexy was activist-attorney Robert Van Lierop who would become an important ally and comrade of Prexy's in the 1970s and beyond. The arrest triggered major changes in Prexy's life, ultimately leading him back to Africa. First, he lost his fellowship, and then he learned of an impending appointment with the Selective Service. Prexy was determined not to fight on behalf of the United States in Vietnam. His plan was to go back to Africa and fight to liberate Mozambique.

2

THE TILT TOWARD INTERNATIONALISM

Race and Ideology in the 1970s

PREXY NESBITT'S BUDDING INTERNATIONALISM translated into a refusal to fight in the American war on Vietnam. Instead, he wanted to join the fight to liberate Mozambique. Upon learning of an impending appointment with the US Selective Service, Prexy made plans to go to Africa. "I want to join the armed struggle," he told Sharfudine Khan, the Frelimo representative to the United Nations. Khan asked the young American about his felicity in local languages: "How good is your Changana? and how good is your Makhuwa?" Khan explained that his help would be appreciated but not in the armed struggle. "This is a Mozambican struggle," Khan said, "but we could definitely use your help as we build schools and create a program for education, which we view as critical as the armed struggle." Prexy left for Frelimo's base in exile in Dar es Salaam, Tanzania, after participating in the protests at the Democratic Convention in Chicago that summer.[1]

Prexy was drawn to the internationalism of the Mozambique Liberation Front (Frelimo)—a socialist-leaning project of anti-imperialism that emphasized solidarity across lines of race, religion, and nationality. Internationalists insisted on the right of national self-determination yet also valued transnational solidarity, given the power imbalance between newly decolonized nation-states and the globalizing spread of American and European political and economic interests. Internationalism was above all a route away from colonial-capitalism toward a postcolonial vision of economic redistribution and social justice. Radical imaginings of new forms of local empowerment, cooperatives, and development became popular among anticolonial insurgents who had witnessed the first wave of decolonized nation states grapple with continuing subordination to the dictates of foreign actors. Internationalism imagined a break from neocolonialism and a new path to develop the global South. National liberation leaders of the 1970s continued the earlier quests of Patrice Lumumba and Kwame Nkrumah to forge regional unity and push for meaningful independence, free from Western control.[2]

In 1969, the conservative Republican administration of Richard Nixon embraced an approach to southern Africa that was dubbed "the tilt toward white supremacy." Foreshadowing Ronald Reagan's policy of "constructive engagement," Nixon and his national security advisor Henry Kissinger endorsed the easing of arms embargoes on South Africa and Portugal, weakening sanctions against Rhodesia, and increased economic and political contacts with South Africa. Nixon overtly and covertly supported the Portuguese dictatorship, most notably with a 1971 deal that sent $430 million in exchange for continuing US access to military bases in the Azores. Portugal's membership in NATO tended to neutralize US criticism of its colonial possessions: "NATO in the Cold War was far more important to the United States," according to a top government official, than was pressuring Portugal to free its colonies.[3] At the same time, with 150,000 of its citizens deployed as soldiers in Africa, the Portuguese regime was becoming destabilized and weakened by its costly and demoralizing commitment to a dying colonial empire. Dissidents in the army—with an outpouring of civilian support—would ultimately topple the dictatorship in 1974.

Undoubtedly, many Americans supported Nixon's efforts, but significant numbers voiced opposition. After the debacle in Vietnam and revelations of government lies, many Americans feared another war in the global South in the name of countering a seemingly ever-present threat of communism. The successes of the Black freedom struggle put pressure on Washington's defense of apartheid South Africa. The contradiction between the morality of one and the immorality of the other would become more glaring in the 1980s with the Reagan administration's more whole-hearted embrace of the white minority regime. But in the 1970s, many radical activists coming out of the antiwar and Black liberation movements moved beyond criticizing American support for empire and apartheid to a more robust identification and solidarity with those organizations and nations fighting for decolonization and majority rule.

These individuals, their overseas travel—including personal exposure to African freedom struggles—their print culture, and the organizations and networks they formed comprised a US internationalist movement that allied itself with the internationalism of the ANC, PAIGC, Frelimo, SWAPO, and the MPLA. Socialist nations, Scandinavian countries, and most importantly "the frontline states" of Tanzania and Zambia were critical architects of internationalism, providing economic aid, arms, military training, and shelter for the national liberation struggles and exiles.[4]

With Prexy's journey as a through line, this chapter traces this left internationalist constellation, paying careful attention to debates around race and ideology. I describe a rising organizational capacity of the Black American left; the critically important role of Amilcar Cabral, the Cape Veridian leader of the PAIGC, and Walter Rodney, the

Guyanese scholar who spent many years in Tanzania and Jamaica, in influencing African American activist opinion; and the pivotal struggle around Angola. A Black Left (re)asserted itself in the early 1970s and clashed with both Black nationalists and white liberals in determining which groups to support in the liberation struggles across southern African. Contentious debates were the order of the day.[5]

Black nationalism offered a different approach to international solidarity in the late 1960s and 1970s. At this juncture, Black nationalists, excepting revolutionary Black nationalists, such as the Black Panther Party, promoted a Pan-Africanism that celebrated traditional African cultures; looked to anticolonial leaders free of European mixture; and often distrusted communist or socialist affiliation. US Pan-Africanists tended to favor African leaders who articulated messages recognizable to African American audiences in the Black Power era. This contrasted with Pan-Africanist currents on the continent, such as those represented by Tanzania's President Nyerere, which were grounded in strategic geopolitical analysis, rising critiques of neocolonialism, and a greater openness to socialism. Challenging for many US Pan Africanists was the fact that the ANC, Frelimo, and MPLA opened membership to all opponents of colonialism—including people of Asian and European descent—and embraced what they called a "nonracial" vision in their armed struggle against white settler regimes and Portuguese colonialism. As Samora Machel put it, "we always say we are fighting a system and not the individuals within it." The goal he argued, was not to "establish Black power in place of white power," but to "destroy the colonialist state."[6]

Frelimo had succeeded in uniting various Mozambican groups, but differences remained about how to oust the Portuguese and build a new society. As in many anticolonial movements, divisions emerged based on region, ethnicity, and political outlook. In a contentious struggle in 1968, three dissenting figures became lightning rods: Frelimo vice president Uriah Simango; Lazaro Nkavandame, a leader from the

Makonde ethnic group in the north; and Mateus Gwenjere, a Catholic priest. The tensions were various, but different views about tribal empowerment and social and political customs stand out.[7] Nkavandame opposed Frelimo's embrace of a guerilla war that aimed to mobilize and politicize the masses, but he had also been "under suspicion of appropriating funds from Frelimo's commercial activities." In December he was implicated in the murder of a Frelimo military commander and while "awaiting trial in Tanzania, he succeeded in escaping and fleeing to the Portuguese."[8]

Father Gwenjere stirred up conflict at the Mozambique Institute in Dar, encouraging the notion of abundant overseas scholarships among the Mozambican students there and sowing resentment over the Frelimo requirement of a year's service in the armed struggle.[9] Prexy met some of these students and recalls their antipathy to getting military training. "Their view was that they could just come to Frelimo and get scholarships in the United States or Europe."[10] A student protest in March 1968 at the institute precipitated its closure, and Gwenjere even persuaded the Tanzanians to expel white Mozambican teachers there as alleged spies. After an "acrimonious debate" the Central Committee censured him, and many of his supporters fled to Kenya.[11]

Meanwhile, a group of Makonde exiles stormed Frelimo's headquarters in Dar, killing the telecommunications chief. The Portuguese secret police, the PIDE, had infiltrated Frelimo and a shadowy revolutionary named Leo Milas turned out to be a Black American suspected of being with the CIA. He was notable for pushing a Black nationalist line; publicly critiquing the role of Jorge Rebelo, an Indian from Portuguese Goa, on the Central Committee; and complaining about the white wife of Mondlane who ran the Mozambique Institute. "The two factions held very different visions of an independent Mozambique," according to Allen and Barbara Isaacman, US scholars who taught in Mozambique after independence. "Simango and Nkavandame adopted a nationalist position under which an educated black elite would rule, as Malawi and Kenya were governed." Mondlane and the Frelimo Executive Committee feared this would lead toward neocolonialism and advocated, instead, a society "responsive to the needs of peasants and workers, that would attack poverty and underdevelopment through the transforming capacity of education, science and technology." Ultimately, Gwenjere and Nkavadame's schemes failed and both left Frelimo—but Simango remained and would prove to be much more divisive in the months to come.[12]

Frelimo's Second Congress took place in July 1968 in the liberated areas of northern Mozambique. This extremely important event turned a liberation struggle of scattered students, refugees, and exiles into a popular mass movement that began to engage the needs of ordinary peasants. Frelimo convened long communal meetings run by collective decision-making in the liberated areas, an approach to governance that would continue after independence. The decisions by the 1968 congress strongly affirmed a commitment, not quite to socialism, but certainly to the transformation of the colonial society and economy; a continuing emphasis on including and educating peasants in the war against colonialism; a commitment to the empowerment and mobilization of women in the struggle; and a focus on fighting the system of colonialism rather than the Portuguese themselves, including an openness to ethnically and racially diverse Mozambicans joining Frelimo. The increasing number of Africans in the colonial army, Frelimo argued, cast doubt on skin color as a reliable indicator of political commitment.[13]

Prexy Nesbitt waited out the Frelimo conflict in London, where Eduardo Mondlane had arranged for him to work with the Committee for Freedom of Mozambique, Angola, and Guinea-Bissau headed by the historian Basil Davidson and with the British Anti-Apartheid Movement, which shared office space with the ANC in exile. These four months in London turned out to be another serendipitous time during which Prexy forged relationships with extraordinary figures that had lifelong reverberations. "Like the ANC people had done in Dar, in London, the ANC people took me under their wing," Nesbitt recalled. Prexy sang with the ANC choir "to hang out and get to know people." ANC leaders Stephanie and Albie Sachs were in London—Albie, a future justice on the Constitutional Court in post-apartheid South Africa, would be the target of an assassination attempt during his subsequent exile in Mozambique. Stephanie brought Prexy along to an anti-Vietnam war protest in Paris where he met James Baldwin. In London he also got to know the South African novelist, Bloke Modisane, and spent time with leading AAM figures Ethel de Keyser and Alan Brooks.[14]

Prexy's time in London gave him the chance to get to know Selma and C. L. R. James, who introduced him to the West Indian community and deepened his understanding of Marxism. A legendary Trinidadian writer and theorist, James and his British wife Selma took Prexy beyond the circles of the Anti-apartheid Movement and the ANC. "He was so eloquent. He impressed me so much," Nesbitt recalled of C. L. R. Through the James', Prexy met the editor of *Race and Class* and the cultural theorist Stuart Hall. "Everyone knew C. L. R. and Selma," Prexy recalled.[15]

Prexy finally made it to Tanzania, but the dissension within Frelimo, had not been fully resolved.[16] He walked into a tumultuous environment, suffused with intrigue, and yet overflowing with inspiration and commitment among the legions of comrades. Just as in the United States, discussions of race and politics pervaded Dar es Salaam in the late 1960s. Kwame Ture, a Black Power advocate formerly known as Stokely Carmichael, had recently come through, arguing for a strong Black consciousness. In contrast, Mondlane urged Prexy "not to base his politics on race." Nesbitt noted that his time in Dar es Salaam distanced him from the Black nationalist fervor back home and inspired him to identify as an internationalist.[17]

Mondlane and Prexy were scheduled to meet on February 3, 1969, to discuss how Prexy might assist with education in the liberated territories of Mozambique. But early that morning Mondlane had retrieved a package—a book of Marxist philosophy—that exploded in his hands, ending the life of this extraordinary person. The investigation pointed to PIDE operatives and their local conspirators, as a "bomb inside a book was a favorite gift of the PIDE to its enemies."[18] On route to their meeting, Prexy ran into a distraught and overcome Pam Beira dos Santos, wife of Frelimo vice president Marcelino dos Santos who gave him the news. Everyone was stunned. "It was a devastating blow," Prexy recalled. The funeral brought together the anticolonial leadership on the continent, including Julius Nyerere, Agostinho Neto of the MPLA, and Amilcar Cabral. "I was present in Dar es Salaam when Eduardo's lifelong friend and comrade, Reverend Ed Hawley (coincidentally my family's pastor who buried my mother, my sister, and my father) officiated over the funeral of Eduardo. He summed it up well, saying that for Eduardo Mondlane, 'Beyond the sword was always the vision of the higher goals, of justice, righteousness, truth, and love; violence was but a regrettable but necessary means to these higher goals.'"[19]

"In many respects, Eduardo had it all," Prexy later wrote. "Like Amilcar Cabral (and Eduardo's successor, Samora Machel), he had a commanding intellect coupled with a real feel for and commitment to ordinary people and their needs. He was a big man who was constantly growing intellectually and politically. Like so many of the great leaders," Prexy reflected, "he respected elderly people, embraced and loved children, and read voraciously. Only 48 when he was blown up, similar to Martin Luther King and El Hajj Malik El Shabazz," Mondlane "was only beginning to blossom with his ideological beliefs and ideas."[20]

After Mondlane's assassination, Uria Simango declared himself president, but the forty-person Central Committee decided that leadership should be shared by Simango, Marcelino dos Santos, and Samora Machel. Like the other dissidents, Simango was uneasy with the internationalism and interracial cosmopolitanism of many on the Central

Committee, which included a few mixed raced Mozambicans. In a stunning move, he published a manifesto accusing his comrades, including Mondlane, of monstrous deception: of spying for the Americans and even colluding with the Portuguese. He lost his bid for power but traveled the region seeking to subvert Frelimo's stature and, after the fall of colonialism, even joined a PIDE effort to seize control of the country. He was expelled from Frelimo and later executed.[21]

Since the Mozambique Institute remained closed in the aftermath of Mondlane's assassination, Prexy helped do English translations for *Mozambique Revolution*, a magazine edited by Jorge Rebelo. Working with Rebelo "became a university for me. He taught me patience. He taught me how to be so informed that you always would have the upper hand in a discussion."[22] Like many Frelimo leaders, Rebelo was a poet. Indeed, expressive arts and culture would play a major role in forging national unity after independence. Many of the leaders of the Portuguese colonies in Africa wrote and read poetry and loved Black American poems with African themes. Rebelo and Marcelino dos Santos enjoyed listening to Prexy recite the famed Langston Hughes poem "The Negro Speaks of Rivers."[23]

Prexy's time in Tanzania was cut short by an urgent call to return to the United States when his mother was diagnosed with late-stage cancer. Sadie Nesbitt's death was a crushing blow and kept Prexy close to home. For him, Mondlane's murder and his mother's death would always be linked memories. But his commitment to Mozambique's independence remained strong. Not long after returning home, Prexy hosted Armando Guebuzo, Frelimo Minister of Education, and Sharfudine Khan, their representative to the United Nations, at Malcolm X College on Chicago's west side. They showed footage of Frelimo's Second Congress, including "scenes of a mass meeting of 10,000 people held under heavy foliage," in order to shield them "from American-made Portuguese bombers overhead." The event was meant to encourage active American engagement. "Use this occasion," the flyer declared, "to create your own ties of solidarity and support with the struggling people of Mozambique."[24]

In May 1970 Frelimo's Central Committee elected Samora Machel as president. Born in the Gaza Province to a peasant family, Machel was educated in a Catholic mission school and trained as a medical assistant. Machel met Mondlane during his 1961 trip to Mozambique. In March 1963, expecting to be arrested for subversion, Machel travelled across Swaziland and South Africa to Botswana, then on to Tanzania to join Frelimo. Later that year, Machel was tapped to lead the second group of Frelimo fighters sent to Algiers for guerilla training. Upon assuming power in 1970, Machel deepened Frelimo's commitment to Marxist-Leninist ideology. He acknowledged the support of progressive European nations and leftist activists and strengthened Frelimo's ties to the Soviet bloc.[25] While Mondlane was Prexy's entry point into Frelimo and his strongest influence, Prexy would be committed to Machel's leadership and particularly to his famed personal discipline. "There was an acute sense of discipline, which had a tremendous influence on me," Prexy recalled. "I never tried marijuana and didn't drink for many years and that was the influence of Frelimo and being identified with Frelimo."[26]

Back in Chicago, Prexy was determined to build greater awareness about the atrocities of Portuguese colonialism. Portugal relied upon foreign support and investments to maintain its overseas empire. American corporations, such as Gulf Oil, had huge operations in oil-rich Angola, and the Nixon administration showered Portugal with economic and military support, but most Americans knew little about Portuguese colonialism or the extent of American involvement. In 1970 Prexy was arrested for passing out leaflets at a soccer match between Poland and Portugal. "A westside teacher was arrested at Soldier's Field for distributing a leaflet supporting African freedom movements in Portuguese Africa," the *Chicago Defender* reported. Kermit Coleman, an African American lawyer with the American Civil Liberties Union, represented him. Charged with disorderly conduct and obstructing an officer, Prexy was held for five hours—although "witnesses claimed the arrest was of a 'political nature.'"[27] In court, the police officer testified that Prexy was handing out anti-imperialist literature. As Prexy recalls, the judge was taken aback. "Mr. Nesbitt," he asked, "would you explain to me what this was about?" Prexy happily obliged, welcoming the opportunity to "explain the crimes of Portuguese colonialism" in a "room full of Black people in a Cook County courtroom." In the end, the judge dismissed the case but advised Prexy: "You have a powerful tongue. Be careful how you use it."[28] And the *Defender* helpfully broadcast his message in their reporting: "according to the leaflet, U.S. arms, aircraft, and napalm, given through NATO, are being used by the Portuguese to suppress African freedom fighters."[29]

Around this time, Prexy learned from a cousin that her father, his uncle Russell, a government employee, had been pressured by the FBI into providing information about Prexy's associations and activities. Greatly upset about this revelation, Prexy informed his father and asked him to confront his brother and demand an end to the surveillance. That never happened. For the sake of family unity in their shared household, Prexy's father declined to confront Russell. For Prexy though, this introduced a rift in the family that would never heal.[30]

The 1970s is a forgotten heyday of the global left, especially in Africa. Historian Elizabeth Banks finds that "African anti-colonialists pursued diverse forms of socialism, ranging from Marxian-inspired scientific socialism to more populist genres of 'African socialism.' Socialism was invoked both as a theory to explain colonialism and as a concrete doctrine of economic development and nation-building that de-emphasized ethnic and regional affiliations."[31] This description aptly characterizes many of the groups vying to end Portuguese rule. Amilcar Cabral, an agricultural engineer educated in Portugal, became very popular globally as he waged a successful armed struggle in his country. He developed a strong following among both Black American nationalists and leftists for emphasizing the importance of culture in achieving social transformation, his waging of a successful armed struggle, and his emphasis on tailoring socialist development and nation-building to the needs of the global South. To build support for the PAIGC, Cabral made thirty-one trips abroad in 1971 alone.

In contrast to Angola and Mozambique, Guinea-Bissau was not a settler colony: there were no white members of the PAIGC. Cabral founded the PAIGC in 1956 and, interestingly, was also a co-founder of the MPLA, along with Angolan Agostinho Neto whom he had met in Portugal—another instance of the colonial metropole becoming the meeting ground for anticolonial resistance. A creative Marxist, Cabral was admired for his organizing skills, deep appreciation for local culture and ordinary people, and his theoretical acumen. His writings, as well as speeches abroad, were key in promoting the internationalist left, beginning especially with his appearance at the Tricontinental Conference in Cuba in 1966.[32]

Prexy Nesbitt first met Amilcar Cabral at Mondlane's funeral in 1969 and saw him next at a 1970 conference in Rome. Shortly before the conference, Cabral visited New York but Prexy, sick, asked his sister Roanne to go in his place. "I asked her to write down every word Cabral said. My sister was very, very striking." Roanne had become a top model in New York, one of the first Black women to break through with an elite modeling agency. She went to every talk Cabral gave, and finally Cabral publicly asked, "Who is this woman writing down my every word?" They laughed and she told Cabral that her brother would also be in Rome. And not long after, at the hotel in Italy, "Cabral saw me walking toward him and said, 'Prexy, you're here, camarada.'"[33]

Sponsored by the Italian Communist Party, the Rome conference on resistance to Portuguese colonialism, brought together hundreds of activists and deepened internationalist ties. Notwithstanding their socialist leanings, CONCP leaders—Cabral, Marcelino dos Santos for Frelimo, and Neto for the MPLA—also had an audience with the Pope.

Figure 3. Amilcar Cabral addressing the United Nations Committee of 24 in Guinea, April 10, 1972. Courtesy of Stephanie Urdang.

"I'm sure that was Cabral's idea," Prexy guessed. "It just rings of Cabral." Crucial for Prexy's own political education, Cabral identified with the African American struggle, yet also advised: "We have our own unique circumstances. You have your unique circumstances. You must base your struggle on the concrete conditions of the people."[34]

Lawyer and activist Robert Van Lierop, whose parents hailed from Surinam and the Virgin Islands, founded the Africa Information Service (AIS) with Prexy in Harlem in 1970. "That organization had a short life, but it was a significant life," according to Nesbitt, in part "because we hosted Cabral." Syracuse University invited Amilcar Cabral to give the Eduardo Mondlane Memorial Lecture in October 1972; before going up to Syracuse, Cabral visited the AIS's office in Harlem where he met with 120 people from a range of Black organizations.[35]

To this audience of Black activists, educators, writers and artists, Cabral offered insights that challenged the dominant political mood in the United States. Like other internationalists waging liberation wars in the 1970s, he disavowed simple analogies across struggles even as he championed the ethic of solidarity and sought support from Black Americans. Cabral began by unpacking his greeting: "Naturally if you ask me between brothers and comrades what I prefer—if we are brothers, it is not our fault or our responsibility. But if we are comrades, it is a political engagement. Naturally we like our brothers but, in our conception, it is better to be a brother and a comrade." In combatting colonialism, he explained, "we don't make progress if we combat the people themselves. We have to combat the causes of racism." He stressed the importance of responding to the unique circumstances of lived conditions across the African Diaspora in forging a plan for revolutionary change. Moreover, he refused to celebrate the fact of armed struggle: "Maybe I deceive people, but I am not a great defender of the armed fight. I am myself very conscious of the sacrifices demanded of the armed fight."[36]

Prexy and Van Lierop later drove Cabral to Lincoln University in Pennsylvania, where the university's president bestowed an honorary doctor of law degree and lauded Cabral for his strides in ousting the Portuguese. Cabral's military strategy had liberated three-quarters of Guinea by 1972, creating the foundation for the PAIGC's decision to proclaim a new nation in a year's time. Cabral was flanked on stage by Charles Diggs, a member of Congress from Detroit who championed African freedom, and Amiri Baraka, Owusu Sadauki, and Mark Smith, key East Coast African American advocates of Pan-Africanism.[37]

Tragically Cabral did not live to see the fruits of his extraordinary commitment. Local proxies of the Portuguese secret police assassinated him on January 20, 1973. But he deserves credit for catalyzing a left-wing military coup and popular uprising in Lisbon in 1974 that decisively reshaped the balance of forces in southern Africa. His goal of "forging a nation by means of the struggle" found vindication when war-weary Portuguese soldiers, overextended in Guinea-Bissau, overthrew the Lisbon regime. Tragically, Prexy's sister Roanne also lost her life in 1973. She was slain by her estranged husband, shocking and devastating the family. The coincident timing of the murders of Cabral and Roanne would intensify Prexy's commitment to internationalism and African solidarity.[38]

Bob Van Lierop of the AIS introduced many American activists to the hopes and dreams of Frelimo. Influenced by Malcolm X's shift toward human rights and support for African liberation struggles, Van Lierop embarked on a long trip to Africa after graduating from law school in 1967, where he met the commanding and charismatic Mondlane. Mondlane greatly prized cultivating new supporters, including Americans—indeed Frelimo was the rare national liberation group of this era that received aid from the United States, China, and the Soviet Union. Even with their socialist aspirations, they took non-alignment seriously. Mondlane encouraged Van Lierop to make a film about Frelimo to generate support among ordinary Americans. Mondlane's assassination redoubled Van Lierop's resolve to make the film.

In August and September of 1971, in fear of Portuguese bomb attacks, Van Lierop traveled with Frelimo guerillas to film in liberated territory in Mozambique. Back home, he quit his job at a prestigious law firm and waited tables at a jazz club in Greenwich Village, to free up his days to edit what would become *A Luta Continua*, a pathbreaking thirty-minute documentary film explaining Portuguese colonialism and Frelimo's armed struggle to an American and international audience.[39]

Released in 1972, the title, *A Luta Continua*, borrowed a phrase first coined by Mondlane as a slogan for Frelimo but which was later adopted by anti-imperialist activists in struggles worldwide. Screened globally and in the United States, the film effectively conveyed three major ideas, according to historian Carla Stephens: "Mozambican nationalists are fighting a guerilla war against Portuguese colonialism, the nationalists have a plan to build a better society for their people, and the United States, its NATO allies, and multinational corporations are complicit in the continued oppression of the Mozambican people." According to another scholar, the film "played a vital role in shaping American views of transnational anti-imperialism" and promoted an internationalist perspective to African American audiences. The film highlights Frelimo's efforts to build a new nation in the liberated territories, bringing health care and education to the villages and emphasizing the importance of women to national liberation. "To die a tribe and be born a nation" was a Frelimo slogan embodied in the nine ethnic groups that composed the guerilla army. But such nationalism also celebrated ethnic culture as Frelimo incorporated various ethnic dances and songs.[40]

Meanwhile, immersed in solidarity organizing in Chicago, Prexy helped launch three new groups: the South Side–based African American Solidarity Committee, which published the monthly newsletter, *African Agenda;* the largely white North Side Chicago Committee for the Liberation of Angola, Mozambique, and Guinea (CCLAMG); and the West Side US Out of Angola Committee. CCLAMG sponsored over one hundred screenings of *A Luta Continua,* including at "Southern Africa Solidarity Day" in December 1972 at the Lincoln Park Presbyterian Church, which featured representatives from Frelimo and the MPLA, Van Lierop, South African exile-poet Dennis Brutus, Sharfudine Khan and Nesbitt for a series of workshops, music and food with over three hundred in attendance. Prexy described how Portugal, with US and South African financial backing, was displacing African populations and bringing in white settlers to build damns in Angola and Mozambique designed to benefit the apartheid economy. Showcasing the solidarity across the region, the event raised funds and donations for the Organization of Angolan Women. The long list of sponsoring organizations illustrated the breadth of anti-imperialist organizing in an era of large-scale protests against the US war in Southeast Asia.[41]

The film helped build a diverse constituency for Africa solidarity work. Requests to CCLAMG for screenings, "were evenly divided between black, school or college and religious communities, with presentations to multiracial audiences almost equaling those provided to African Americans."[42] Prexy recalls that a screening at the predominantly Black Dunbar High School on the South Side became a "tremendous opportunity" to teach about Mozambique to a large audience of ordinary people. In addition to Khan, also present on that occasion was Joaquin Chissano, a future president of Mozambique.[43] At another event at Dunbar High School, in early 1973, ANC President Oliver Tambo and African American activist Angela Davis spoke at the founding of the Communist Party–supported NAIMSAL, the National Anti-Imperialist Movement in Solidarity with African Liberation. While most of the left's focus was still on ending the war in Southeast Asia, these events illustrate a simultaneous effort to bring attention to struggles in southern Africa.[44]

Veteran activist Bill Minter noted that *A Luta Continua* "became an important organizing tool for peace, solidarity, and anti-imperialist groups around the country" and that it "has made a special contribution to the mobilizing of millions of United States citizens against US-supported colonialism in Mozambique and South Africa, so much so that the title itself has become part of the movement's vernacular." The film educated an activist generation and helped lay the groundwork for much wider internationalist organizing in the 1980s.[45]

In another initiative, Prexy joined the Africa Research Group (ARG), "an independent organization with a radical perspective on imperialism and revolution in Africa," which had been founded in Cambridge, Massachusetts, in 1968 by students and recent graduates radicalized by the war in Vietnam. Founder Daniel Schechter explains that, in writing an article for *Ramparts* analyzing CIA involvement in sub-Saharan Africa, he came to see the need for greater research on African political economy. But the group, "convinced that the policy objectives and strategic interests which led to war in Asia could involve the United States in war elsewhere in the Third World," were mainly concerned about US military intervention in Africa. According to Schechter, "America's alignments with apartheid and counterrevolutionary forces in Africa seemed to us particularly pernicious and destined to suck us into an explosive confrontation which the American people knew little about and would not support if they did." The ARG wanted "to put the problem of African liberation on the map of American political consciousness" by refocusing their academic skills toward political engagement.[46]

The ARG produced studies, pamphlets, leaflets, and newspaper and magazine articles. Their work proved directly useful to the liberation struggles: "We were able to get American scientists to undertake some research on the American-made herbicides which the Portuguese Air Force was using in Angola. The request for this information had come from the Popular Movement for the Liberation of Angola." The group disbanded in 1972 but left an important legacy, and Danny Schecter went on to play a major role in the anti-apartheid movement as a journalist and media-activist.[47]

They dissolved at this early juncture in the struggle because members wanted to put their energy into activism rather than research, but dissension around race and gender also played a role. There was "an undercurrent of racial anxiety," Schechter wrote. "From its inception, the group was overwhelmingly white, although it did have black members and African supporters." Evidently, some in the group "became nervous once it was clear that Africa was becoming a 'black issue' and that the black community is the social force in the United States with the potential for exerting the most leverage against US intervention on the continent. Individuals within the group began to feel uncomfortable as whites working on African issues, especially when challenged about their motives, no matter how rhetorically, by blacks." Prexy was one of two Black members of the ARG. He recalls Black nationalist objections but remembers as well that a rising feminist consciousness among women members may have contributed to the break-up of the organization. Patriarchal attitudes and behavior were widespread among the men. "Some of the women in the ARG really didn't like Danny's machismo and arrogant 'I am the leader' style."[48]

ARG wanted to share its archive with a Black-led solidarity organization, so it chose the Africa Information Service. Activists with the Pan-Africanist Youth Organization for Black Unity, likely one of the pressure points on ARG to dissolve, were evidently disappointed not to get it.[49] In a major loss, the archive was destroyed. The AIS had moved from Harlem to a lower Manhattan building, which housed progressive organizations. "We moved the whole collection down there," Van Lierop said. At one point, while abroad, he lent his office to a Zimbabwean liberation activist. "Unfortunately, the rent wasn't paid," so the landlord moved to repossess. Shortly after returning home, Van Lierop actually dove into a dumpster when he saw a "container full of books and records" being "hauled away." He ended up retrieving a few items. For Prexy, the episode was always tainted. "They took it all. The story is that the maintenance people threw it out. I have never believed that to this day. I think there was an infiltrator in one of these organizations who saw to it that this stuff was confiscated or destroyed."[50]

Another small initiative that punched above its weight was the African American Solidarity Committee (AASC) founded in 1971 by Prexy, Otis Cunningham, Linda Murray, Harold Rogers, and others. From 1972 to 1977 it produced a monthly newsletter that disseminated coverage and analysis of events and struggles in the Third World, but especially in southern Africa, from a Black anti-imperialist perspective. It became an indispensable and rare source of such information across Chicago, moving via Communist and other networks to a much wider readership. It reprinted speeches from leaders of the ANC, MPLA, and Frelimo and offered detailed analysis of US and European foreign policy and corporate activity. And it gave extensive coverage to the liberation movements and the global internationalists immersed in solidarity work. They printed letters from leaders of African liberation movements praising the newsletter.

They produced the *African Agenda* (beginning at Prexy's kitchen table) with support from the Communist Party–affiliated NAIMSAL. Harold Rogers and Otis Cunningham were close to the party. Prexy never joined the CP although he was around its circles. "Many people assumed that I was in the party, because one of the people who everybody admired and loved was Ishmael Flory (a legendary Black Communist Party leader) and Ish knew my family."[51] Harold Rogers taught for many years at Chicago City Colleges. He was active in the local Black Studies movement as well as the Chicago chapter of the Coalition of Black Trade Unionists. Black women in the AASC included Aisha Ray and Linda Murray, who would become a prominent physician in Chicago. Otis Cunningham recalls that men's voices dominated the discussions while the women did the work. "Obviously you had to have machismo in the organization, given the historical period," but he contends that it was more subtle than in some other groups, in part because of the incipient feminism articulated in the internationalist movement and embraced, at least formally, by many of the liberation movements, especially the ones they supported. Moreover, *African Agenda* "did a number of special issues on women, both domestic as well as international."[52]

The AASC was small but Rogers' connections to the ANC via Communist networks, and Nesbitt's connections to the groups fighting Portuguese colonialism meant that their influence exceeded their size: they hosted numerous visitors from southern Africa and injected an internationalist perspective into the Black public sphere in the city. About a thousand folks, including NAIMSAL founders Mildred and Willie Williamson, turned out for an appearance by ANC president Oliver Tambo at Dunbar High School. Cunningham vividly recalls their petition drive at an Operation PUSH expo where they collected thousands of signatures over four days calling for the expulsion of South Africa from the UN.[53]

To raise consciousness about southern Africa, internationalists stressed a shared struggle, but they also faced the challenge of cultural translation and the need to promote an appreciation for distinct histories. African Americans sometimes pushed back against what they viewed as the ANC's naive advocacy of nonracialism. One time Otis Cunningham brought ANC activists to Chicago's Black radio station WVON. "The ANC described itself as a 'non-racial movement,' and callers urged them not to trust white folks," Cunningham recalled. He came to feel that "African Americans oftentimes think they know more than other people of color around the world who are in struggle. African Americans think their struggle is more advanced and think they are in a position to tell others how to proceed." In contrast, Cunningham tried to convey that "each struggle has its own historical conditions."[54]

In addition to organizing among African Americans, Nesbitt organized with white leftists to raise consciousness and find ways to materially assist African liberation struggles. Multiple sources influenced Nesbitt's approach to race and organizing, including foremost his family's influence, but critical as well were African liberationists, especially his early childhood encounters with Eduardo Mondlane. "Liberation movement leaders in Africa in this period," Nesbitt wrote, "particularly the ANC and the leading movements against Portuguese colonialism, were very clear that the enemy was not individual white people as whites, but the systems of colonialism and racism."[55] And yet, Prexy notes the practical impossibility of working interracially in Chicago in the 1970s. Black Chicagoans harbored a skepticism of working with whites in this hyper-segregated city, even if, in Prexy's view, some of this distrust was born of what he saw as provincialism and an isolationism that could become a feedback loop. "I think I was very influenced by South Africans and the Mozambicans and Cabral. My philosophy was basically whoever is prepared to give concrete solidarity to the struggles, that's who I organized."[56]

His approach in the 1970s was to organize separately, although he personally bridged the racially divided movement. "The challenge was, on the South Side I'm working with the African American Solidarity Committee, which is all Black. On the North Side, there's CCLAMG, which is all white except for me, and maybe one other person. But in any event, I'm the only one going between both organizations." Prexy would spend hours mulling over the names of the many organizations that he founded or co-founded in this era. He wanted an acronym that in his perspective, sounded African. "I would lay in bed thinking. CIDSA, Coalition for Illinois Divestment from South Africa," and COBALSA and later CCISSA. "I always look for an African sound." CCLAMG included people from the Committee of Returned Volunteers, largely ex–Peace Corps and church people, including Mimi Edmunds, who was in graduate school at Northwestern.[57] Edmunds recalls that Prexy provided critical analysis of African struggles and was a very effective communicator: "The words came easily. The metaphors came easily. Prexy was imposing, he walks into a room and commands your attention. He's committed. He speaks as someone who deeply, deeply believes in it." Prexy explicitly guided them as white activists: "He kept us on the up and up of being, I don't want to say politically correct, but what's appropriate for us to do. And what's not." Edmunds says their role was "not to educate African Americans. It was to educate our own culture and to change the policy in Washington."[58]

CCLAMG organized support for the MPLA, PAIGC, and Frelimo and maintained an office in a North Side bookstore-event space called the New World Resource Center.[59] It hosted lectures and workshops and conducted material aid efforts, most notably one that sent Vitamin C to Angola, where the widespread use of herbicides and frequent bombings had created "an urgent need for Vitamin C in the liberated areas." Like other activist groups during the Vietnam War, it feared escalation of US war-making in the global south. "We see clearly the possibility of another Vietnam in Southern Africa," a CCLAMG leader told a UN committee. CCLAMG supported the boycott of Gulf Oil. "Consumers are being urged to turn in credit cards and boycott their local Gulf Station," their flyer instructed. Gulf Oil is the largest US investor in Angola, "controlling about 1/2 of all American investment in that country." Prexy recalled doing "many, many demonstrations against Gulf Oil Company," whose handsome payments to Portugal buttressed colonialism. He attended a Gulf shareholder meeting at their Pittsburgh headquarters, but after a threat to their lives, the local police literally put them on a Greyhound bus back to Chicago.[60]

At the same time, on the predominantly Black West Side of Chicago, Prexy organized the U.S. Out of Angola Committee at St. Mary's, a Catholic school where he taught popular adult education classes in the evenings. "It was a hotbed of political activity," Prexy recalled, with many movement people on the staff. Prexy was once fired for inviting a radical organization on campus, but student protests led to his rehiring.[61]

The robust antiwar movement and US defeat in Vietnam nurtured an anti-imperialist sensibility among many Americans in the 1970s. The fact that the most popular national liberation movements in southern Africa were on the left strengthened a left perspective within the American solidarity movement. But this was a fluid era, and nothing was preordained. It's important to recall, for example, that the leading African solidarity organization operating in the US, the American Committee on Africa (ACOA), and its longtime leader George Houser, were deeply shaped by Cold War liberalism. Moreover, the dominant strain of Black radicalism in this period remained Black nationalism, rather than socialism—notwithstanding the strong left currents in Black political culture. And yet, what turned out to be influential for the trajectory of US solidarity work was the fact that many southern African leaders were skeptical of Black American cultural nationalism. They had come to socialism, hopefully and purposefully, wanting an escape from the tentacles of neocolonialism and from continuing Western control in the aftermath of formal decolonization.

Fractious organizing around Angola revealed some limitations of Black nationalist–inflected Pan-Africanism and created more space for a left-internationalist outlook that would strongly shape ensuing solidarity work in the United States. In oil- and mineral-rich Angola, three national liberation movements—the MPLA, Unita, and FNLA vied for power before and after Portuguese colonial rule collapsed in 1974. Seven million people lived in Angola, a society shaped by a long history of slave trading and then a forced labor system under colonialism that compelled Africans to work in diamond mines, coffee plantations, and other projects belonging to white settlers or foreign investors. Desiring more foreign exchange to finance its wars against freedom-seeking Angolans, Portugal invited in corporations including Gulf, which in 1966 discovered oil in the Cabinda region.[62]

Anticipating the end of colonialism and in search of pro-US leaders, the Kennedy administration began to fund Holden Roberto, the anticommunist Zairean-based leader of the FNLA. Jonas Savimbi, who served for several years under Roberto, broke with him and founded Unita in the mid-1960s and developed secret links with, at first, both Washington and Pretoria. Neither Unita nor the FNLA spent much energy fighting the Portuguese: the MPLA did that. The MPLA came to control considerable territory before independence, where it established rudimentary health, educational, and agricultural programs.

In addition to political outlooks—language, class, ethnicity, and region also shaped affiliation. Angolans tended to see the MPLA as the more cosmopolitan party: its leaders were primarily Kimbundu-speaking urbanites, and some were mixed race or Western-educated or influenced. By contrast, Unita tended to attract more rural Angolans, particularly Ovimbundu speakers, and their politics were more traditionalist and masculinist compared to the MPLA. The differences were genuine, but it's also important to acknowledge the degree to which international machinations and intrigue, not least from the CIA, Portugal, and South Africa, shaped the crises in Angola around the time of independence and well beyond. Unita became a more sizeable and lethal force after independence and, with lavish funding from South Africa and the US, caused havoc and bloodshed in independent Angola for decades.

Before exploring the struggles that broke out in Angola with the collapse of Portuguese rule, I turn to the internal conflicts it inspired within US solidarity groups. The American Committee on Africa, according to historian Sheila Collins, introduced "the leaders of emerging African independence movements to the world"; or as another scholar put it, the "ACOA was nearly ubiquitous in its support of African liberation, creating coalitions with a multitude of disparate organizations—from religious and human rights organizations to student and black freedom movement groups to political, educational and cultural societies."[63]

The ACOA was led for years by George Houser, a white American Cold War liberal and the son of Methodist missionaries, who grew up abroad and worked for civil rights before founding the ACOA. But a new generation of left-leaning activists—in conjunction with the powerful ideological currents of African liberation—would push the ACOA to the Left in the 1970s and 1980s. The ACOA hired Prexy in January 1970 as their Chicago field organizer, shortly after he had returned home from Tanzania. Several young progressive church people (including the writer and longtime Africa-solidarity activist William Minter) raised funds for a one-year Midwest field organizer, whose mission included organizing in Black communities, and urged Houser to raise the funds to continue his employment. But Houser never did so. "I think that was partly because he had decided . . . that I was not loyal enough to him, that I was raising cane about different issues." Those issues were race and global politics. Even as Prexy did political work in multiracial or predominantly white settings, he was always consistent in his stance, and this sometimes cost him his job.[64]

The Black members of the ACOA board and staff were increasingly assertive in this era of Black radicalism and anti-imperialism. Nesbitt, along with ACOA board member Bob Van Lierop and two other African Americans, New York organizer Blyden Jackson and Charles Hightower, who led the staff at the Washington Office on Africa, an ACOA affiliate, provoked a series of challenges within the organization. After a group of African American leaders took out a page in the *New York Times* voicing support for Israeli actions in the Middle East, Hightower wrote to several signatories decrying their support for a nation that provided various sources of aid to apartheid South Africa. In turn, ACOA leadership chastised Hightower for expressing a personal opinion using his ACOA title. In September 1970, Nesbitt confronted the Executive Board regarding this matter and regarding the difficulties faced by Black staff in the Black community who were tasked with representing an organization headed by a white executive director. Furthermore, due to its Cold War origins, the ACOA was suspected of receiving funding from the CIA. Heightening this suspicion was the ACOA's continuing support for CIA-backed Holden Roberto despite the fact that, according to Nesbitt and others, the MPLA was the most viable liberation movement in Angola. Surprisingly, ACOA president Peter Weiss endorsed the concern about the ACOA's political direction, and offered to step down to be replaced by a Black leader. The conflicts resolved with no changes to the leadership, but with a clear shift toward the more left liberation movements. By 1971, the ACOA supported the MPLA exclusively in Angola and invited MPLA president Agostinho Neto, PAIGC president Amilcar Cabral, and ANC leader Oliver Tambo for speaking tours in the United States. Moreover, a few more traditionalist executive board members were moved to the national committee, while progressives Bella Abzug, Charles Rangel, Shirley Chisholm, and Ronald Dellums were nominated as new members of the board. The ACOA also embraced more assertive tactics, including "protests against the federal government and multinational corporations," which would accelerate in the years ahead.[65]

Tense battles around Angola and other African liberation struggles also took place within the broad orbit of Black radicalism and the specific orbit of Pan-Africanism. A Black Power–inflected Pan-African Movement flowered in the late 1960s and peaked at the Sixth Pan African Congress (6PAC) in June 1974 in Dar es Salaam. Owusu Sadauki, director of Malcolm X Liberation University in Greensboro, North Carolina, visited Tanzania in 1971, and returned with a message from Samora Machel urging Black allies in the United States to organize support for African liberation back in the United States. This led Sadauki and others to organize annual African Liberation Day demonstrations to cultivate Black American identification with and support for struggles on the continent. The first ALD demonstration in May 1972 drew forty thousand in Washington, DC; a year later tens of thousands attended events in thirty cities.[66]

The success of the first African Liberation Day demonstrations led to the creation of the African Liberation Support Committee (ALSC), which brought together a big tent of Black radicals who mostly self-identified as Black nationalists or revolutionary Black nationalists. In an important development, the ALSC pivoted toward Maoist thought as the popularity of Chinese communism surged in the early 1970s. Significant turnouts for African Liberation Day demonstrations reinforced the sense that support for African liberation was an important unifying thread for Black American activists. But at the same time, points of ideological tension were emerging. In 1973 and 1974, differences among Pan-Africanists over who to support in southern Africa, especially in Angola, sharpened.

While not many activists were fully informed on the gradations of Angolan politics, Unita leader Jonas Savimbi and his backers had identified mobilizing racial affinity among Black Americans as a key strategy of gaining Western support.[67] The dark-skinned, charismatic Savimbi embraced the mantle of Black nationalism and sought to leverage Unita's history with American missionaries. "Already by 1971, I knew that supporting Unita was a mistake," Prexy recalled. He and Bob Van Lierop had attended a "very contentious" conference that year in West Germany, where Prexy forged ties with Scandinavian solidarity activists that would last decades. The Swedes pushed hard for exclusive financial support to the MPLA. According to Nesbitt, they presented "extraordinary documentation" on the differences between the three groups, and especially damning was their evidence of Unita's secret collaboration with Portugal to undermine the MPLA.[68]

Prexy shared this information with Black American supporters of Unita. The New York–based Interreligious Foundation for Community Organization led by the Reverend Lucius Walker had hired Prexy to develop an organizing institute. Prexy tried to persuade Walker and IFCO–board member Owusu Sadauki to jettison Unita in favor of the MPLA, but to no avail. (This institute was short lived. Less than a year later, a group of staff members aired a series of grievances against Walker, including sexual harassment. Walker fired everyone on the spot, including Nesbitt.) In a similar effort, Nesbitt, along with fellow AIS activists Van Lierop and Craig Howard, convened a meeting with Harlem supporters of Unita to share this information. "I know one of them had a pistol," Prexy recalled, "but there were other people who had pistols too, because it was a very tense meeting."[69]

"In the midst of all this," Prexy relates, "we started having run-ins with the nationalists in Chicago." But a talk at Roosevelt University in 1975 by Guyanese historian Walter Rodney undercut Black nationalist support for Unita. "That changed the whole picture in Chicago," Prexy recalls. Because Rodney gave a "class analysis of the Angolan struggle and why it was critical to look at the Angolan struggle in terms of the historical development of Angola, and not look at it in terms of African American development."[70]

Jimmy Garrett, who ran the Center for Black Education in DC, was a Black nationalist moving to the left, partly due to the influence of C. L. R. James, with whom he spent considerable time in the 1970s. Garrett participated in the turn toward African solidarity among young Black radicals. In late 1971, he visited Tanzania, the home to scores of African liberation organizations in exile. "We saw a lot of the ideological struggles that were going on. And a lot of very fervent and aggressive brothers, particularly brothers who had been in the US (and now lived in Tanzania), supported Unita because it fostered from their point of view, a more nationalist or Black point of view, whereas MPLA was seen to be made up of mulattos." Garrett's first personal encounter with an MPLA leader was in Dar where he met an MPLA representative, who ended up marrying Geri Augusto, an African American woman. According to Garrett, this MPLA leader was brilliant. "He could speak like five languages. But he explained MPLA in a way that made it work. And then my relationship with MPLA grew from there." Still, Garrett vividly recalls that activists in his circle, veterans of the southern civil rights movement, thought differently. "Courtland Cox and Charlie Cobb supported the first stage of Pan-Africanism as 'black men rule,'" without factoring in the political and economic agenda of these rulers.[71]

Rivalries and rearrangements among the global superpowers—the United States, China, and the Soviet Union—shaped their funding of African liberation movements, and likewise impacted the strategies of solidarity organizations. The rapprochement between the US and China in the early 1970s precipitated a further wedge between China and the USSR, escalating into a sharper divide in the ensuing years. These developments especially influenced the Youth Organization of Black Unity, Baraka's Congress of African People and the ALSC, which all saw support for Marxist-Leninist-Maoist thought increasing.[72]

The African Liberation Support Committee became consumed with debates between nationalists and those moving to a pro-Chinese Marxist-Leninist position. Even though Black Maoists believed fervently in the Third World character of their struggle, Black cultural nationalists persisted in labeling them as pawns of the white left. In a prominent shift, poet and activist Amiri Baraka embraced Marxist-Leninism, breaking with the cultural nationalists, who were led by such stalwarts as Chicago poet Haki Madhubuti. As an effective umbrella organization, the ALSC essentially collapsed after 1974.[73] Strikingly, many of the nationalists and Maoists in the Pan-African orbit still found common cause in their support for Unita, which was backed for a short time by China to counter the Soviet Union and Cuba's support for the MPLA. "The cultural nationalists saw Unita as a black organization," Jimmy Garrett recalled, and the pro-China side thought "the most important opposition should be to the Soviet Union and not to the US."[74]

Notwithstanding these fractures, the ALSC and other Pan-Africanists helped to organize the Sixth Pan African Congress in June 1974. The organizers did not invite Prexy and Bob Van Lierop, a slight that Prexy chalks up to political differences. But ultimately, because the American delegation "had such a confrontation over these ideological questions, with Frelimo, MPLA, and PAIGC . . . our views were represented, so we didn't feel so bad."[75]

Many observers stressed the disarray, unpreparedness or political naivete of the American delegation to Dar, even as scholars in more recent years have highlighted 6PAC's success in cultivating Black women leaders who would play important roles in the anti-apartheid movement.[76] Here I stress the political disconnect between many in the US delegation and the delegations from the continent, where the currents of left-wing internationalism were very strong. The event also showcased the tensions and inequalities that emerge when activists convene with heads of state. According to one participant, "the militant, yet extremely articulate group of delegates, from the very beginning of the 10-day conference, knew they were in the wrong ballpark."[77]

A decision made before 6PAC likely put the Americans at a disadvantage. Caribbean heads of state facing internal dissent had pushed 6PAC host and Tanzanian president Julius Nyerere—admired by internation-alists and nationalists alike—to make most 6PAC delegations state sanctioned. Black Americans were the exception—and would be welcomed—but not Caribbean dissidents who had pushed so hard to make it happen. C. L. R. James, key in the planning stages, and a lead-ing critic of the Eric Williams administration in Trinidad and Tobago, refused to attend as a result.[78]

Ebony magazine editor and historian Lerone Bennett, part of the US group, wrote an insightful account. Bennett felt that the Africans bent over backwards to belittle the racial affinities and identifications of African Americans while the Black Americans found it hard to conflate colonialism with what the Africans termed "racialism." Bennett noted that the 180-member US delegation comprised almost half of the entire congress, yet as a single delegation the Americans had one vote and arrived without position papers or a clear plan. They met a strong, vocal, and organized African left, who in the end, seemed to have rede-fined Pan-Africanism: "When the dissecting and defining ended, it was not entirely clear whether the concept had been given new life—or whether it had been defined out of existence by delegates who denounced 'the Utopian idea of returning to promised lands' and rejected a 'purely racial' struggle of Africans and people of African descent in favor of a worldwide struggle by the oppressed black, brown, yellow and white peoples of the world." And yet, despite the many challenges of cultural and political translation, many lives were altered that June in Dar es Salaam and many new relationships were forged.[79]

Reading accounts of the event, Prexy was struck by the difference in orientation between the Americans and the Africans. "There were plenty of African Americans who were interested in socialism or anti-capitalism, but they're not trying to organize nation states outside of the sphere of influence of the United States, right?" He noted that Afri-can liberation leaders in these years were studying ways to avoid neo-colonial arrangements and "the tentacles of imperialism." They wanted to find ways to develop and get support "outside of this Western sphere of influence."[80]

This became a turning point in US Pan-Africanism. Geri Augusto, a Black American activist who moved to Dar to help organize 6PAC, powerfully articulates the influence of African struggles and perspectives on her consciousness. Africans, she said, "changed my head around. By the time everybody showed up in June 1974 . . . I was already thinking like a Southern African about the various political questions." She immersed herself in the milieu, read literature on imperialism and learned Kiswahili. "By the time my brothers and sisters got there with their arguments, I said to myself, this is an argument for the Western hemisphere. It is not an argument that fits here. To the extent that it fits, I think they're mistaken."[81] Stark grew critical of the idea of race as a proxy for politics. "I knew Agostinho Neto (president of MPLA) was married to a Portuguese woman, but that's not an argument for a national movement. I just saw things in a more complex way, so that an argument of 'I'm married to a black woman' doesn't tell me anything about your politics or what economics you hope to have. And they based it pure and simple on China backs Unita, the Soviet Union backs MPLA, a very simplistic reading."[82]

Geri Augusto married the MPLA representative in Tanzania and lived there and later in Angola from 1973 to 1991. She edited *Resolutions and Selected Speeches of the Sixth Pan African Congress* for the Tanzania Publishing House. In her view—one shared by others—"the cleavage left a bitter taste . . . the contestations that took place among the North American delegation, both during the organizing phase and the conference itself, fractured the liberation support movement." Her mother, Florence Tate, "was a big Unita supporter" back in the United States. "And we didn't have much contact with each other for years. Probably part of it was because I just wasn't here. But she relates to me that it was an extremely bitter and acrimonious fallout."[83]

The collapse of the Portuguese dictatorship in 1974 was a turning point for southern Africa and the trajectory of the Cold War. The leaders of both MPLA and Frelimo were internationalists, desiring democracy and freedom for themselves and the region. Chiefly, they wanted an end to apartheid and majority rule in Namibia and Rhodesia, meaning that they might offer bases and sanctuary to the liberation movements, as Tanzania had been doing for years. As a result, South Africa greatly feared the prospect of these movements assuming state power.

In Angola, "hoping to avert a bloody conflict," the MPLA agreed to a transitional coalition government until elections could be held after independence in November 1975. The FNLA and Unita broke the agreement. In March, US-backed Zaire dispatched troops into northern Angola to bolster a possible path for the FNLA, and in August, South Africa launched a military invasion of Angola from the south.[84] Both the US and South Africa began sending covert aid to the FNLA and Unita, who sought to topple the fragile new government led by the MPLA's Agostinho Neto. "We are working with South Africans to shape a common destiny," Jonas Savimbi would say. In a striking intervention that reshaped southern African politics for years to come, Fidel Castro—who had sent troops and doctors during the previous decade to Algeria, Congo Brazzaville, Zaire, and Guinea-Bissau to assist liberation struggles, immediately organized the shipment of thirty-six thousand troops from the faraway Caribbean nation. By April 1976 the Cubans and the fledgling Angolan army had repelled the South Africans; with Soviet weapons and support, the Cubans would stay and defend Angolan sovereignty against a continuing threat of South African and Unita warfare until 1991.[85]

Back in the United States, a large group of activists organized pressure on the US government, which they feared would militarily intervene. As the Southern Africa Committee in New York saw it, "Kissinger, and the US interests he represents are fundamentally opposed to the establishment of free, politically and economically independent societies in Southern Africa. They have a rich prize to defend—and defend it they will, with ferocity." But the transitional Ford Administration held back. After revelations of the many lies by American presidents regarding US war-making in Southeast Asia, the US Congress began to take a more independent role in shaping US foreign policy. In the 1970s and 1980s it more readily asserted itself as a third branch of governance.[86]

For their part, the South Africans were angry at the Americans who did not come to their rescue; and the US was embarrassed by the Cuban triumph. "Cuba is a red flag in the U.S.," a top National Security Council official flatly stated. "Anything they do, we hate." According to historian Piero Gleijeses, "humiliating one superpower and repeatedly defying the other, Cuba changed the course of history in Southern Africa."[87]

Walter Rodney visited the United States in April 1976 and helped shift Black American opinion against Unita. In a speech at historically Black Howard University, Rodney carefully analyzed how various African nations and diasporic Africans reacted to the scramble for power in Angola. "This particular confrontation with imperialism is different from the situation faced by Ghana or Nigeria twenty years ago," he suggested. "In that epoch it was possible to say we are merely fighting for national independence. After we get our independence, we will address ourselves to a variety of other questions." The ensuing years, however, saw the rise of neocolonialism and continuing poverty and underdevelopment for ordinary Africans in former colonies, demonstrating the importance of tying political independence to social transformation and of supporting nationalist groups with strong critiques of both colonialism *and* imperialism. While imperfect, Rodney argued, the MPLA had demonstrated a clearer commitment to societal transformation than either of its rivals. Rodney analyzed how Roberto and Savimbi had already created alliances with regional and global forces of neocolonialism and imperialism, and primarily sought the departure of the Portuguese and their own ascension to power.

Walter Rodney offered a sympathetic analysis of why many Black Americans were drawn to Unita but still considered it a major error. Like Cabral, Rodney brought a perspective that unsettled and reshaped Black American analysis. In contrast to the MPLA, which had not devoted much attention to cultivating support in the US, Unita saw Black Americans as a ripe audience. "They simply appealed to the growing Black consciousness by saying 'Inside of Angola we stand for the elevation of the Black man to a position of dignity and rule, and the MPLA stands for the elevation of whites and mulattoes over the indigenous African people,'" Rodney said. These arguments were appealing, especially at a time when "brothers and sisters were going through that terrible period of self-identification, of self-recognition, of purification and the like, trying to extract themselves out of the dominant white culture." But Rodney pushed his audience to rethink this basis of support for Unita. "To declare for Blackness," he said, "is one of the easier things to do." He argued that colonial racial classifications, marriage partners, and the like were not the basis for mature political thinking. Invoking the work of Frantz Fanon, Rodney argued that "national consciousness is clearly a liberating force, but at a certain point it can provide (blinders) . . . and constitute a barrier for further understanding of the real world." He then turned his critique to those who imagined Unita "as a Maoist movement" fighting "Soviet Socialist Imperialism." But in choosing to privilege superpower politics, Rodney declared, these advocates ignored the needs of Angolans. Echoing Cabral, he asked, "How does that relate to Angola with its specific characteristics"? He implored those in the audience "who have talked for so many years about Pan-Africanism" not to turn their backs on the more revolutionary forces.[88]

While some Black Americans may have continued to support Unita, they declined as a vocal source of support after 1976 and, in any event, were overshadowed by the rising conservative backing of Savimbi. The MPLA, for its part, gained greater traction among African Americans as seen in the strong Black mobilization against an effort by Roy Innis, a vocal Black nationalist who was on a journey to the right, to sign up Black military veterans to fight with Unita. (The right-wing cultivated mercenaries for southern Africa during these years.) Activists united nationwide to denounce Innis's call, expressing outrage that Black Americans would be called upon to fight for a group backed by apartheid South Africa.[89]

As noted, an exception to this trend was Geri Augusto's mother Florence Tate, a communications specialist active in the Black freedom struggle who became a staunch advocate for Unita. Her first trip to Africa, she recalled, was "exhilarating, emotional and life changing." Moved by Unita's efforts to connect with African Americans and by the group's base in the countryside, Tate was undeterred by revelations of their alliance with apartheid South Africa. She reports being "denounced, shunned and accused of working with the CIA and South Africa." This break with longtime movement coworkers was very painful for Tate, who "chose to continue to support the people with Unita." Key to her decision were personal relationships and a sense of identification: Unita "represented the 'Black' Black people—those in the southern part of Angola who were rural, agrarian folks," rather than the urban, educated Angolans, including the mixed-race Africans and Portuguese in Luanda. "I should note," she later reflected, "that my support of Savimbi began a long time before he deteriorated into a madman. Though it was the opinion of many that he had always been a madman, I never saw signs of it."[90]

Jimmy Garrett journeyed to Angola in January 1976 for a conference of 250 people from seventy nations to strategize ways to build support for the MPLA. Garrett wrote about it for the *Black Scholar*, a journal that closely chronicled Black activist debates. Garrett unpacks how the colonial system organized people according to their proximity to the "Portuguese civilization" via heritage, education, or culture. In contrast to observers who sanitized this system by comparing it favorably to other colonial modes, Garrett termed it "a profoundly dehumanizing chapter in the history of imperialism." Much of the article focuses on the opportunism and treachery of the FNLA and Unita. "It is clear," Garrett argues, "that it was the MPLA which carried out the main struggle against Portuguese colonialism." Garrett describes how US arms and money to FNLA and Unita, with Zairian and South African support, escalated the death and destruction experienced by ordinary Angolans. He summons his readers to think more deeply about what beyond simple nationalism should replace colonialist structures in southern Africa. To Black Americans, he urges a rethinking of the conflation of MPLA "mulattoes" with antiblack sentiment. "We were blinded," he writes, "by our own simplistic notions of Black nationalism."[91]

MPLA chose not to spend precious resources building support among citizens of a country historically positioned against it. But the threats the new nation faced after independence brought forth a surge of organizing by Americans. In February 1976, the MPLA hosted a gathering in Havana of American supporters from nineteen organizations and seven media outlets, including *Freedomways*, the *Black Scholar*, the *Sun-Reporter*, and Baltimore *Afro-American*. Organizations included progressive labor unions, the National Conference of Black Lawyers, ACOA, the National Council of Churches, and solidarity committees from around the country like CCLAMG. Prexy was there and wrote about it. "None of us will forget the seriousness and bereavement in the delegation's voices when they described life in Luanda as that capital faced the South African US-equipped blitzkrieg from the south and the forces of the FNLA/Unita from the north," he wrote.[92]

An MPLA leader spoke of their desires for nation building; solidarity with the peoples of Zimbabwe, South Africa, and Namibia; and why they saw a form of socialism as essential to the needs of an extraordinarily underdeveloped society. Asked about the role of women, he offered, "If we do not struggle for the freedom of women we would not be struggling for our own freedom." Women are subject to two

Figure 4. Havana Seminar with the MPLA: Willis Logan, Africa secretary of the National Council of Churches, foreground; Prexy Nesbitt, second from left; and Brewster Rhoads from the Coalition for a New Foreign and Military Policy, right. Courtesy of Christine Root for the Washington Office on Africa.

colonialisms, he explained; one was the Portuguese and the other was "their oppression by man." He explained that women had joined the struggle in great numbers and had made the anticolonial struggle a fight for their freedom as well. But he acknowledged the enormous work that would be required to forge "equality of rights between both sexes" in the new nation.[93] The Americans adopted seven goals coming out of Havana, including gaining US recognition of Angola, nation-building support (organizing medical aid, fertilizers, educational support), averting a US economic boycott and organizing against American military aid to Zaire or South Africa.[94] This solidarity network organized demonstrations to bring media attention to their efforts. An impressive group of one thousand demonstrated against US intervention in Angola in New York City in early 1976 while Prexy's West Side group, the US Out of Angola Committee, helped organize a march of a couple of hundred people down State Street in Chicago. The marchers carried signs and chanted "US-CIA Hands off Angola" and "MPLA."[95]

Carrying forward the momentum from Havana, a wide range of progressive organizations, everyone from the ACOA to NAIMSAL, formed the National Angola Support Committee and hosted a convening, "Angola: From Cabinda to Cunene, One People, One Nation," in Chicago in May 1976. Nesbitt co-chaired it with Patricia Murray of the National Conference of Black Lawyers. According to Prexy, the three MPLA representatives who journeyed to Chicago had a tremendous impact on the three hundred people who attended.[96] The diversity of attendees illustrates the extensive national concern over events in Angola, as well as a budding and expanding internationalist network. They included, among others, the Chicago Women's Liberation Union, *Black Scholar* magazine, Harambee Inc. (with Kathryn Flewellen, a leading organizer of 6PAC), the Bay Area Namibia Action Group, the Cuba Resource Center, the Black Military Resistance League, the Campaign for a Democratic Foreign Policy, CCLAMG, AASC, the Minority Women's Task Force, the Madison Area Committee on South Africa, the Patrice Lumumba Coalition (a very important Black internationalist group based in Harlem, led by Elombe Brath who would soon join the Board of the ACOA), and the Puerto Rican Solidarity Committee.[97]

The convening coincided with the Cuban rout of the South Africans, Unita, and FNLA forces in Angola. "Now I don't know how many agents infiltrated that thing," Nesbitt recalled. "But undoubtedly, it was infiltrated because it was a hot issue. Cuba's involvement made it very hot. Kissinger hated what the MPLA stood for." The conference focused on dispelling myths about Angola, fostering support for the new nation, and organizing material and medical aid. It called on the US to cease all military action against the new nation either directly or through third parties.[98]

As it happened, on the heels of defeat in Vietnam, Congress was in no mood to be pulled into another Third World conflict framed as a fight against communism. Named after its sponsor, Senator Dick Clark of Iowa, the Clark Amendment, barring US aid to insurgents in Angola, was signed into law in June 1976. As it turns out, in defiance of congressional restraints and despite its public assertions to the contrary, the CIA had been secretly aiding the insurgents all along. The chief of the CIA's task force on Angola felt so betrayed by what he saw as a needless conflict fueled by the wounded egos of American leaders, he resigned and published an explosive account of CIA machinations in Angola.[99]

In the summer Prexy became interim coordinator of the new national Angola Support Steering Committee but attempts to sustain it quickly fell apart. There was no paid staff, and long-standing groups like the ACOA and AFSC had their own ways of doing the work. And while the 1976 Angolan support effort encompassed liberals, Black nationalists, and leftists of various stripes, who could all gather amicably for a conference, the ideological differences would make sustaining a single national organization much more challenging. Still, the solidarity work continued in pockets, in local areas, especially out of places like New York and Chicago with preexisting southern Africa solidarity organizations.[100]

Complicating the prospects for sustained solidarity work was the fact that ultimately, Angola decided not to invest in building a solidarity movement in US. President Neto concluded that the socialist bloc was a much more likely source of support—and certainly the fact that the CIA was funding and coordinating efforts with the FNLA and Unita played a role. In a 1979 trip, Prexy met with many Angolan officials who "repeatedly admitted that they erred in not devoting more attention to stating their case to the people in the United States, as did both Frelimo and the PAIGC." Sadly, American aid to Savimbi escalated in the Reagan era and the Clark Amendment was repealed in 1985.[101]

Prexy infused his solidarity work in the United States in the 1970s, with insights learned overseas, including an openness to transnational exchange; an investment in education alongside advocacy; and a commitment to working at the grassroots yet with a clear focus on changing American governmental and corporate policies. A major lesson was that the fight for freedom in southern Africa—whether in the former Portuguese colonies, Namibia, or Rhodesia—exceeded South Africa yet depended upon the abolition of apartheid. As long as apartheid survived, it posed a grave threat to the prospects for peace and justice in the whole region. The clashes over race and ideology in the Pan-African/internationalist movement of the 1970s were bruising, but they also awakened many activists to the concrete details of the multiple struggles in southern Africa, seeding the ground for a robust anti-apartheid movement in the years to come.

3

THE GLOBAL AND LOCAL DIMENSIONS OF THE ANTI-APARTHEID STRUGGLE

||||||||||||||||||||||||||||||||||||||||||||||||||||||||||||||||||||||||||||||||||||||||||||||||||||||||||||||||||||||||||||||||||||||||||||||||||||||||||||||||||||||||||||||

BEGINNING IN THE 1970S, Prexy Nesbitt became a leading activist in the global anti-apartheid movement, and over the next few decades helped make Chicago a center of solidarity for southern Africa. A committed internationalist with extensive knowledge of the region, Prexy maintained numerous close relationships with southern Africans on the continent and in exile. A robust anti-apartheid movement arose across the United States in the 1970s and peaked in the mid-1980s. A few major organizations based on the East Coast—the American Committee on Africa, the American Friends Service Committee, the Washington Office on Africa, and TransAfrica—provided guidance to activists nationwide, but local creativity and variation shaped the US anti-apartheid movement. Prexy and his circle brought an anti-imperialist lens, an emphasis on organized labor, and efforts—not always successful—to overcome racially divided organizing. Because Prexy was in such high demand as a speaker nationwide and regularly worked and traveled overseas, he didn't always lead the new organizations that he created or helped to create. One result of the intense level of activity was a broadly shared commitment to collective and rotating organizational leadership.

This chapter charts the course of the US anti-apartheid movement through Nesbitt's local and global sites of organizing. New York, Chicago, and Geneva were key bases, but regular travel to Canada, Sweden, southern Africa and connections with African exiles also shaped Prexy's work. From its formation in 1912, the ANC sought international support and made friends worldwide. Black American advocacy for African independence had deep roots, but a robust movement against settler colonialism and US imperialism in South Africa and elsewhere on the continent took shape in the 1940s. Led by Paul Robeson, Alpheus Hunton, W. E. B. Du Bois and others, the Council on African Affairs lobbied the United Nations for sanctions even before the formal launch of apartheid by the Nationalist Party in 1948.[1] Prexy picked up the anti-imperialist tradition of the council, which fell victim to the red scare, often beginning speeches with quotes from Paul Robeson.

For many American anti-apartheid activists, their bridge to the world went through the United Nations, and particularly the Centre Against Apartheid, which was led for many years by the steadfast Indian-born diplomat E. S. Reddy. "In India, in our generation," he said, "we were all influenced by Gandhi" and "by Nehru, who was a socialist." Reddy began his activism in the US with the Council on African Affairs, but he fostered connections with the ACOA and other organizations. "We had McCarthyism at the UN," he recalled, but noted that the atmosphere improved when "many African countries became members."[2] From 1963 to 1984, Reddy oversaw action against apartheid, a tough assignment as the UN largely went the way of Western leaders in protecting South Africa. Hosting convenings for global activists, Reddy offered the Centre as a gathering place for internationalists. Ironically, as a leader in a global institution, he helped American activists from across the country connect with each other; people who met at his conferences began to collaborate across campuses and regions. It cannot be overstated how important Reddy-organized convenings were to US activists. Counterintuitively, he made the UN critical to the domestic anti-apartheid movement.

At the same time, for Prexy, the Centre Against Apartheid played an important role in nurturing and extending his international relationships and strategic thinking. It was through the UN that Prexy first came to know a cohort of extraordinary scholar-activists who became mentors and comrades: the South African sociologist Ben Magubane, Pakistani political scientist Eqbal Ahmad, and the Palestinian scholar Edward Said. Prexy was deeply inspired by their commitments to an internationalist Third World nationalism. Reddy also supported the travel of scores of visiting southern Africans and connected them to American activists. Nesbitt estimates that close to sixty southern Africans stayed at his family's West Side home during these decades of struggle. The UN nexus helped Prexy foster and maintain old and new ties to the region outside of the Communist Party connections that had catapulted Chicagoans like Harold Rogers and others into ANC circles. As always, for Nesbitt, personal relationships with southern Africans helped to ground and grow his work.[3]

Prexy became very close to another person at the United Nations: Johnstone (Johnny) Makatini, a longtime member of the ANC Executive Committee, who in 1977 became head of the ANC mission to the UN and, in 1983, a director of the ANC's Department of International Affairs. Part of the first group sent out for military training in 1962, Makatini served as an ANC diplomat in Morocco and Algeria and became close friends with Marcelino dos Santos of Mozambique, Agostinho Neto of Angola, and Amilcar Cabral of Guinea-Bissau. His "flair for diplomatic work flowered during his years at the United Nations," according to ANC comrades. He "paid special attention to the solidarity movement in the United States, winning millions of friends and

Figure 5. ANC representative Johnstone Makatini addressing the UN Security Council, March 25, 1977. Courtesy of Stephanie Urdang.

supporters for our struggle." Prexy became a highly valued interlocutor and key point of connection in the US.[4]

Likely because Prexy had become close to many ANC people in London, the ANC began shipping him copies of *Sechaba*, the East German produced magazine covering the ANC's overseas struggles. "I'd get five hundred to a thousand copies of *Sechaba* in big bags that came from the GDR." He tried to tell the ANC that he couldn't possibly deliver all of these. "My station wagon was always filled with *Sechabas*"; he couldn't keep up with the volume and he knew he was under surveillance. "The FBI was all over the stuff in Chicago." He worried about the attention they drew to him as he was continuously hosting visitors from southern Africa. He decided to change the delivery address to his family's summer compound in Wisconsin, until an uncle there said the post office was overwhelmed.[5]

It's crucial to understand that anti-apartheid activists in the United States were not only organizing to change South Africa: first and foremost they were organizing to change the United States, the leading financial backer of the apartheid state. Since World War II, South Africa had become a major source of strategic minerals for the US and Europe: cobalt, copper, magnesium, uranium, and diamonds. Moreover, the US government regarded South Africa as a staunch ally in the fight against global communism and followed its lead in labeling the ANC a subversive organization. The US, especially under the right-wing administration of Ronald Reagan, felt kinship with a white-ruled regime fending off claims to Black equality. As anti-apartheid organizations methodically detailed, American support enabled the survival of apartheid. By 1982, US investment in South Africa amounted to about $14 billion. American activists fought to change government policy—but also came to target many other institutions helping to sustain the apartheid regime, such as banks and corporations.[6]

A 1959 call from the African National Congress was decisive in shaping the ensuing thirty years of US and international solidarity work. ANC president Chief Albert Luthuli urged the international community to impose sanctions on South Africa, arguing that "the economic boycott of South Africa will entail hardships for South Africans. We do not doubt that. But if it is a method which shortens the days of bloodshed, the suffering to us will be a price we are willing to pay."[7] The United Nations General Assembly reinforced this demand in January 1979 with a vote to end to all new investments and loans to South Africa. But the United States used its veto in the Security Council then and many times over the ensuing years to block economic sanctions. Most activists went further than the UN call and pushed for the withdrawal of all investments and loans to the South African government, parastatals (government owned enterprises), or corporations. To pressure US banks and corporations to cease ties with South Africa, activists pressured individuals, unions, municipalities, states, churches, and universities to withdraw all accounts from banks that lent to South Africa and to divest their holdings from corporations that engaged in business there.

The fight against apartheid is often likened to the fight against Jim Crow, but the anti-apartheid struggle had a more explicit economic analysis, condemning racial capitalism rather than simply racial segregation (even if many ordinary American critics of apartheid may not have shared this critique). As ANC president Oliver Tambo put it in 1985, the ANC desired "a mixed economy with major industries controlled by the state. This country is very wealthy," but it was concentrated in the hands of a few multinational conglomerates. "Now, the situation cannot remain like that," he declared, "there's got to be a certain amount of redistribution of this wealth so that the bulk of the people will benefit."[8]

The global anti-apartheid movement was deeply responsive to events inside South Africa. On June 16, 1976, twenty thousand school children in Soweto marched to protest the government's new policy requiring the use of Afrikaans as the language of instruction in their schools. The protest was part of the larger Black consciousness movement led by Steven Biko and others. Police violently attacked the march killing or wounding hundreds of children—many of whom were shot in the back. The Soweto massacre sparked grief, outrage, and a new resolve by South Africans to aggressively free themselves from apartheid. Thousands of young people left South Africa to join the ranks of the liberation movements in exile. The media ran the images of the brutal killings around the world, arousing international outrage and ushering in a new period of more intense and regular attention to apartheid and struggles against it. As the ACOA put it, "the increased militance of South Africa's black population awakened the American public to the full reality of apartheid."[9]

Over the next decade, activists in the United States intensified their effort to show the full extent of American complicity with apartheid via research, picket lines, legislative campaigns, and ultimately, mass protest and civil disobedience. Financial reverses in the 1970s and the extraordinary cost of making war internally and in the region in the 1980s made the apartheid state increasingly dependent on foreign lending. The roster of American corporations involved in South Africa was long and distinguished: Chase Manhattan, Citibank, Manufacturers Hanover, and scores of other banks lent billions to South Africa; Mobil and Shell Oil sold petroleum products to the police and military; Ford and General Motors sold vehicles to the police and military; and IBM and Control Data sold computers to the government, including for use by the military and prisons. In 1977 alone, US banks lent South Africa $2.27 billion, a third of its overseas loans.[10] This "intervention to support apartheid and racism," Prexy Nesbitt told a reporter, is "a particularly heinous undergirding of racism because that capital is the very capital that makes it possible for the South African government to spend over 40% of its revenue on armaments and defense."[11] It's striking to consider that in ten years' time, two hundred American corporations would leave South Africa.[12]

THE BANK CAMPAIGN

Several months after Soweto, in February 1977, the ACOA and Clergy and Laity Concerned (CALC) launched the Campaign to Oppose Bank Loans to South Africa with Prexy as one of two national coordinators. Prexy recalls that this partnership with CALC rankled Houser, who preferred to work alone. Global events had elevated left-wing voices in mainstream organizing, and CALC, part of a still-robust Christian left and founded by close clergy allies of Martin Luther King Jr., was known for its vigorous resistance to US militarism.[13] Prexy and others were trying to push the ACOA away from its Cold War roots toward a closer affinity with anti-imperialists on the continent and in the United States. At this juncture, for example, white labor leftist Moe Foner and Black left organizers Elombe Brath and Michael Simmons had joined the ACOA's Board.

Prexy plunged into the work. Based in New York, COBALSA quickly developed scores of affiliates nationwide and in Canada and used demonstrations, delegations, education, and various pressure tactics to push for change. They urged individuals and organizations to withdraw checking, savings, payroll, and pension accounts, and deposit then in banks that did not do business in South Africa. Main targets were Bank of America in California; Continental Bank and First National Bank in Chicago; and Citibank, Chase Manhattan, Manufacturers Hanover Trust, and Morgan Guaranty Trust in New York.

Pretoria's answer to the cry for justice after the Soweto massacre was more violence. On September 12, 1977, security forces killed Stephen Biko, the most prominent anti-apartheid activist in South Africa and leader of the Black consciousness movement. Protests erupted worldwide. US Senator Dick Clark said his death "fit a pattern of outright racial repression conducted by an authoritarian state which permits unconscionable acts on the black community."[14] Prexy sought to direct some of the outrage over Biko's assassination to American enablers of apartheid. "The guilt in the murder of Biko, and the many other Black South Africans," Prexy insisted, "must also rest on the 400 or so American corporations and banks whose investments and loans provide the foundation of the South African apartheid system."[15]

Michael Weeder, an Anglican priest in Cape Town and later a dear friend of Prexy's who went on to succeed Desmond Tutu as Dean of St. George's Cathedral, remembers the devastation of losing Steven Biko. "For us at that point in the early '70s Nelson Mandela was an abstraction, and so Biko was our dream incarnate, he was our vision," Weeder recalled. His murder "had a tremendous impact on us because we often said that there is a black president in the making. Before there was a Nelson Mandela, before there was an Oliver Tambo, or a Thabo Mbeki, there was a Steve Biko."[16]

With his personal and family ties to the labor movement, Prexy was particularly effective in gaining union support for the bank campaign. Left-leaning unions would be a leading force in the anti-apartheid movement in New York City and California, especially, and they were the first to pull their funds. The United Electrical Workers withdrew $4 million from Chase Manhattan Bank. The Furriers Joint Council terminated an $8 million payroll account and a $16 million pension account with Manufacturers Hanover. "We have contacted other unions to do the same thing and they have reacted sympathetically," said their leader. "By using their pension funds, which are a major source of investment funds in this country," he said, unions "can have an effect on the banks."[17]

Progressive unionists were outraged when they learned of their financial support for apartheid. Cleveland Robinson, secretary general of District 65 of the Distributive Workers Union and an organizer of the March on Washington, said to Prexy, "You're telling me that our union monies are helping to finance that killing of those children right now in South Africa?" Prexy vividly recalls Robinson picking up the phone and without hesitation, giving the order. "You know that account we got at Chase? Take the money out of it right now. I want it out by the end of the day." District 65 also announced a withdrawal of millions of dollars from Manufacturers Hanover at a large demonstration. Fifteen years later Cleveland Robinson would speak alongside Nelson Mandela in New York City.[18]

The legendary Chicago labor leader Charlie Hayes became a major supporter of anti-apartheid work. A longtime leader in the progressive United Packinghouse Workers of America (and its successor union Amalgamated Meat Cutters) and the first trade unionist ever elected to Congress, Hayes served ten years in Mayor Harold Washington's former House seat. Prexy first met Hayes at the Women's Center of the Methodist Church near the UN, where Prexy's good friend Don Will ran seminars on Southern Africa. "He had me there once with Charlie

Hayes. And Charlie and I really hit it off because Charlie realized that I had worked with his old buddy Cleve Robinson. So, he and I just became bosom buddies." Hayes convinced his union to withdraw funds from Continental Illinois. Prexy had another connection to Hayes through Henry and Moe Foner, New York trade unionists with long ties to the Left, whom Prexy had gotten to know through the bank campaign. The Foner brothers had joined the Communist Party during the Depression and were early victims of the red scare. A further connection was through Prexy's uncle George, a lawyer who traveled in Popular Front circles. "They all knew my uncle," Prexy recalled. "They'd all say, 'Oh, yeah, George. We knew George.'"[19] Ray Rogers of the Amalgamated Clothing and Textile Workers Union was another early supporter of the bank campaign. Rogers was "an effective COBALSA activist," Prexy recalled, "who initiated the tactic of organizing bank employees to join the demand. This was particularly successful in Seattle." Rogers also shared one of his union's staff members with COBALSA—Nomonde Ngubo, a South African exile who proved a powerful speaker against apartheid on her many trips across the country. This sharing of resources characterized and strengthened the movement.[20]

The bank campaign highlights the leading role organized labor played in the anti-apartheid movement—a theme that in Prexy's view has fallen out of popular memory. As the divestment movement began to accelerate over the coming years, unions fought hard for city and state divestment, especially in the Northeast, Midwest and West Coast. The public employees union, AFSCME, with a large Black membership, was instrumental in pushing Michigan, Connecticut, Massachusetts, Maryland, Philadelphia, and Washington, DC, to divest pension funds from corporations and banks doing business in South Africa. Mandela repaid their support by speaking to an AFSCME convention in Miami months after his historic release from prison.[21]

Unions also supported the struggle by flexing their muscles in the workplace. In Oakland, Leo Robinson of Local 10 of the International

Longshore and Warehouse Union (ILWU) called for a boycott of South Africa immediately after the Soweto uprising, and for the next two decades Robinson and West Coast dockworkers were staunch activists in the anti-apartheid movement. On Easter Sunday in 1977 Local 10 members boycotted a ship loaded with South African cargo. A few hundred people "cheered the workers while hoisting banners including one that said, 'Apartheid is Crucifixion.'" A year later, the local collected food, clothing, medicine, and other essentials; they "convinced shipping companies to donate two containers, and loaded the goods for South Africans in exile in Tanzania, where the ANC had a huge training camp." By the 1980s, the West Coast unionists, controlling docks from Vancouver to San Diego, refused to load or unload ships doing business with South Africa. Prexy collaborated with Leo Robinson and the ILWU often, and as in so much of his organizing, personal relationships facilitated his access to key people. ILWU treasurer Leon Goldblatt's daughter Lee had been part of the same small group of American teens that did homestays with Swedish families in the early 1960s, and she and Prexy remained friends for years. The ILWU shaped currents in the Bay Area, and in 1979, Berkeley became the first US city to divest. Many years later, before a roaring crowd in Oakland, Nelson Mandela thanked the ILWU for being on the frontlines of the movement.[22]

A few churches also began to align their money with their values. One result of the Black Power movement, and especially of James Forman's challenge in the "Black Manifesto," was the creation of a host of caucuses or initiatives in Protestant denominations focused on racial justice. These created a clear path for anti-apartheid organizing. "The Methodists had the Black Methodist Federation for Social Action," Prexy recalled. "The UCC had a Black caucus, the Unitarians had a Black caucus. Those caucuses and individuals around them, very early, became very involved with southern Africa work." In 1977, the National Council of Churches Governing Board voted to "undertake the withdrawal of all funds and closure of all accounts in financial institutions that invest or make loans to the South African government and business."[23]

Interrelating local and global injustice was core to anti-apartheid organizing and pivotal to the bank campaign. Prexy invoked a shared transatlantic history of bank racism to mobilize Black Americans. The slogan "'redline South Africa and not New York!' (or Boston or Chicago or Washington)," he said, "captured people's rage at banks that wouldn't make loans for them but would provide massive capital to sustain a brutal, white supremacist system in Africa."[24] A COBALSA forum, "Runaway Banks: The Misuse of Our Money at Home and Abroad," with state assemblyman Al Vann and US representative Stephen Solarz, chair of the subcommittee on Africa, publicized a study finding that "for every $1000 deposited in Bankers Trust, Chase Manhattan, Chemical, Citibank or Manufacturers Hanover Trust by Harlem residents, that community receives $4.61 in home mortgage loans. Yet a pervasively white, wealthier community in Brooklyn—the Flatlands—receives $138.66 for every $1000 deposited."[25] A few years later, in the fight for divestment by the city of Chicago, Prexy highlighted the US-South African connection in a very tangible manner: "The Chicago Police Department buys its radios from Motorola; street sweepers and fire trucks are purchased from Ford Motor Corporation; and the City is negotiating with Westinghouse for developing the 'people mover' at O'Hare. All three of these companies are heavily involved in South Africa and directly contribute to the support of apartheid."[26]

Bank of America lent about $200 million to South Africa. California's "stop Banking on Apartheid" campaign, led by the Quaker activist Miloanne Hecathorn, organized thousands of people, including many students, to leaflet at hundreds of Bank of America branches on November 17, 1978. Prexy spoke at their rally in San Francisco. Bank of America was not a new target for anti-apartheid protesters in California; someone had set fire to a branch in Santa Barbara in 1970. Under immense pressure, Bank of America stopped making loans to the government of

South Africa in 1980. Many of these California student activists later moved into the labor movement bringing their internationalism into that sector as the divestment movement peaked in the mid-1980s.[27]

Anti-apartheid organizers relied heavily on speakers, newsletters, films, pamphlets, and other material to educate Americans on events in southern Africa. During a trip to the Bay Area, Prexy showed the documentaries *Namibia: A Study in Colonialism* and *South Africa: A Rising Tide*, which "depicts the uprisings in the black townships; extensive military build-up; US support of apartheid; South African undermining of Zimbabwe and Namibian independence." The films made the critical point that the anti-apartheid struggle was part of multiple interrelated struggles in the region. Speakers from southern Africa always reinforced this point.[28] This information flow was crucial, if extraordinarily outmatched by Pretoria's well-financed, sophisticated propaganda machine, or as one scholar termed it, "a worldwide media and lobbying operation run with military precision." The United States was a particular target, and Pretoria repeatedly strove to find and pay little-known Black Americans to defend its homeland system. During this era, South Africa spent hundreds of millions of dollars to "improve its image" and taint its critics as communist subversives.[29]

Activists faced unique challenges in trying to build a mass movement while staying faithful to an anti-imperialist outlook. The US left was coming out of an era of schisms and sectarianism, which the solidarity movement endeavored to avoid. A memorandum by the Southern Africa Collective in California illustrates such thinking: "We want to reach out beyond the left to mobilize the largest possible number of people behind our two principles of unity: 1. End all US military, economic and diplomatic support for South Africa and Rhodesia. 2. Support self-determination for the people of southern Africa. We want to create a broad coalition of black groups, trade union activists, church people and everyday folks who join forces with the students and southern Africa activists who are already in motion," they declared. "At all times, we must be conscious of reaching out to a wide range of people—in our leaflets, speeches, radio appearances, etc. No rhetoric, no ultra-radical posturing. We are trying to build a genuine coalition that will be taken seriously—one that has political clout and can begin to make an impact in this country." There was advice on how to conduct a successful rally. It "should be well-organized, informative, clearly understood to all passersby, entertaining and snappy. No long-winded, rhetorical speeches."[30]

The memo advised steering clear of the reflexive American critiques of communism: "As we said at the last meeting: No anti-Soviet, anti-Cuba raps allowed at the rally." They would "go against the politics of the Patriotic Front (in Zimbabwe) and SWAPO as well as the ANC and many leaders of the Black Consciousness Movement. It would also confuse and misdirect many of the people we are trying to reach in this country, who are already anti-communist and anti-Soviet enough. Our task is to take on the US—the main danger and obstacle to . . . liberation in southern Africa." This memo of practical advice reveals how left-wing currents in southern Africa influenced the approach of a burgeoning American social movement.[31]

In addition to his work as an organizer, Prexy was always an analyst, sometimes even a critic of the movement's work. One example is his critical appraisal of using shareholder power to cease future engagement in South Africa. This tactic was favored by many religious denominations and was championed by Tim Smith, leader of the Interfaith Center on Corporate Responsibility. In contrast, COBALSA urged total withdrawal of international finance from South Africa, not just the cessation of new lending. In 1978 in response to shareholder activism, Citibank pledged to no longer originate new loans to South Africa. Asked for comment, Prexy called "the Citibank action 'a significant step in the right direction.' He added, however, that until Citibank barred all loans to South Africa—to Government or private borrowers—'we view it as a participant in the apartheid system.'"[32]

Two years later Prexy more forcefully criticized shareholder activism, describing it as an option available to a privileged few and not helpful in building a mass movement that might engage greater numbers of Black people. He acknowledged the successes of the tactic but urged "that shareholder activism now assume a secondary role to the greater task of mass-oriented educational and mobilizational work." Or perhaps "the annual pilgrimages for the shareholder voting" could "be coordinated with mass activity. As five or six individuals or institutional investors vote on the inside, five or six hundred should be marching on the outside." He cited a 1978 meeting with the Motorola Company in suburban Chicago as a missed opportunity to relate shareholder work to Black perspectives and needs. "When asked about their activities in South Africa—which included selling radios for South African police vehicles—company executives defended themselves by saying that they weren't selling the South African police their best equipment, only their second-best equipment! They kept their best equipment for the Chicago police department!" He cited the assassinations of Black Panther leaders Fred Hampton and Mark Clark and continuing police violence against Black Chicagoans as a way to bridge the global to the local and build consciousness in Black communities.[33]

Prexy was committed to coordinating strategy across national borders, guided by an ethic of comradery. The UN Centre Against Apartheid hosted meetings for the bank campaign with activists from Canada, Britain, and Europe, who shared strategies and information that were pivotal to their successes. Moreover, Prexy maintained direct contact with African struggles and collaborated with international activists at global convenings. He visited Tanzania, Mozambique, Botswana, Zambia, and Kenya for the ACOA in the spring of 1978 and witnessed the change afoot in the region. "The May 4th raid on SWAPO at Kassinga, Angola, by the South African fascists, the FNLC uprising and the Western-initiated Pan African Security Force for Zaire, the acceleration of the armed struggle in both Zimbabwe and South Africa, the processes of consolidating 'people's power' in Angola and Mozambique, all these events and others constituted a most historic moment in which to be traveling through southern Africa," he wrote. On the same trip, he stopped for meetings with solidarity organizations in London, Geneva, Lisbon, and Rome and gave many radio and newspaper interviews about anti-apartheid activities in the United States.[34]

IPS

When the Institute for Policy Studies (IPS), a leftist think tank in Washington, DC, offered Prexy a position to help lead an Africa research group, he left COBALSA. Prexy felt constrained by ACOA leader George Houser, who he thinks felt threatened by his leadership and connections in southern Africa and by his success in pushing the ACOA more to the left. Houser would step down as executive director in 1981, passing the baton to Jennifer Davis, a white South African whom Prexy greatly admired and worked well with. At IPS, he again experienced tension with white male leaders who appear to have been challenged by his independence and outspoken antiracism. "What I didn't know at that point, but later found out was that IPS had a history of difficulty working with Black employees," he recalled. According to Prexy, Ivanhoe Donaldson of SNCC had worked there and left for this reason. But during his brief stint with the IPS working with Kevin Danaher, who later founded, with Medea Benjamin, Global Exchange, and the young researcher Elizabeth Schmidt, Prexy continued to deepen his international ties while maintaining his involvement in the bank campaign and other divestment efforts.[35]

As protest-driven interventions in the marketplace, sanctions and divestment sparked controversy. Organizations like universities, banks, and corporations vigorously defended their autonomy over investment decisions, but given the moral weight of the anti-apartheid position, these groups dissembled, saying that sanctions wouldn't work and would hurt Black South Africans in the process. In contrast, one study of the potential impact of sanctions pointed to likely success, finding "that South Africa is trade and credit dependent and is thus vulnerable to selective sanctions which can disrupt the most dynamic and advanced sectors of the economy." It suggested that sanctions could be applied in a way that inflicted pain on the white elites rather than the Black majority.[36]

In a move that provided corporate America with a rationale for continuing to invest in apartheid South Africa, Leon Sullivan, a Black clergyman and board member of the General Motors Corporation, created the Sullivan Principles, a template of enlightened practices for US companies to follow in South Africa. This became a way around the rising demand for US companies to divest their holdings from South Africa, and not surprisingly many corporate and political leaders embraced it. The first defense in various divestment campaigns was typically: "We'll sign the Sullivan Principles." According to Prexy, "the story of Leon Sullivan and his contribution to prolonging the apartheid saga is another illustration of how crucial the communication links were to the effective functioning of the global anti-apartheid movement. . . . His principles were globally analyzed, debated, and rejected within months of their first appearance, and the potent little booklet *Decoding Corporate Camouflage* by Elizabeth Schmidt was circulated widely and internationally before being banned by the South African government."[37]

Alongside the rising rejection of the Sullivan Principles by Black American clergy and their condemnation by Black South Africans, Schmidt's report helped discredit them in liberal circles. Prexy witnessed one particularly dramatic turning point: in 1979 Leon Sullivan addressed the Summit of Black Religious Leaders on Apartheid. In the packed room, Johnny Makatini, the Black South African head of ANC's International Affairs, stood up and told Sullivan, "You may have created many principles; I have but one principle and it's freedom." Well, Prexy recalls, "the place erupted." Indeed, Sullivan himself later renounced his own principles, coming to see that they stabilized rather than challenged the apartheid regime. He became a proponent of sanctions.[38]

In 1976, agents of the regime of Augusto Pinochet murdered Chilean dissident Orlando Letelier and American Ronni Moffit in a car bomb in Washington, DC. The two had worked for the IPS, which began offering an annual award in their honor. IPS leaders proposed Andrew Young as the first recipient, but Prexy and his group objected over Young's work to "outflank and manipulate liberation movements" for the Carter administration. A Howard University student working as an intern at IPS evidently organized fellow students who vowed to picket the on-campus venue for the event if Young was chosen for the honor. But in Prexy's view, IPS leaders "felt that I was the one who organized Howard Black students to picket against the Institute. Robert Borosage reportedly said, 'The Howard students couldn't have thought of this. That had to come from Prexy.'" As it turned out, the first recipients of the Letelier-Moffit Human Rights Award in 1978 were Samuel Rubin—father of ACOA board member Cora Weiss—and the Reverend Ben Chavis who did important work exposing Jonas Savimbi's hypocrisy and brutal methods in Angola.[39]

WCC: GOING GLOBAL

In late 1979 the World Council of Churches (WCC), a bastion of progressive Protestantism and staunch supporter of the global solidarity movement, hired Prexy to direct its Programme to Combat Racism (PCR), an initiative funded by Scandinavian churches and nation states, that made grants to liberation movements and antiracist initiatives worldwide. The WCC launched the PCR after a 1968 address by James Baldwin, who stood in for the recently slain Martin Luther King. A year later, Oliver Tambo, president of the ANC, and Bishop Trevor Huddleston, a leading white British voice against apartheid, spoke in place of Frelimo president Eduardo Mondlane who had been invited but, like Dr. King, had been assassinated between the invitation and the event. Two of the most principled and inspiring global Black leaders were invited to address the WCC within a year of each other, and both were murdered. In an eerie echo, in 1979 the WCC invited Walter Rodney to speak, but his tragic assassination led WCC president Philip Potter to ask the newly hired Prexy to take his place. Prexy demurred and suggested Randall Robinson instead, an up-and-coming anti-apartheid activist who had cut his teeth in various organizing campaigns at Harvard.[40]

Prexy first met WCC leaders at a conference in West Germany in 1971. He and Bob Van Lierop got into "a huge confrontation with the World Council of Churches staff" over Western support for two dams Portugal was building in Angola and Mozambique. "We argued about the World Council of Churches continuing to give support to Unita," the CIA backed group vying for power against the Portuguese in Angola. "I think some of the WCC staff were so impressed with us that they then invited me to work with them."[41]

Marked by controversy, achievement, and risk—including even a covert trip inside South Africa—Prexy's time at the WCC solidified his leadership role in global solidarity movements. The first controversy was internal and showed that the council was not living up to its commitments. A 1979 report by the UN Committee Against Apartheid named banks that did business with South Africa, including ones with WCC deposits, a revelation which contravened the council's own commitment not to invest in "institutions that perpetuate racism." UN and WCC consultant Beate Klein's extensive research on banking practices revealed novel ways in which banks were concealing their activities in South Africa. She and Prexy worked together to persuade the WCC to withdraw their funds from three banks. At a press conference with journalists from around the world, WCC leaders announced the decision to remove church funds from two Swiss and one German bank. "It was a bombshell," Prexy said, because in Switzerland, there are "two things you don't mess with: chocolate and banks."[42]

Figure 6. Prexy Nesbitt, director of the World Council of Churches' Programme to Combat Racism. Courtesy of Prexy Nesbitt.

In 1969 the WCC decided to financially support national liberation organizations that were engaged in armed struggle, a move which led to active participation in the anti-apartheid struggle by clergy worldwide. The African National Congress was not the only group fighting to end apartheid from exile. The Pan Africanist Congress (PAC) was another South African organization leading a struggle that attracted international support, including from the World Council of Churches. But the PAC was undergoing intense leadership turmoil after the assassination of the charismatic and highly regarded David Sibeko and expulsion of Potlake Leballo and because of strained relations with governments in the region, so the WCC sent Nesbitt to conduct a first-hand review. Prexy traveled to Zambia, Tanzania, and Mozambique to interview government officials, activists, and church people. "I concluded in my report that the PAC was an ineffectual liberation movement and that the World Council should not give it any money" that year. He determined that financial corruption, administrative weaknesses, and internal divisions undermined the PAC's ability to mount an effective campaign and noted that internal conflict had led to "armed encounters with some fatalities amongst the contending factions and against host government officials." He recommended that WCC support go to the ANC, which despite its banned status, he found to be "both ideologically and organizationally prepared to benefit from the labor militancy, student protest, and other social forces rising up in South Africa." In the aftermath, PAC leaders flew to Geneva for a combative showdown with council leaders. "The PAC blamed me personally for their failure to receive a grant, so for the next year I had to face various PAC warfare." The China-backed PAC mobilized its allies worldwide, including many Maoist groups, to attack the WCC, and Prexy specifically.[43]

Prexy's report on the PAC exemplified for him what he was most proud of in his long relationship with southern Africa: his honesty in calling the shots: "I was very clear about what I had seen." The fracturing and eventual decline of the PAC would prove him correct. And yet his assessment also dovetailed with his support for a multiracial approach in the anti-apartheid movement over a Black nationalist approach. This political background shaped the reaction to his report. "Some African Americans, for example, supported the PAC because the PAC believed in a Black struggle in South Africa. . . . So I got attacked." But Prexy's stance was supported by many on the continent including the Tanzanians and the Organization of African Unity's Liberation Support Committee. The worst personal attack happened at a conference in West Germany when a PAC member assailed Prexy as the "Black Craig Williamson"—a reference to a white South African police agent and assassin who had infiltrated anti-apartheid groups. Williamson managed to get a position at a European philanthropy where he urged a shift in their funding away from the Black consciousness movement toward the ANC so he would be able to spy on the ANC and set up leaders for arrest. At the conference, "the anti-apartheid groups throughout Europe were furious" and demanded a halt to the proceedings until an apology was issued. "It was a huge brouhaha," Prexy said. "And he was forced to apologize."[44]

At the WCC, Prexy came to more deeply appreciate the Christian left. A dramatic example of their solidarity was a 1983 "illegal" trip by Nesbitt into South Africa to attend a secret convening to update South Africans on developments in the liberation struggles in Angola, Mozambique, Namibia, and Zimbabwe. These were places white South African soldiers were being sent to fight, but because the government censored information, importing such knowledge was dangerous—"if you had a piece of paper that said SWAPO on it, that's illegal." The hosts were Black and white nuns—the latter mostly Irish.[45] Due to concerns over listening devices implanted in the vehicles of attendees, the nuns arranged for cars to be parked near the chapel and for the playing of loud classical music to drawn out the discussions. But they still didn't trust having sensitive discussions anywhere indoors, so they talked at night on the roads. "We had intense political discussions in the pitch black, walking around this nunnery." Prexy vividly recalls the anxiety that gripped the place. After a few days, it was abruptly decided that Prexy and a Kenyan man who had been leading workshops on Paolo Freire, needed to be smuggled out early the next morning. An Irish priest drove the two men, disguised as nuns, into Lesotho.[46] In another covert initiative, Prexy tried to help South African cleric Allan Boesak develop a clandestine way to communicate with ANC people in Zimbabwe. The assassination of Joe Quabi, former Robben Island prisoner and the ANC representative in Harare, stanched the effort, but Prexy and Boesak would work together in the years ahead.[47]

Figure 7. Martha Biondi, James Thindwa, and Allan Boesak together in Chicago, 2012. Courtesy of Martha Biondi.

Prexy first met Father Michael Weeder, an Anglican priest who would become Dean of St. George's Cathedral in Cape Town, in Geneva. The WCC brought Weeder to Geneva, where he and Prexy bonded over a shared love of jazz. Designated by the government as Coloured, Weeder rebuked the apartheid aim of getting Coloureds to look down upon Black South Africans. Weeder later married Bonita Bennett who founded the acclaimed District Six Museum in Cape Town, and the couple have remained longtime friends of Prexy's. Prexy also got a chance to get to know ANC president Oliver Tambo when the WCC hosted him on a visit to Geneva. Tambo gave testimony at a United Nations office there on the ANC policy that they would not kill captured South African combatants.[48]

The apartheid state was not only ruthless in murdering ordinary and prominent critics of apartheid within South Africa; it was also ruthless in killing exiled freedom fighters. Many ANC leaders abroad were murdered in the 1970s and 1980s. Prexy was close to several. Ruth First, a white South African leftist, was assassinated in Mozambique on August 17, 1982, not long after a visit to Maputo by Prexy.[49] Prexy greatly admired First, whom he had first met in London in 1968 along with fellow exiles Stephanie Kemp, Joe Slovo, and Albie Sachs, figures Prexy would work with for decades. "Ruth was always very patient and supportive," even though "I must have set a record for asking uninformed and naïve questions." First's commitment to the struggle, including her willingness to die for a free South Africa, confirmed for Prexy the importance of the ANC's nonracialism. Ruth "modeled for me being both brave and nice to people at the same time." He also admired her political acumen and independence: "She was the finest of the fighters, who had a much broader political perspective than so many people narrowly tied to the party and to the Soviet line on everything."[50]

Prexy hosted scores of visitors during his time in Geneva and continued his extensive global travel. In a memorable trip to Africa, he was joined by his father, "Baba Prexy," who "was the hit of the trip, warmly received by all" in Mozambique, Zambia, Kenya, and Tanzania. They both thought of how much his late sister Roanne would have loved the trip and the chance to have worked with African children.

THE FIGHT FOR DIVESTMENT IN CHICAGO AND ILLINOIS

The 1980s brought a dramatic halt to the sense that the international anti-apartheid movement was making gains in beginning to isolate South Africa. The election of Ronald Reagan gave white rule a new lease on life with his administration's policy of "constructive engagement," which meant continuing to invest in South Africa on the pretext of urging reforms. During Reagan's efforts to strengthen US–South Africa ties, American investment became even more crucial to the survival of the apartheid regime. In December 1984, US financial involvement in South Africa, including direct investment, bank loans, and shareholdings, totaled some $14 billion.[51]

A new constitution went into effect in 1983 that granted a segregated role in parliament to Coloureds and Indians but completely excluded Black South Africans. An "explosion of political resistance" followed. "In a total rejection of apartheid," wrote activist Richard Knight, "black South Africans mobilized to make the townships ungovernable, black local officials resigned in droves, and the apartheid regime sent thousands of troops into the townships to quell 'unrest.'" In 1985 President P. W. Botha declared a state of emergency.[52]

Anti-apartheid activists around the world accelerated protests, demanding total isolation and repudiation of the regime. The blunt racism of Reagan's domestic and foreign policies fueled protest in the United States. The Reagan white house, according to one scholar, "plunged into a full-scale partnership with the racist regime. It increased military and nuclear collaboration, eased restrictions on the exports of U.S. goods to South African security forces . . . and approved the largest loan in South African history, just as the country was declaring war on students, workers, and neighboring countries." Reagan also engineered the first IMF loan to the apartheid state since 1975.[53]

Prexy returned to Chicago from Geneva and took a job organizing for the UAW while trying to catalyze a greater degree of anti-apartheid work in the city and the region. In 1983, Prexy, Cheryl Johnson-Odim, Carol Thompson, and Kevin Thompson founded the Coalition for Illinois Divestment from South Africa, or CIDSA. CIDSA members were both individuals and organizations, drawing unions, students, lawyers, churches, and an array of social justice organizations to fight for divestment in Chicago and Illinois. CIDSA members lobbied politicians, organized symposia, gave speeches, produced a quarterly newsletter, hosted delegations of South Africans, and organized demonstrations and picket lines. They understood that educating Illinoisans about conditions in southern Africa and US complicity with apartheid was a precondition to success, so they devoted considerable energy to disseminating educational materials and hosting speakers.

CIDSA was multiracial, with Black leadership, and had male and female co-chairs. Prexy lamented what he saw as the insular racial politics of Black Chicago, which in his view produced an unfortunate distrust of interracial organizing. While he certainly understood the roots of this distrust and sympathized with the dilemma, he had become committed both pragmatically and in principle to the multiracialism encouraged by the liberation movements in southern Africa. On this point, he doesn't think it's a coincidence that key Black leaders in CIDSA were not from Chicago; both Basil Clunie and Cheryl Johnson-Odim hailed from New York City.

Cheryl Johnson (later Johnson-Odim) moved to the Chicago area for doctoral study in African history at Northwestern. She first met Prexy in 1972. "Prexy always brought a kind of a gravitas to whatever he did or does, and part of that gravitas is the fact that he's brilliant. Part of the gravitas is the fact that he has done work in the movement all over the world, and so he's always been an internationalist. You don't always find that, at least in those days." Johnson recalled that she and Prexy "bonded because we were both Black and progressive" and shared a similar sense of what the movement was about. "Its destination was never everybody gets a nice house; it just wasn't about that." They co-chaired CIDSA. "We trusted one another," Johnson-Odim reflected, "but working in CIDSA certainly increased the bond because we were working together all the time for several years."[54]

Johnson-Odim took note of the experience Prexy brought to organizing. "He had so much street cred around the world, and he brought all of that to CIDSA." She also chaired the Chicago committee of TransAfrica, a Washington-based African American foreign affairs advocacy group, and would later serve as the national chair of Trans-Africa's local affiliates. For Johnson-Odim transnational dialogue was essential, stressing that "you need to be in contact with people who are on the front line." CIDSA strove to be continuously engaged with South Africans and "in some ways take [their] cue from them."[55]

A white woman from Palatine, Illinois, active with Clergy and Laity Concerned and Christians for Socialism, Carol Thompson began her anti-apartheid activism in the effort to defend exiled South African poet Dennis Brutus from deportation. And then "everything changed" when she met Prexy. Thompson's church was one of only two in the entire country that contributed funds to the WCC's Programme Against Racism. Most US Protestant denominations fiercely opposed sending money to national liberation groups engaged in armed struggle. She recalls having coffee with Prexy and marveling at their many connections overseas. "So that's when we formed CIDSA." Describing her role as "the chief cook and bottle washer," Thompson did the behind the scenes work of making newsletters, phone calls, and packets of literature as well as handling the books and finances. Her spouse Kevin Thompson was also actively involved and brought his professional experience in technology to serve the movement's work. Thompson credits her Black comrades with challenging her to confront white privilege more deeply in both American life and movement organizing.[56]

Basil Clunie, a child of Jamaican immigrants, graduated from City College of New York, where he had been active in anti-apartheid organizing while a member of the Organization of Afro-American Unity, formed by Malcolm X after his departure from the Nation of Islam. Clunie moved to Chicago in 1968 to attend graduate school. His friend Cheryl Johnson told him about CIDSA and Clunie eagerly joined, making lifelong friends and comrades.[57]

A concise, illustrated CIDSA pamphlet shows their efforts to convey basic yet politically sophisticated information. Why focus on South Africa?

South Africa is the only country in the world today where white supremacy is written into the constitution. A white minority in South Africa benefits from the oppression of the black majority through a social and economic system known as apartheid. In this system 87% of the land is reserved for the 16% of the population which is white. Over 3.5 million blacks—Africans, Asians, and 'coloreds' (people of mixed descent)—have been forcibly relocated under apartheid; over 2.5 million Africans have been resettled to remote, barren areas known as 'homelands.' In these 'homelands' 50% of all children die before the age of five. Officially, blacks are not citizens of South Africa, cannot vote or form political parties. Some independent black trade unions exist, but they operate under strict government control and their leaders are frequently harassed, detained and tortured. Malnutrition, high unemployment, and a lack of all political rights are the reality for black people in South Africa, while white South Africans enjoy the highest standard of living in the world.

And what did this have to do with Americans?

350 American corporations now support the South African economy through direct investments and trade. In 1980, U.S. exports to South Africa jumped by 50% to make the U.S. the largest trading partner of South Africa. U.S. multinational corporations and banks have over $14 billion shoring up the South African economy; they control 43% of the South Africa's petroleum market, 23% of its motor vehicle sales, and 75% of its computer business.[58]

Over several years state legislators Carol Moseley Braun and Woods Bowman introduced divestment bills in Springfield that went nowhere, even as Johnson-Odim testified in Springfield on the ways that divestment could be done in a fiscally responsible manner. CIDSA's discovery that a new state office building in downtown Chicago was being built with South African steel at a time when the large steel plants on the city's South Side had recently closed handed activists a powerful new strategy. Activists had long tried to connect local injustices to international injustices—both to deepen understanding of the globally enmeshed character of racial capitalism and to reach people emotionally. As Basil Clunie put it, "letting people know that Americans were being put out of work at the same time that essentially slave labor was helping to build steel that was being used in our state office building made a big effect with people in many different local communities."[59]

Clunie headed CIDSA's Steel Task Force and organized a large demonstration at the May 1985 dedication of the State of Illinois Building. Clearly embarrassed by the discovery, the governor claimed that only two beams of South African steel were used. "Contrary to the Governor's line," CIDSA wrote, "at least 30 to 40 beams of steel from South Africa were used in the construction of the building. The exact number of beams, of course, is not important; the use of any South African steel symbolizes the bitter irony of using the tax money paid by Illinois residents to support the South African steel industry while massive numbers of area steelworkers are unemployed." Moreover, banks were enabling this capital flight to South Africa: "Continental Illinois Bank has participated in a $300 million loan to the Iron and Steel Corporation of South Africa, while doing nothing to prevent the local Southworks plant from closing its doors."[60]

CIDSA organized tours to pressure the legislature. In April 1985 with sponsorship from the ACOA, WOA, and the AFSC, CIDSA activists, including Prexy, toured Illinois with twelve nationally known South Africans and South Africa experts. They visited thirty-five Illinois cities and towns, giving presentations and press interviews.[61] Black South African speakers were vital to piercing South Africa's propaganda against sanctions. Dumisani Kumalo, an exiled South African journalist who joined the ACOA staff and became instrumental to their work in the 1980s, linked divestment to human rights in an address to a large University of Illinois audience. Dumisani stressed the moral contradiction involved in US financial support of the South African regime: "I ask people in this country if they want their universities to make

Figure 8. Cheryl Johnson of CIDSA with Dumisani Kumalo, projects director of the ACOA, December 1983. Courtesy of Jim Cason and Cheryl Johnson-Odim.

money, and they tell me yes. Then I say, well why not invest in cocaine, or pornography? They tell me those are wrong, and I ask, then why invest in racism? What is the difference? Where do you draw the line?"[62]

These voices became even more important as South African authorities cracked down with alarming severity at South Africans' attempts to protest. In the latter half of the 1980s, more than thirty thousand people were imprisoned without charges, and scores of United Democratic Front and Congress of South African Trade Unions (COSATU) leaders were tried on charges of sedition and treason for conducting peaceful protests.[63]

CIDSA members appeared on the local PBS public affairs program *Chicago Tonight*, explaining and urging divestment. The *Chicago Defender* covered their work. But just as often activists had to strategize to overcome the biased local media coverage. A very effective tactic was showcasing the voices of visiting southern Africans who narrated their own struggles for self-determination against colonial or minority rule. This proved crucial in countering what Clunie describes as the "Cold War lens" of the *Chicago Tribune*.[64] After a *Tribune* editorial claimed divestment would hurt Black South Africans—a group it had no record of ever defending—CIDSA's Carol Thompson fired off an indignant letter, clarifying that the economic pressure was aimed at white South Africans, a group who "enjoyed the highest standard of living in the world," with the goal of pushing them to negotiate "with the Black majority for full and free political and economic participation" in their nation.[65] Likewise, West Side alderman Danny Davis replied to radio station WBBM's claim that a city ordinance would interfere with the federal prerogative to make foreign policy, with the reminder "that change is essentially a bottom-up process and I shudder to imagine what our country would be if we always waited for the federal government to shape, mold, and direct public opinion."[66]

A CIDSA community forum showcased the internationalist solidarity that was a major component of the US left during the Reagan years. The event, One Struggle, "brought together South Africa, Central America, and Caribbean activists to discuss the similarities in these regional conflicts as well as the Reagan administration's foreign policies toward these areas." The forum was held in the Latino neighborhood of Pilsen in the morning and a South Side Black church in the afternoon. As ever, anti-apartheid activists focused on the wider region, emphasizing that the apartheid state was a threat to not only Black South Africans but to the possibility of independent nations being able to thrive on its border. The WOA's Jean Sindab declared that the "root cause of famine in Africa is not climatic conditions, but the wars which have resulted in billions of dollars in damage in Angola caused by South African attacks and millions of deaths in both Angola and Mozambique." Reagan's policy of constructive engagement, she insisted, was actually "an alliance with South Africa." Sindab assailed the focus on "Soviet expansionism" as a diversion tactic by the US media and noted that Washington had recently extended a warm welcome to Jonas Savimbi, leader of the group waging war on the elected government of Angola, as he whipped up a "red scare" to win greater covert aid. John Saul, a Canadian scholar who had lived in Mozambique, said the US-supported counterrevolutionary guerrillas there aimed to "kill the dream, not just the revolution."[67]

In addition to public speaking and organizing, Prexy regularly wrote for a public audience. In 1986 he penned *Apartheid In Our Living Rooms: U.S. Foreign Policy and South Africa*, a fifty-eight-page "comprehensive primer on current conditions in South Africa" that exposes the long arc of US presence in South Africa and assesses American policy across southern Africa.[68]

Chicago's first Black mayor, Harold Washington, offered significant support to the anti-apartheid movement which peaked during his time in office. Washington faced jarring and overt racial vitriol on the campaign trail and in office. On the eve of the 1983 primary, Edward Vrdolyak, a powerful Democratic alderman, reportedly told precinct captains, "It's a racial thing, don't kid yourself. I'm calling on you to save your city, to save your precinct. We're fighting to keep the city the way it is."[69] Washington won but faced years of opposition by members of his own party in the city council. Mayor Washington was very supportive of the city's growing anti-apartheid movement. After he threatened to pull city funds from the First National Bank of Chicago and Continental Illinois Bank, both banks halted sales of the Krugerrands, South African gold coins, whose sale abroad raised significant revenue for the regime.[70] Mayor Washington welcomed many visiting southern African liberation leaders, bestowing official honors on many who were at the same time deemed terrorists by the Reagan administration. In the words of labor activist Kathy Devine, the movement "was rolling on a high" with Harold Washington as mayor. She especially recalls a visit by Archbishop Desmond Tutu. "I'll never forget the day in 1985 when Harold and Bishop Tutu stood together and said the doors of City Hall are now open to the people of South Africa." Prexy and Harold Rogers organized a big event at City Hall in 1987 where Oliver Tambo, president of the ANC, was given a key to the city. "That was a coup," since the State Department still characterized the ANC as a terrorist organization. Tambo arrived with one security person, but the Afro-American Patrolman's League, a Black caucus of the Chicago Police Department, provided additional security. Tambo spoke at Operation PUSH's headquarters on the South Side where the audience of over nine hundred gave him a "rapturous welcome."[71]

Mayor Washington also greeted a delegation from the South West African People's Organization (SWAPO) from Namibia, which was under illegal occupation by South Africa. Men and women from SWAPO and the Ndilimani Cultural Troupe flanked the mayor for a photo at City Hall. For Prexy, the contrasts were dramatic and sharp. This was the era of the "council wars"—where conservative aldermen lined up to block the progressive African American mayor's initiatives. And at the same time, dancers from SWAPO performed in front of the City Council.[72] Indeed, internationalists were all over the Washington administration. Cheryl Harris, an active member of CIDSA who would become a very influential legal scholar, was a lawyer for the city. She later married Prexy's dear friend, the exiled South African poet Keorapetse (Bra Willie) Kgositsile. Attorney Tim Wright, whom Prexy first met at the UN in the 1970s, served in multiple capacities: as special counsel, director of Intergovernmental Affairs, and commissioner of economic development. "Harold and I were extremely close," Wright noted. "He was my mentor. He taught me politics." Wright would later participate through the National Lawyers Guild in the negotiations around South Africa's first post-apartheid constitution.[73]

Prexy even came to work for the mayor during his tragically brief second term. "How do I know you?" the mayor asked Prexy during his job interview. "Well, I was the one who testified in City Council in favor of divestment," Prexy replied. "Clearly you're somebody I want on my side!" the mayor exclaimed, assigning Prexy to a four-person team dubbed the Mod Squad who reported to the mayor on community relations and hot spots in the neighborhoods. Mayor Washington often showed up at the annual South African Women's Day backyard barbeques at the West Side home of Ronelle Mustin, which became a gathering place for the Black left anti-apartheid network. Despite the vitriol heaped on the mayor and his tragic death in office, Prexy contends that Harold Washington's leadership ultimately transformed racial politics in Chicago.[74]

THE FREE SOUTH AFRICA MOVEMENT

A wave of civil disobedience beginning in late 1984 accelerated a change in US public opinion toward South Africa and increased pressure on Congress to pass sanctions against the apartheid regime. TransAfrica catapulted to the frontlines of the anti-apartheid movement when its leader and three prominent African Americans were arrested on the day before Thanksgiving in 1984 to protest "constructive engagement" and a massive crackdown in South Africa. In response to the biggest work stoppage in the nation's history, the Pretoria regime had sent thousands of troops into Black townships, killing dozens and arresting thousands, including thirteen Black trade union leaders. Randall Robinson, Mary Frances Berry, Eleanor Holmes Norton, and Walter Fauntroy were arrested after sitting-in at the South African embassy, sparking what became known as the Free South Africa movement. Civil disobedience spread wherever there were South African consulates—including in Chicago. The daily picket lines at consulates gave thousands of people a new way to get involved, and over five thousand nationwide were arrested. In turn, the explosion of college student protest later that spring proved a tipping point. The call for divestment was mainstream and growing. Even Republican politicians got arrested at the embassy in Washington.[75]

In Chicago, Black women launched the local Free South Africa Movement (FSM). Their savvy organizing led to the first trial in the country of activists who had been arrested and charged—an event in which activists succeeded in reversing the equation by putting apartheid on

Figure 9. Prexy Nesbitt speaking at a divestment rally at the University of Illinois Urbana-Champaign, April 7, 1986. Courtesy of Jeff Machota and Prexy Nesbitt.

trial instead. The FSM helped expand the local movement, bringing in greater Black leadership and grassroots involvement, especially from Black nationalists wary of joining the interracial CIDSA. On the day of the embassy arrests in Washington, Salih Booker of TransAfrica telephoned Cheryl Johnson-Odim, urging her to "get something going" in Chicago. She began phoning key Black activists—notably Alice Palmer, Bob Starks, and Conrad Worrill, and they convened a meeting at the institution where Starks and Worrill both taught—the Center for Inner City Studies, part of Northeastern Illinois University and a hub of organizing on the South Side. Hundreds came—including Black nationalists, union organizers, church leaders, veterans of the civil rights movement, and seasoned anti-apartheid activists.[76] Jeremiah Wright, pastor of Trinity United Church of Christ, who had put a Free South Africa sign in front of his church in 1980, came and would play a key role in galvanizing anti-apartheid sentiment in Black Chicago. Incarcerated ANC leaders would later say that word of his early solidarity had reached them and bolstered their morale. The women activists in the Church and Society Committee at Trinity, including Iva Carruthers, became leaders in the anti-apartheid movement transnationally. Carruthers found that Black Chicagoans could readily relate to apartheid because of the intensity of the segregation there. "It was up South for real," she said. A lifelong antiracist strategist and organizer, Alice

Palmer was working in African American student affairs at Northwestern when she became a leader of the Chicago FSM. On the morning of the first demonstration, she huddled with Johnson-Odim at a hotel across from the consulate in the heart of downtown Chicago mapping out a strategy for daily picket lines and civil disobedience.[77]

The first demonstration took place on December 6 in front of the South African consulate on Michigan Avenue. "There must have been a thousand people," Johnson-Odim recalled. And "it was one of the coldest days of the year." They planned a high-profile arrest. Ora Schub, a white lawyer (and pioneer in the later restorative justice movement) went inside pretending to be an ordinary traveler in need of a visa. African American TV reporter Art Norman accompanied Schub in her task, as she discreetly left the door ajar for Jacqueline Jackson, Congressman Gus Savage, and State Senator Richard Newhouse to sneak in and conduct a sit-in. They were arrested, but South Africa undermined their publicity goal by refusing to press charges against such well-known figures. The daily demonstrations went on for well over a year but peaked shortly after Harold Washington's inauguration.[78]

Another planned arrest took place on a chilly day in January 1985 with about a thousand demonstrators, including folk singer Pete Seeger and several ANC representatives. Several people entered the building, were arrested, and spent the night in jail including Addie Wyatt, legendary labor, faith, and political leader; Bob Lucas, veteran of the civil rights movement; and Heather Booth, a white New Leftist, founder of the Jane Collective, and later influential figure in Democratic Party politics. Another group was arrested on February 2. Mayor Washington was happy to drop the charges, but both groups wanted a trial because they planned to put the apartheid state on trial. The defense team relied on the rarely used theory of "the law of necessity" to argue that apartheid was so heinous that the fifteen defendants had a right and obligation to do whatever they could to halt it. They brought in witnesses to describe the horrors of apartheid, including US Senator

Paul Simon and South African poet Dennis Brutus. The jury was persuaded and acquitted the defendants: one juror even asked how she could join the movement! "Reagan's policy is doomed," declared the Rev. Orlando Redekopp upon their victory.[79]

Alice Palmer and scholar-activist Fannie Rushing were particularly outraged at a *Chicago Tribune* story about how "wonderful it was for children in South Africa." The *Tribune* offices were across the street from the consulate. A South African woman with the ANC stood in front of the consulate and read the names of children who had been killed in the struggle while demonstrators carried a coffin up and down the sidewalk. At first, Palmer recalled that people came out of the *Tribune* building and just pointed and laughed. "But we kept it up day after day. And finally it got to be embarrassing to them." An executive with the paper met with Palmer, Rushing, and the South African activist. Alice insisted that he directly address the ANC activist: "We said don't talk to us; tell her why you are publishing photographs saying how wonderful it is in the midst of apartheid. This woman represents the mothers and sisters and daughters who were murdered. Tell her." That was the end, Palmer recalled. "They never printed any more of those photos."[80]

By the mid-1980s, the Free South Africa and divestment movements had transformed consciousness across the United States. In his 1984 presidential run, Jesse Jackson frequently condemned US support for apartheid, helping to reframe the alliance as a "moral disgrace" rather than a strategic necessity. Students were forcing universities to contend with their relationship with apartheid, getting major publicity and beginning to win key battles nationwide, most notably at Columbia University in New York. Prexy spoke at over four hundred campuses in those years, visiting every state except Mississippi.[81]

Prexy inspired scores of young people. He first met Heeten Kalan, a South African of Indian descent, in British Columbia in the mid-1980s. Kalan's student club had invited Prexy to give a talk. Prexy spoke more informally with students later that evening. "There were about three hundred students around this fireplace," Prexy recalled. "We talked and talked and talked. And the questions and the comments were just unbelievable. The depth of them, the sophistication of them." Heeten moved on to Dartmouth where he met his future wife, Jenny Dahlstein, a student from Sweden, and they joined the robust divestment movement. Prexy visited a few times during their campaign. "He's such an engaging speaker and he spoke not just from the heart but with a lot of personal experience and knowledge," Jenny recalled. "And it's just different to hear from someone who's been to all these places, met people who are involved locally on the ground, in these different movements. It adds a whole other dimension to what you might read in a book."[82]

Prexy shared news with Heeten and Jenny about other campus struggles and connected them to the ACOA and other groups. "Prexy was one of the bridges we had to the broader anti-apartheid movement," Heeten noted. "I mean it's in college that I knew about people like Bill Minter and Imami Countess and Jean Sindab and what they were all doing." For his senior thesis, Heeten conducted an oral history of the Black South African Trade Union Movement from 1973 to 1979, and many of the people he interviewed became government leaders, including Cyril Ramaphosa.

After college the couple continued working closely with Prexy, including producing *Baobab Notes*, a newsletter Prexy had begun, which included original writing alongside summaries and reprints of news and views on southern Africa. Heeten and Jenny put it together it in their small Boston apartment for several years in the 1990s, with Prexy still part of the editorial team. Jenny recalls laughing at the letters they'd get saying, "Dear Editorial Department, or Dear Publishers, or Dear Subscription Department." *Baobab Notes* reached a large audience. Heeten is still surprised when he hears someone "waxing on about how great it was. To this day I'm still blown away when people talk about the *Baobab Notes* and how they looked forward to it and how it was their connection to that region."[83]

Prexy did many educational speaking tours for the AFSC during these years. "I remember one we did in Texas; I'll never forget that one. Bob (Van Lierop) and I were together, I was driving, and a car full of rednecks pulled up next to me. And these guys spit at me. Spit all over my arm. And I lost it for a minute. Bob said, 'Let's just get out of here. They've got too many people.'" They sped up and got off at the next exit. "I shot off, then shot back on, on the other side. Bob was right. They wanted to provoke."[84]

Coming together as Artists United Against Apartheid, cultural workers added their power to the movement. After learning about Sun City, a South African resort catering to wealthy whites, US musician Steve Van Zandt organized an international boycott. The song "Ain't Gonna Play Sun City," created by fifty-four leading jazz, rock, and hip hop singers, including Bruce Springsteen, Miles Davis, Bonnie Raitt, George Clinton, Peter Gabriel, and Run-DMC, raised over a million dollars for anti-apartheid organizations. Danny Schecter, an activist journalist whom Prexy first met in the African Research Group in Cambridge in the early 1970s, was with ABC's 20/20 at the time, and teamed up with Van Zandt to organize the boycott and enlist the artists. When Van Zandt demurred from asking his bandmate Springsteen to join the effort, Schecter had no qualms. Likewise, when Van Zandt hesitated to approach the legendary Davis, Schecter got him on board. Danny invited Prexy to watch a studio session in New York. The "person that stole the show that night was Miles Davis, who came in high as a kite" and did "this incredible piece of music." Schecter later made a documentary and wrote a book about Nelson Mandela.[85]

DIVESTMENT

By the mid-1980s, the movement was winning divestment in states, cities and campuses across the country, moving public opinion and increasing pressure on Congress to act. Ultimately CIDSA's education and pressure campaigns, alongside the moral witness of the Free South Africa Movement, succeeded in pushing the city and state to pass divestment legislation. Chicago passed an ordinance in May 1986 that barred the city from depositing funds in banks that do business with South Africa and barred contracts with corporations involved in South Africa or Namibia. In 1987 Illinois finally enacted a bill barring future investments in South Africa. The laws were not sweeping and comprehensive; they were full of compromises and loopholes. And yet, in Prexy's view, "it was important to build public support" and to change the image of the US internationally from a pro-apartheid state to one with a thriving and growing anti-apartheid population. The new laws "sent a message to South Africa that the people of Illinois want no part in the profit of apartheid." CIDSA saw its work as part of the grassroots consciousness raising and groundwork that pushed Congress to finally act.[86]

These were years of dramatic developments. In January 1985 Senator Edward Kennedy went to South Africa to show his support for the ANC; he visited the banned Winne Mandela and tried to visit Nelson Mandela, but was rebuffed. "Behind these walls are men who are deeply committed to the cause of freedom in this land," Kennedy said as he led a dramatic protest in front of Pollsmoor Prison.[87] In March, Ted Koppel's daily television show *Nightline* devoted a week to South Africa. *Nightline* had become appointment TV for the movement—and Koppel's coverage would continue to grow. In the spring students at Columbia University blockaded the main administration building for weeks—sparking similar protests nationwide. In August, South African President P. W. Botha "dealt constructive engagement yet another blow" with an incendiary speech. "I am not prepared to lead white South Africans and other minority groups on a road to abdication and suicide," he declared. Afterwards, Archbishop Desmond Tutu said, "the chances of peaceful change are virtually nil." Later that month, international banks refused to renew South African loans, and a South African business delegation met with the ANC in Lusaka.[88]

A Republican filibuster defeated sanctions in 1985, but the following June the House passed a strong bill sponsored by anti-apartheid stalwart Ron Dellums. Movement strategists focused on moving moderate Senate Republicans to their side to gain the necessary supermajority. ACOA leaders saw Kansas Republican Nancy Kassenbaum, chairwoman of the Senate Foreign Relations Committee on Africa as susceptible to pressure. They enlisted Prexy to crisscross the state with Nomonde Ngubo, a South Africa trade unionist. They made forty stops to mobilize constituent pressure on Kassenbaum. "I drove everywhere, and we stayed in hotels, cots, and couches, and ate meals that people gave us. It was organizing in its most wonderful moments, because you're so tied with people." Prexy stresses how important it was for Americans to hear the voices of South Africans directly impacted by apartheid. "You know what got people most excited? It wasn't my speaking. It was her speaking; it was her singing. People would flood places to come and hear her sing." As it happens, after a ten-day visit to several African nations in the early fall, Kassenbaum "abandoned her support of constructive engagement."[89]

The Senate passed a weaker sanctions bill in August, but its veto-proof majority brought the House on board producing a historic act of congress to isolate and punish the apartheid state. In September, the White House announced that President Reagan would veto the sanctions bill despite a warning from Senate sponsor Richard Lugar that "we really need to be on the right side of history in this case." Sure enough, Reagan vetoed the bill, but in October in a stunning rebuke of "constructive engagement" and a major foreign policy defeat for the White House, Congress overrode his veto.[90]

For veteran internationalist Bill Minter, "Reagan's veto made a Senate bill that I and other activists felt was a weak one far more significant. When the Republican Senate and the Democratic House both overrode the veto, a clear message was sent to South Africa—the people's representatives within the government of the United States had trumped the executive branch and had taken control of the character of the sanctions that would be imposed." By overturning Reagan's veto, the movement had finally succeeded in turning what the right had long framed as a Cold War geopolitical issue into a straight moral question. "After decades of work, activists had been successful in making votes on apartheid become referenda on racism."[91]

After sanctions took root, and many began to envision the end of apartheid, new internecine strife began to consume South Africa. Oliver Tambo, the legendary ANC president living in exile in London, visited Chicago to acknowledge the importance of this center of anti-apartheid ferment and progressive Black political power. He met with Mayor Washington, who declared January 24, 1987 "South African Freedom Day" and presented President Tambo with a key to the city. Tambo spoke at Rainbow/PUSH with Jesse Jackson, whose 1984 presidential campaign had made divestment a priority and whose 1988 campaign would feature calls for sweeping change in US policy toward southern Africa. He met with US representative Charlie Hayes, an outspoken critic of apartheid. At the Center for Inner City Studies in Bronzeville, a base of the Free South Africa Movement, Tambo made a prediction which sadly turned out to be true: "We believe that in that brief period which stands between now and the collapse of that brutal system there's going to be a most vicious confrontation between those who seek freedom and peace and those who live by violence upon Blacks and other oppressed people." He warned that Inkatha leader Buthelezi was making a power play in the changing political situation in South Africa: he had abruptly turned against the ANC and was unleashing violence against UDF forces and counseling submission to the regime.[92]

On the eve of winning sanctions, Prexy contemplated new directions for the movement in a piece for *The Black Scholar*. He wanted readers to grasp the degree to which the apartheid state was waging campaigns of terror against independent nations on its borders. The fight for Angolan, Namibian, and Mozambican peace and freedom, he argued, was critical to the fight against apartheid, and vice versa. He warned that Washington was free to fund these other wars even as sanctions tied its hands in South Africa. The Clark Amendment barring US support for Angolan rebels was repealed in 1985. "The Frontline States, particularly Angola, form the backbone for the liberation movements. They have provided supplies; they are the source of a rear base for the ANC and SWAPO; they are sites where apartheid's victims can be brought." As a result, he explained, South Africa, with US cooperation, "has given military assistance to counter revolutionary forces operating within the borders of Angola and Mozambique." Bills currently before Congress asked for millions for Unita in Angola and the Mozambican National Resistance (MNR) in Mozambique. "The U.S. anti-apartheid movement must be unceasing in its work to see that these bills are defeated," he wrote. He noted that the Reagan administration had sought to normalize the funding of opposition groups in Nicaragua and warned that aid to Unita and the MNR would only accelerate the drive to normalize regime change in socialist-leaning countries. Prexy called for a pivot from opposition to support: "We must go from being merely anti-apartheid to being supportive of the specific national liberation movements in their quests for the total destruction of apartheid and in their creation of new societies in southern Africa."[93] In the next chapter, I explore how this unfolded in Mozambique.

4

OUR SOPHISTICATED WEAPON

The Forgotten Story of Internationalist Mozambique

> Until the present time the United States has been able, generally, to cloak its exploitative and oppressive role in Southern Africa behind hypocritical public posturing and a sea of ignorance on the part of American citizens. The actual role of the United States, both directly and through its allies, Portugal and South Africa, in destroying the lives and freedoms of African peoples must be made known. If we, as Americans, are to translate professed commitments to freedom and independence into reality, there is only one course open to us: we must support, by all available means, the Mozambique Revolution.

PREXY GREATLY ADMIRED FRELIMO, and that attachment deepened after Mozambique won independence and Frelimo pushed to make decolonization truly transformative. Frelimo consisted of true believers: the core group that waged the long guerrilla struggle would govern for years, and while they remained committed to their internationalism, they revised social and economic policies as conditions warranted. Just as Cuba had become a beacon and destination for many leftists who wanted to help build socialism, so too did Mozambique.

After independence, Mozambique attracted support from internationalists around the world, including extended stays by hundreds of *cooperantes*, who brought their skills to help build and develop Mozambique. But almost immediately Rhodesia and South Africa saw this socialist internationalist neighbor as a threat to their regimes of minority rule, and each took their turn in organizing and training rural terrorists to pillage the countryside, brutalize peasants, burn villages, and create as much havoc as possible to rollback development and destabilize the government. A harrowing history, barely reported upon and mostly forgotten in the United States, the counter-insurgency, like the one in Angola, shows how South Africa's ruthless regime—albeit with willing local partners—brought death and destruction to the whole region. Mozambique mobilized a network of allies in the US to press its cause in Washington.

SAMORA MACHEL AND INDEPENDENT MOZAMBIQUE

Exhausted from the long colonial wars and restrictions on their freedoms by a fascist regime, Portuguese soldiers toppled their country's dictatorship in June 1974, paving the way a year later for Mozambican independence. Mozambicans celebrated and savored the moment. "We do not hide the difficulties," Samora Machel declared, but "for the first time the Mozambican people have a government of their own, a government of their representatives, a government to serve them."[1] On the eve of independence, "thousands of Mozambicans flocked to the streets in order to wait for the strike of midnight. As the bell tolled, a new flag was raised and power passed from the Portuguese interim government to Samora Machel," the first president of the new Republic.[2]

Frelimo faced immense challenges. Most managers, doctors, merchants, technicians, administrators and other trained personnel left upon independence. Many departing Portuguese sabotaged property.[3] As Eduardo Mondlane had long stressed, Frelimo's task was literally to create Mozambique and forge a national identity out of the ten major ethnic groups with their own languages, customs and culture. Colonial

Figure 10. Poster of Samora Machel, celebrating the independence of Mozambique. Courtesy of Anti-Apartheid Movement Collection, Archives and Special Collections, Columbia College Chicago.

Mozambique had been structured to service outsiders. Internal transport links were recent. The coup in Lisbon surprised Frelimo which had to quickly plan for postcolonial leadership. The Portuguese had prevented Frelimo from gaining traction in the middle and southern sections of Mozambique, so it had to introduce itself to millions of people.

Mozambique would have to figure out a new relationship with South Africa, a white supremacist nation on its border with an advanced military, which had dominated the colonial economy. Portugal had "leased" Mozambican workers to South African mining companies, and South Africa had paid Lisbon for use of the port at Maputo. At independence, half of Mozambican foreign exchange came from these labor payments and port fees.[4] What would replace them? Adding to the challenge was the ambition of Frelimo's vision. They promised free access to education and health care; women's equality; the reorganization of agriculture and other work away from exploitative and extractive arrangements toward cooperative and collectivist experiments.

Frelimo dramatically expanded access to education. Graça Machel, the spouse of the president and only woman in a top post, served as Minister of Education until 1989 and fought to implement universal education. Frelimo quickly built scores of schools and Tanzania sent teachers to help staff them. Children learned in the mornings and adults attended in afternoon and evening shifts. They made remarkable strides. Machel aimed to "turn the country into a school in which everyone learns, and everyone teaches."[5]

They made similarly rapid gains in health care. "By 1978, most of the population had been vaccinated against smallpox, polio, and measles, and by the early 1980s, twelve hundred rural health posts had been built and staffed," a physician involved noted; "over eight thousand health workers were trained and employed." With only about forty physicians for eleven million people, Mozambique reached out to supporters abroad, mostly in the socialist bloc, and recruited several hundred health care professionals who delivered care but also trained Mozambicans. The Portuguese word for these visitors with technical expertise was *cooperantes.*[6]

Women across the global south leveraged anticolonial struggles to improve their position in society and renegotiate gender roles. Sometimes this brought post-independence gains; often it did not. Women played an important role in the armed struggle, and Frelimo created the Organization of Mozambican Women (OMM) in 1973. Samora Machel spoke eloquently about the multifaceted nature of women's subordination and stressed that "the liberation of women is a fundamental necessity for the Revolution, the guarantee of its continuity and the precondition for its victory."[7] And yet male dominance defined the new nation even as Frelimo challenged such traditional practices as bride price, polygyny, and female initiation rites. Frelimo's top leadership was male, and while the creation of public childcare, and the nationalization of health and education provision certainly benefited women, specific gender concerns and issues were downplayed. "As in other countries, socialism and feminism did not always make a neat package," according to one scholar, "but in articulating a politics that posited an end to oppression, it did bring about improvements for women."[8]

American peace activist Medea Benjamin passed through Mozambique and her observations from an OMM meeting illustrate the challenges: "Despite the efforts of Frelimo to make changes regarding gender, the bride price still existed as did polygamy. Parents objected to sending daughters to school. Frelimo was actively fighting these practices. They expelled men who had been/were polyamorous, fought against the bride price, and greatly decreased prostitution (nearly eliminated). Women were being taught construction, cultivation, sanitation, and nutrition skills."[9]

Frelimo was committed to an expansive sense of national belonging. "No one fought for a region, race, tribe or religion," Frelimo insisted. "We all fought and are still fighting for the same nation, for the single ideal of liberating our land and our people."[10] But Frelimo's rejection of "racialism" should not be mistaken for color-blindness or a refusal to see the entrenched nature of white supremacy. Machel insisted that that "all superiority and inferiority complexes created and reinforced by centuries of colonialism must be completely eliminated." Whites, Asians, and mixed-race people must "wage a profound internal struggle and eliminate the attitudes of superiority and paternalism towards blacks." But Machel was under no illusions that forging this new society would be easy. It would take "a conscious effort to change attitudes and habits, a deliberate effort to make people of the different races which make up our people, live together in harmony."[11]

In the context of weak national bonds, promoting cultural expression helped foster unity. Vivid colors, dance, poetry, music, and murals were everywhere. "There was a very poetic side to Samora that is found in the culture of the Mozambicans," Prexy recalls. "They're all poets. It's always fascinated me that all these leaders wrote poetry. All of them. And Samora was not an exception, he wrote poetry too."

Frelimo's love of poetry moved Prexy, who grew up in a household where poetry was sacred and the prominent poet Robert Hayden was virtually a member of the family.[12]

At the center of Frelimo's vision was an economy free of exploitation, but delivering on this vision was tough. Mozambique started from a position of tremendous underdevelopment yet considerable revolutionary zeal. In 1977 Frelimo formally embraced Marxist-Leninism, although in some respects its moves replicated configurations it inherited from the Portuguese. Frelimo's plan prioritized industrialization, state farms, and communal villages. A major state farm in the Limpopo Valley resembled the Portuguese *colonato* which had displaced peasants from their lands; similarly, Frelimo's communal villages were built on former *aldeamentos*, the fortified villages the Portuguese had forcibly relocated peasants to during the war.[13] The state farms turned out to be a dismal failure, due to inexperience, poor management and machinery, and lack of enthusiasm among the peasants.[14]

Frelimo's profound challenge was in finding ways to reorient Mozambique's economic activity away from the apartheid state. This meant trying to reduce the reliance on wages earned by sending Mozambicans to work in dangerous South African mines; keeping the energy generated from the Cahora Basa damn, the largest hydroelectric power plant in southern Africa, which the Portuguese built toward the end of their rule, inside Mozambique rather than sending it to South Africa; and working with other frontlines states to reroute the lucrative flow of regional trade through Mozambique's ports rather than South Africa's. These proved to be uphill battles. Not only was South Africa the economic giant in the neighborhood; it was also the bully. As Prexy put it, "Mozambique was never in the position to develop independently of the stranglehold that the apartheid economy had on it. The reality that so much of the income of Mozambique was based on servicing the apartheid regime, especially in terms of mining, created a very difficult situation."[15]

As one Frelimo leader put it many years later, "Sanctions are the most effective way of putting pressure on the apartheid regime. But Mozambique itself will never be in a position to do so mainly because we are more dependent on South Africa than it is on us. South African sanctions against *us*—such as cutting back the number of Mozambican miners, reducing use of our ports and railroads—have had a catastrophic effect on our foreign exchange earnings."[16]

And still, Frelimo's foreign policy was steeped in "its internationalist duty of solidarity." In a 1977 address to the United Nations, President Machel promised Mozambique's full compliance with sanctions against Rhodesia. This cost the young nation an estimated $150 million per year. Above all, Samora declared, apartheid must end: "The existence of this regime, hostile to humanity, creates intolerable tension and constitutes a threat to the peoples of Africa."[17] There could be no truer statement, as South Africa's eventual turn to the "total strategy" to defend apartheid would lead to disastrous and deadly regional wars.

While an image of an AK-47—paying homage to the armed struggle—is on the Mozambican flag, peace was the dream of Mozambicans, indeed of most southern Africans. "Mozambique defends the principle of universal disarmament and of the immediate cessation of the arms race," Machel declared to the UN. He emphasized the responsibility of the West for repairing the injuries of colonialism. Responsibility he declared, "falls in particular on the highly developed countries, whose development process was achieved at the expense of those countries which today are the most backward." Machel voiced support for a "new international economic order" that fostered relations of economic cooperation among developing nations.[18]

"The commitment that Frelimo gave to ZANU [Zimbabwe African National Union] was the highest level of solidarity you can give," Prexy reflected, referring to one of the national liberation groups fighting to end white-rule in Rhodesia. "There would never have been an independent Zimbabwe had it not been for Frelimo bringing ZANU into the northern parts of Mozambique and opening the way for ZANU forces to fight the Smith regime," he noted, underscoring the importance of the ZANU military base in Mozambique. "They also gave ZANU a discipline and sense of how you conduct a liberation war. Josiah Tongogara, the man who should've been the head of Zimbabwe, instead of Robert Mugabe, if you ask me, was a special student of Samora Machel's. He was a wonderful man, a wonderful soldier. I got the pleasure to meet him in Northern Mozambique."[19]

Cash-strapped and impoverished, Mozambique paid a high price for this solidarity. It halted Rhodesian trade through its second-largest city Beira, forgoing crucial revenue, and it hosted over 150,000 Zimbabwean refugees, while facing violent Rhodesian reprisals. And in a development that would ultimately devastate Mozambique, Rhodesia and former members of the Portuguese army helped to form a group to terrorize Mozambicans; it was known as the Mozambique National Resistance (MNR) and later referred to by its Portuguese acronym, Renamo.[20]

Mozambique also supported the African National Congress (ANC), which kept an office in the capital Maputo, and engaged in military training in the north, which angered Pretoria. In many respects, though, Mozambique's sheer existence as an independent, antiracist, socialist, Black-ruled nation constituted an affront. South Africa dramatically reduced its recruitment of Mozambican mine workers, depriving families in the southern half of the nation of a leading source of income. After South Africa wrongly accused Mozambique of concentrating "sophisticated weapons" on its border, Machel hurled back, "the only thing the regime has to fear is our example." The sophisticated weapon, he declared, "is guaranteeing all citizens the right to study, culture, health, justice, progress, to the benefits of society. The sophisticated weapon is putting our resources into carrying this out and not into the manufacture of weapons, the production of death."[21]

Lisa Brock, a scholar-activist in Chicago and longtime friend of Prexy's, lived in Mozambique in the 1980s while conducting research for her dissertation and spent time with the ANC exiles there. It was very dangerous for them. "I met tons of South Africans. They were literally a government in exile. I met Joe Slovo, who ended up becoming a major hero. I met Chris Hani, and Albie Sachs, who ended up becoming a Constitutional Court Justice, and helped write the constitution." Sachs gave Lisa rides to the university in the same car that later blew up and almost killed him. "It was a scary time." Lisa intended to work with Slovo's wife, Ruth First, but she had been assassinated by a letter bomb.[22]

With pressing domestic needs and already controversial internationalist commitments, Frelimo avoided entanglement in superpower rivalries, embracing a genuine stance of non-alignment in the hope of getting aid from all sides. The USSR supplied some military aid, but Frelimo turned down a Soviet request for a naval base on its shores. Mozambique's relationship to the USSR was vexed—it resented the paternalist judgement by the Soviets that it hadn't reached the correct stage of development for certain investments, such as a steel plant. And in 1981, the USSR denied Mozambique full membership in the Council for Mutual Economic Assistance, or COMECON, a major Eastern Bloc economic alliance. At the same time, Mozambique signed an important commercial pact with China, even as it was critical of China's role in Angola and of its 1979 invasion of Vietnam.[23]

Socialist countries supplied doctors, planners, and teachers and gave scholarships for thousands of Mozambicans to study abroad. There was some Cuban assistance in agriculture and planning, but economic aid from socialist countries was far less significant than the military aid. Most economic aid came from Scandinavian countries. "It was consistent and always there," Prexy recalls. By the early 1980s, with insufficient economic support from the Eastern Bloc, Mozambique strove for closer ties with the West. Frelimo also hoped that Western investment might generate pressure on South Africa to not support Renamo.[24]

COOPERANTES, PART I

To compensate for the exodus of skilled workers after independence, Mozambique recruited professionals to come and stay for two years or so. These *cooperantes* hailed from Eastern and Western Europe, Cuba, Scandinavia, Chile, Canada, and the United States. Samora called them "militants who share a common cause and have put personal considerations in second place in order to help with National Reconstruction." Prexy met "a wonderful group of Chileans," who came after the US-backed coup of the socialist president Salvador Allende.[25]

Two American cooperantes who moved to Mozambique not long after independence illustrate the risks and rewards that came with this very tangible solidarity. Roberta Washington, who was a Black graduate student at Columbia in the early 1970s, studied with the renowned architect Max Bond. Bond, who designed scores of buildings in postcolonial Ghana, took students on a trip, which had a huge impact on Washington. "That trip changed my life, and although it was just Ghana that we saw, it was so informative. I came back wanting to do something in Africa like Max did."[26]

Back in New York, she went to a screening of *A Luta Continua*. "I was convinced by the film that it was Mozambique that I was looking for. I just fell in love with the leaders, and I fell in love with what they showed of the country." Her friends introduced her to Bob Van Lierop. "When they become independent," she told him, "I'm going to work there." He connected her to the Southern Africa Committee, a predominantly white solidarity group. "It took me years to feel like I belonged," Washington reflected. One evening while she was editing the group's newsletter from their small West 27th Street office, the FBI showed up, asking vague questions for which she gave equally vague responses. She never saw them again.[27]

At a reception near the United Nations, leaders of the newly independent Mozambique asked the roomful of activists if anyone wanted to come

Figure 11. Roberta Washington, left, with fellow cooperante Wendy Simmons, Maputo, Mozambique, 1980. Courtesy of Wendy Simmons.

live in Mozambique and a dozen hands shot up, including Washington's. She sent in her resume and didn't hear anything. A year later, at another reception, Joaquin Chissano said "I never got anything from you." So, she sent the information again and more time passed. At yet another reception, she finally learned that not having translated her resume into Portuguese was the problem. In the end, it was Chissano himself who translated her resume into Portuguese. Finally, in 1977 she was off to Mozambique. On the plane Washington realized that the Portuguese she had been studying "was more suited to Brazil than Mozambique," and upon arrival she encountered challenge after challenge. "But the fascinating part of it was that people came to Mozambique from all over the world." There were Brazilians, Chinese, Swedes, and Cubans. "My best friend was this other architect from the Philippines. A guy from Italy taught me how to ride a motorcycle, because I couldn't get a car." In addition to the Chinese, Cubans, and Soviets who were there on assignment, she estimates that 150–200 cooperantes overlapped with her.[28]

Roberta Washington stayed for four and a half years. She designed houses, health centers, schools, nurseries for cashew nut factory workers, and teacher-training schools. "But to say my first year was rough, would be an understatement," she recalled. "The Public Works Ministry assigned me to work with the last Portuguese architectural firm to remain in Mozambique." Working in that office, she said, "felt like being in Mississippi." She was later transferred to the Maputo Province Public Work's Office, where she ran the architectural department. Her greatest satisfaction was "being able to design things and see them go up where before there was nothing." At Portuguese language classes she got to know other cooperantes: "Throughout my whole time there, those people were my friends."

However, Washington avoided the US embassy in Maputo. "I think there was some edginess between cooperantes and people at the embassy," she recalled. "It's like our government wasn't on the side we thought they should be." After her first year in Mozambique, Roberta was excited to be flying home for a visit. But she ran into paperwork issues at the airport. She tried but couldn't send a telegram to her family who were to meet her in New York. Arriving home from work one day soon after, she saw a car with two white men inside sitting in front of her apartment building. "One of them jumped out and approached her, 'Are you Ms. Washington? We're from the embassy.' 'What's going on?' I asked." He handed her an envelope with a telegram in it and drove off. From Secretary of State George Schultz, it said, "Call your mother." Washington later learned that her friend at the American Embassy had overheard diplomats discussing the case of a Black American whom no one had ever heard of lost in Mozambique; her friend made the decision to give them Washington's address.[29]

Another cooperante, Stephen Gloyd, a physician from Seattle, arrived in early 1979 to find incredible underdevelopment. "I was sent to an isolated town along the Zambezi River as the only doctor for a district of seventy-five thousand people. We got electricity for two hours at lunchtime, then again in the evening. With about ten very good nurses, we were responsible for all health care in the district and a community health-worker training center." He was sent to another position a year later with even more difficult conditions. But the comradery and spirit amongst the workers and people motivated and sustained him. What made it hard were the first stirrings of warfare. "Our vehicles were frequently attacked and many of my colleagues were killed. Landmines were everywhere; about once a week we would treat somebody with a landmine injury."[30]

A few years later, Gloyd returned to Seattle where he became involved in anti-apartheid organizing and efforts to stop US support for Renamo. He and others launched the extraordinarily important Mozambique Health Committee, which sent many American cooperantes to Mozambique, including a doctor-nurse married couple, Paul and Andy Epstein. In camps for Zimbabwean refugees, the Epsteins discovered a horrific technique of torture used by the Rhodesians and later South Africans: poison was put in the clothes of refugees, causing extensive bleeding and then death. The World Health Organization confirmed it was warfarin, an anti-coagulant used to poison rats. The South Africans would use this and other chemical agents against anti-apartheid leaders.[31]

CONTRADICTIONS AND CHALLENGES

Samora Machel was famously puritanical and allergic to corruption. He drove a hard line within the party, warning on the eve of independence that "power and the facilities which surround rulers can easily corrupt the firmest man." Frelimo leaders must "live modestly and with the people" and reject "material, moral and ideological corruption, bribery, seeking comforts, string pulling, [and] nepotism" as "characteristic of the system which we are destroying."[32] Frelimo went through a period of intense internal debate in the early 1980s. A highly self-critical report found that growing signs of elitism and corruption risked alienating them from their peasant-worker base. People were ousted; roles changed. Machel's government launched a campaign against corruption in the state bureaucracy, including at ports, airlines, and the housing agency, and a year later extended the campaign to the military and police forces. Many complaints of abuse had been lodged against the police, some of which were holdovers from the colonial era. By 1982, four hundred police and security officials had been dismissed.[33]

Corruption was not the only challenge. Some of Frelimo's policies had inspired discontent among the people. Frelimo emphasized state planning, but the peasantry wanted autonomy. Machel believed in modernization, but he "was too honest with himself and too committed to his people to maintain an unalterable stance," according to another Frelimo leader, and in 1978 Machel enabled a shift to more family farming.[34] At the Fourth Congress in 1983 Frelimo acknowledged the failure of the state farming projects in the Limpopo valley and resolved to shift toward smaller scale production. Supporters of Mozambique admired Frelimo's willingness to adapt and change strategies as conditions demanded. "Frelimo has been able to innovate African Marxism (even) while it's under siege and fighting for sheer survival," noted John Saul, a Canadian social scientist and longtime Frelimo supporter.[35]

This flexibility was also demonstrated in foreign affairs. Mozambique made overtures to the US as it became clear that the USSR would not be able to provide sufficient economic investment or protect it militarily. As early as 1978 Machel had reached out to the West, and in the 1980s, he launched "charm offensives" in both London and Washington.[36]

War ravaged Mozambique in the 1980s and early 1990s, reversing many of the nation's early gains in health and education and exacting a devastating toll on human life and social well-being. After Zimbabwean independence in 1980, South Africa took over the training and funding of Renamo, and not long after, war enveloped the whole country. In 1984 Machel described the toll of a war, which was tragically only beginning: "Our people had their houses destroyed, their granaries looted, their crops pillaged and flattened, their cattle stolen and killed, their tools burnt and destroyed. The communal villages and cooperatives, the schools and clinics, the wells and dams built by the people with so much love, effort and sacrifice became targets for the enemy's criminal fury. The bandits have murdered and kidnapped peasants. This is the enemy's cruel nature—kill everything, steal everything, burn everything. The children who witnessed atrocities . . . will grow up with the nightmare of their tragic memories. Men and women who have been permanently mutilated and maimed, both physically and psychologically will be the living evidence of the cruelty of the war waged against us."[37]

Renamo cultivated disgruntled or dissident Mozambicans or those who fostered regionalist political ambitions. "Renamo's supporters were united by their opposition to Frelimo and did not share any other political platform," according to one scholar. While failed Frelimo policies may have brought Renamo some support, wrote another, "Renamo's plundering, brutality and terrorism quickly alienated most of the rural population who, above all else, wanted to be left alone."[38]

THE NKOMATI ACCORD AND ESCALATION OF ATROCITIES

Mozambique faced multiple crises in the early 1980s that severely damaged the economy: Renamo terrorism, misguided economic policies, and a calamitous drought. In 1984 South Africa was able to pressure it into signing the Nkomati Accord which bound South Africa to cease aiding Renamo and bound Mozambique to halt support for the ANC. This turnabout shocked many, but Machel took the risk, hoping this would finally bring peace to Mozambique. But as it turned out, the South Africans would double-cross Frelimo.

On October 19, 1986, Samora Machel, two government ministers, and thirty-one others were killed on route from a summit in Zambia to Maputo when their plane crashed in South African territory. It was widely seen as an assassination. A transcript from the 1998 South African Truth and Reconciliation Commission, declassified in 2016, "strongly corroborate(s) previous evidence indicating that the apartheid security forces caused Machel's plane to crash, thereby eliminating one of colonialism's most outspoken foes."[39] Maureen Reagan, daughter of President Reagan—but politically liberal—and the Rev. Jesse Jackson had met with President Machel in Maputo not long before his death. Incredibly impressed, Reagan returned home ready to press for US support for the beleaguered nation, but she and Jackson, shocked and distraught, returned for his funeral instead.[40]

Machel's assassination left the nation devastated and grieving. Prexy arrived a week later and found that "everyone was just in tears." Nelson and Winnie Mandela remained staunch friends and supporters of Samora Machel—notwithstanding Nkomati—and Nelson Mandela implored prison authorities to allow him to attend Machel's funeral. In all his years of imprisonment, "it was the only occasion on which he asked to leave South Africa," but his request was denied. Leaders of dozens of African nations and national liberation movements attended the funeral. In his funeral oration, Marcelino dos Santos pledged to "build the Mozambique of your dreams, a developed and prosperous country, the socialist Mozambican motherland. Viva Samora! A Luta Continua!"[41] In a further outrage and final assault on Samora Machel, South Africa violated the Nkomati accord from the get-go and continued to organize, train, and supply Renamo.[42]

Machel's death precipitated a prolonged crisis—the Soviet-led socialist bloc was soon to implode, Mozambique's own dream of socialism was unraveling, and Renamo atrocities were worsening. Scholar-activist John Saul posed the stark question: "Mozambique's socialist experiment, thrust forward by the long years of guerrilla struggle and increasingly based on a Marxist approach to social transformation, began with high hopes at independence in 1975. It now lies in tatters." What happened? He cited many factors but blamed "the South African war of destabilization," which, he argued, "functioned as a 'counter-development' strategy."[43]

RENAMO IN WASHINGTON

Right-wing forces in the United States were lobbying the Reagan administration to back Renamo but were hampered by infighting: It turns out that two Mozambican exiles in Washington, Luis Serapiao and Artur Vilankulu, each claimed to represent Renamo. "Conservatives strongly supported the Renamo guerrilla movement," said National Security Council Africa adviser Herman Cohen. "There were a lot of them in the defense department and the CIA. Secretary Weinberger felt 'Renamo was the wave of the future.'" But surprisingly, Reagan supported the State Department's efforts to improve relations with the Frelimo-led government.[44]

Melissa Wells, Reagan's nominee to be the ambassador to Mozambique, referred to Renamo as armed bandits—the term Mozambicans favored to describe the fighters, because they seemed to have no interest in winning people to their side, only terrorizing them. This outraged Renamo backers—notably Senators Jesse Helms and Steven Symms—who delayed her confirmation for six months in 1987 in an attempt to change Reagan's approach.[45]

Their gambit failed—in part because of Mozambique's successful counter-lobbying but also due to Renamo's escalating violence. In July Renamo killed an estimated four hundred villagers, including pregnant women and many children. Using automatic weapons and machetes, they slaughtered whole families. The crisis worsened later that year when Renamo severely disrupted agricultural production and food distribution, putting three million people at risk of starvation.

A US State Department official reported that "Renamo [had] impeded the movement of goods by hit-and-run attacks on food convoys and the placing of landmines in roads."[46] A 1987 UNICEF report on Mozambique and Angola confirmed that millions are at risk of famine in Mozambique "largely because of the destruction of food crops and transport capacity." Infant and child mortality in both countries was among the highest in the world. The "underlying cause is underdevelopment, compounded by war and destabilization." The report attributed 45 percent of the deaths of children under age five to the effects of conflict, a level they termed "catastrophic."[47]

A UN task force found that "South Africa has sought to destroy the transport routes, the economy, the civil society and the state's ability to serve the citizens of Mozambique—and has used a proxy terror group inherited from Rhodesia as its chief instrument. The economy of Mozambique now operates at levels much less than half of what they would be in the absence of war," it went on, "while almost 1 million Mozambicans would still be alive had even the tenuous 1975–1980 peace with South Africa not been shattered by the latter's escalation of hostilities."

Three thousand Renamo fighters accepted a government amnesty in 1988, and the following year the State Department confirmed that South African support for terrorism continued despite Nkomati and international calls for peace. They termed the devastation of the infrastructure and economy and slaughter of the people as a "holocaust."[48]

THE MOZAMBIQUE SUPPORT NETWORK

To counter right-wing lobbying for Renamo, Mozambique launched a major effort to influence public opinion and policymaking in the United States. Before his tragic death, Machel had urged friends in the United States to build support for the beleaguered nation. Historian Allen Isaacman—who along with his wife Barbara first taught in Maputo in

Figure 12. Prexy Nesbitt, Mozambique Support Network publicity photo, 1989. Courtesy of Prexy Nesbitt.

1978 and returned regularly for years—played a key role.[49] Isaacman urged Frelimo to pay more attention to race when sending Frelimo delegations abroad, especially to the United States, since part of Renamo propaganda was to portray Frelimo as run by white and Asian Marxists rather than Black Africans. Isaacman urged Frelimo to hire an American to fight for their interests in the United States, and he suggested Prexy. "Prexy moved across racial lines with great ease," Isaacman recalled. "And in some ways, he became the embodiment of what a good activist was from the perspective of Mozambique because he brought labor ties, he brought civil rights ties, he just brought his whole history." Indeed, Mozambique hired Prexy as a special consultant to Mozambique to run the Mozambique Solidarity Office (MSO) in Chicago.[50]

In September 1987 eighteen people from seven states met in Washington, DC, to launch the Mozambique Support Network, which eventually grew to encompass over a dozen chapters nationwide. The executive committee consisted of Roberta Washington and Isaacman, who were co-chairs; Bill Minter in Washington, DC; and Lisa Brock in Chicago. Sylvia Ewing served as the administrative coordinator for the Chicago-based national office.[51] The original idea was for Prexy to head it, but as a registered agent for Mozambique, he needed formal autonomy; yet in practice, Prexy's work with the MSO merged and overlapped with the MSN. Two years later, Dr. Loretta Williams and Mackie McLeod of the Boston MSN became national co-chairs. The MSN provided material and political support to Mozambique, while also organizing against apartheid. "We said to defeat apartheid is to defend Mozambique," Prexy explained. "We believed that helping to overthrow the apartheid regime was helping to make it safer for the Mozambican people."[52]

Joaquin Chissano, Machel's successor as president, came to New York and Washington in October to "consolidate Mozambique's friendship with the United States." He met with Bob Van Lierop, George Houser, Randall Robinson, presidential candidate Jesse Jackson—as well as President Reagan and numerous senators and representatives.[53] MSN leaders hosted a reception for him in New York. Chissano addressed the United Nations, vowing to find the truth behind Machel's plane crash, and denouncing apartheid and South Africa's campaign to impose its will on the region. On the last day of his visit, "he received the good news that an amendment introduced by Senator Jessie Helms to cut off aid to Mozambique had been defeated by a 61–34 margin."[54]

As special consultant to Mozambique, Nesbitt worked to heighten American understanding of the danger South Africa posed to the entire region. "For years ahead, Mozambique will need our attention, concern, and support," Prexy declared. "We should respond not with pity or alms, but rather, with a recognition that in helping Mozambique to once again flourish, we are helping ourselves to flourish as well."[55] Prexy spoke in schools, churches, and community groups. From Boston to Seattle and Hawaii to Alaska he educated Americans and offered concrete ways to help. Prexy and Fernando Lima, of the Mozambique News Agency, visited several cities together. In Omaha, Prexy urged folks to call their representatives to press for greater US assistance to Mozambique. "South Africa wants to destabilize Mozambique and its other black African neighbors, Nesbitt said, because 'Mozambique provides a model of a non-racial society that in and of itself is very threatening to a country like South Africa, which is based on white supremacy."[56]

Tragically, on November 25, 1987, Mayor Harold Washington died of a heart attack. Prexy was in Mozambique. President Chissano arranged for him to fly back for the funeral. Washington's support for their young nation and his opposition to apartheid had earned him high esteem in Mozambique. Prexy was devastated by the back-to-back losses of Samora Machel and Harold Washington; it reminded him of the back-to-back losses of Eduardo Mondlane and his mother Sadie Nesbitt and Amilcar Cabral and his sister Roanne Nesbitt. While devastating, these pairings strengthened his internationalist resolve.

The MSN developed a national presence, even if the chapters were typically small. There were initiatives in Boston; New York City; Washington, DC; Atlanta; Chicago; Minneapolis; Madison; Des Moines; Cedar Rapids; Idaho; Seattle; Los Angeles; San Francisco; and Omaha. Prexy stressed the need to build awareness about Mozambique in Black communities. "It's crucial that we begin sending representatives of Mozambique to the South," he told Frelimo leaders, "so that the large Black American population there becomes more of a base." Through former SNCC activists Heather Booth and Congressman John Lewis, Prexy explored prospects in the South, but ultimately the MSN's Southern reach remained limited mainly to Atlanta.[57]

Prexy underwent briefings in Mozambique. Highlights of one trip included "a two-and-a-half-hour dinner with President Joaquim

Chissano and his aide; extensive travel in Inhambane and Zambezia provinces; a meeting with the inter-cabinet working group on North America; meetings with almost all ministers; extensive meetings with the leadership of Frelimo; and a meeting with a multinational group of 'cooperantes' from Holland, Canada, Britain, Sweden, Australia, Italy, Portugal and the USA." He felt "the single most important achievement of [his] trip" was encouraging the production of English-language posters, videos, and news by the Ministry of Information to assist in solidarity work in English-speaking nations.[58] But other trips were harder. "The Mozambicans wanted me to know the Mozambican realities very well. To know them and to represent them in the United States and Canada." They took him to scenes of Renamo violence. "You see something like that, you never forget it."[59]

Prexy deepened his connections with Frelimo. "I strengthened my relationships with all of the leading figures in Mozambique," Prexy said, including Marcelino dos Santos, Jorge Rebello, Joaquim Chissano, and especially with Graça Machel. "Graça had a horrible time trying to deal with the loss of her husband. And whenever I was in Mozambique, I would eat dinner at Graça's house with her and the children." He got closer to Valeriano Ferrao, Mozambique's ambassador to the United States, "a wonderful, wonderful man dedicated to Frelimo and dedicated above all to Mozambique."[60]

In a stunning move, but one which illustrates the depth of the crisis in Mozambique, Frelimo hired Bruce Cameron to undermine support for Renamo in right-wing circles. While Cameron may have had some heft in right-wing circles, he was deeply distrusted among US internationalists. Cameron had recently worked with Oliver North to channel American aid to the contras in Nicaragua. That Mozambique would hire someone with this record astonished many American supporters, including leaders in the MSN who "raised strong objections," after they learned of the appointment. It put them "in a very difficult position" because they had "worked hard to build bridges with the larger and better organized Central America movement."[61] Prexy was more understanding of Frelimo's approach. "It was all part of a strategy to keep the U.S. Government from doing to Frelimo what they were doing to the MPLA. And Cameron was very good. The Mozambicans felt by hiring him, they would be able to reach out to the right as by hiring me, they would be reaching out to the Left and to the Black and oppressed communities." Thankfully Cameron's contract was short, and evidently, he did what he was hired to do.[62]

Mozambique's move to "liberalize" its economy in exchange for badly needed funds would generate controversy within the solidarity community in the years ahead. This direction became clear in 1987 when Chissano approved a World Bank/International Monetary Fund economic rehabilitation program and ordered the privatization of more than 1,200 state companies.[63] Prexy acknowledged an unstated aspect of his hiring. "Knowing that there were going to be some moves made that would upset some on the Left," Frelimo "wanted to build solidarity and support, and an understanding about moves that would have to be made to ensure the survival of Mozambique."[64]

Tours of visiting Mozambicans became the Mozambique Support Network's most effective form of outreach. "We brought Malangatana Ngwenya, the great sculptor and muralist, to the US," Prexy recalled. "He did a mural at a school in Chicago. They ask me all the time, 'When is Malangatana Ngwenya coming back?'" Prexy thinks that because he was so warm and likable he conveyed the humanity of Mozambicans to ordinary Americans.[65] Malangatana later explained how the war had affected his painting. "When South Africa took over backing Renamo—and destroying more than the Portuguese ever destroyed—my painting got more violent, more shocking, with reds that were stronger than ever. To see the schools, the hospitals, the farms the railways—all symbols of hope and growth for our country being destroyed. To see pregnant women, children, men being killed—sometimes two or three hundred in one day, in forty minutes—creates in my heart a sadness that does not stop. When I meet people I laugh, I sing, I dance. When I go to the canvas, I am another Malangatana."[66]

Of all the Mozambican speakers Prexy brought to the US, "Graça was the most effective and most eloquent." Prexy took Graça Machel to speak at the Shrine of the Black Madonna, a popular Black nationalist church in Detroit. "There were five hundred or six hundred people and Graça was so eloquent. She could get so passionate but stay very targeted."[67] At the University of Illinois, Mrs. Machel called education "an instrument of liberation." It's no accident, she said that "education is segregated in South Africa or that schools and teachers are targets of attack" in Mozambique. "South Africa has made liberation a target." South African funded "armed bandits" destroyed over two thousand primary schools between 1980 and 1986. She emphasized the trauma endured by the nation's twenty-thousand orphans who saw their parents get killed and villages burned.[68]

In 1988 journalist Lina Magaia toured seven states and Canada. One of the first Mozambican women to study in Lisbon, Magaia joined the armed struggle. After independence, she worked in agricultural development and witnessed Renamo atrocities, which she documented in the book *Dumba Nengue*. Sylvia Ewing, the MSN/MSO staffer, welcomed her to Chicago, where Magaia spoke at a large Methodist church downtown. Ewing's young daughter, Eve, had a toy phone. "She used to pick up her play phone and say, 'Hello, Mozambique.' Eve loved Lina and wanted to follow her everywhere," including the bathroom! Ewing was struck by Magaia's tenderness and patience toward her daughter despite all that she had seen and endured. "Her story reinforced my faith in the power of culture, writing and communications, all of that together, to make a difference."[69]

The MSN and MSO's public relations offensives changed many Americans' understanding of events in Mozambique. And at the same time, the continuing reports of Renamo atrocities pushed the anticommunist narrative off stage, undercutting the right's attempt to portray the group as a credible and popular opposition force. In 1988 Robert Gersony interviewed hundreds of displaced persons in Mozambique for the US State Department and found "a systematic pattern of human rights abuses, overwhelmingly attributed to Renamo." His finding that it was one of the worse mass carnages since the Holocaust garnered significant media attention. "Rarely does a State Department document evoke a nightmarish Conrad novel," read an editorial in the *New York Times*. "Alas, there's nothing fictional about a news report describing how 100,000 people have been massacred in Mozambique—mainly by Renamo, a rebel group waging a bush war against Mozambique's left-wing regime. Civilians have been shot, knifed, axed, bayoneted, burnt, starved, beaten, drowned and throttled. Nearly a million have fled into exile."[70]

Social scientist and Africa activist Bill Minter interviewed thirty-two ex-Renamo combatants in Mozambique, who had either responded to an unconditional amnesty or had been captured. He reported two key findings: "that a high proportion of the Renamo rank-and-file combatants, probably in excess of ninety percent, is recruited by force, and kept in the Renamo ranks by control mechanisms including threats of execution for attempted desertion." And second, that "the professionally competent Renamo military operations are sustained by regular supplies from South Africa as well as by a centralized system of command, control and communications and a coordinated program of basic and advanced military training."[71]

Mackie McLeod, regional director of the MSN in New England and later AFSC's regional director for southern Africa, participated in a delegation of African American activists and religious, medical, relief, and development workers to Mozambique in 1988. They met with government leaders, survivors of Renamo attacks, and even Renamo "bandits" who had been captured or had turned themselves in. "It's difficult to convey to anyone," he wrote, "what a war of genocide means." To those in his delegation, "it meant the glazed, profoundly weary eyes of thousands of dislocated villagers who had been robbed of *everything* and who were clothed only in the bark of trees. It meant encountering clusters of sick, confused children and infants, orphaned and stunned into silence by the sheer barbarity of their parents' murders at the hands of Renamo bands."[72]

The media finally drew attention to Renamo's forcible conscription of children. The US State Department enlisted Neil Boothby, an American psychologist, to help treat children in Mozambique who had been forced to serve as soldiers for Renamo. Many children—even as young as six years old—had been compelled to participate in the destruction of their villages and deaths of their families. While committed to bringing food, medicine, and therapy to the victims of such trauma, the haunting question "What does one do in a place where maybe 500,000 children have seen their own parents die?" pushed Boothby to shift toward training local healers.[73] "One of the most frightening dimensions of the war," Prexy told a church conference, was the use of children as killers. "Young boys are kidnapped and trained to kill. They are doped up so killing becomes a part of their lives."[74]

South Africa Now, the television show produced in New York by Danny Schecter, devoted several episodes to Renamo violence. One guest, *New Yorker* writer William Finnegan reported that the "national economy was effectively destroyed." And yet, despite everything, he still encountered a spirit of resistance. Graça Machel lamented that "if white children were dying, people would act immediately." Her country's children were traumatized, but "world leaders are not moved by black death."[75]

Sylvia Ewing recalls how Prexy would share devastating images and stories. "It was rough. He shared pictures of people who were burned or just terrible things that had happened." It brought it home. "We are in solidarity with these folks, but I didn't need the motivation to be so graphic, but it was part of our reality check."[76] But at the same time, Prexy was keenly aware of how stories of Renamo brutality could be mobilized to dehumanize Africans. He drew up speaking tips and advice for the MSN: "It is crucial, particularly when sharing visuals of Mozambique to debrief audiences after the viewing. The horror and difficulties of the Mozambican situation either completely overwhelm people or fulfill some of the negative stereotypes and expectations with which they've already been indoctrinated. Hence, it is important to state and re-state the positives and strengths of Mozambique and the Mozambican situation."[77]

New directions in Frelimo's politics were consolidated at the Fifth Party Congress in July 1989 with over seven hundred Mozambicans in attendance. Prexy was there. Allen Isaacman called it "a major turning point in Mozambican history," when "national consensus and unity replaced class struggle and Marxism-Leninism as the dominant political idioms." Isaacman, Roberta Washington, and Loretta Williams attended as MSN representatives. Williams delivered remarks to the congress: "In this difficult moment of your history, we commit ourselves to intensifying our efforts in the United States to increase public awareness, popular action, and concrete legislation in support of the Mozambican nation."[78]

Frelimo pivoted toward "gradual socialism" in rural areas, casting cooperative and collective farming arrangements as voluntary. They sought an "opening up" to a broader range of voices. As President Chissano put it, "We must not only seek to express what the militants feel and want as a social group, but also the aspirations of all the people." Frelimo moved to allow more private involvement in provisioning housing and education, but defended the constitutional guarantees of education and health care, seeing these as the greatest gains of independence. The overall message from the grassroots was support for the government's efforts to negotiate an end to the war.[79]

Rather than moving away from socialism, Jose Luis Cabaco, the External General Secretary, reminded supporters that "our priority has always been to build two things together: our nation and social justice." The war had weakened the state's capacity to provide for the people, propelling this shift: "We have to give greater freedom to the private sectors. Of course, this will create social divisions, which is a matter of concern to us. But we have to do what we can to encourage our people to participate in the creation of wealth for the survival of our nation."[80]

Many friends of Mozambique were more critical about the terms and tentacles of Western aid. "For many donors," the British journalist and Frelimo supporter Joseph Hanlon wrote, "destabilization was the entry ticket—Mozambique did not want or need them before. Now they can recolonize Mozambique and force it to accept new and inappropriate policies. The new missionaries can come in and dispense charity, preaching the gospels for God and capitalism, as they did nearly a hundred years ago. And everyone is happy to blame the victims."[81]

Similarly, a Canadian solidarity group protested that Western institutions had imposed wrenching austerity policies on a war-torn decimated country, noting that since 1987 Mozambique had "experienced the familiar recipe of large currency devaluations, cutbacks in the public sector, [and] reductions in food subsidies and privatization." Inflation spiked and workers took to the streets as the "purchasing power of wages plummeted." At the same time, "some Mozambicans have profited from the war and from structural adjustment. There is now a tiny but thriving business class and, more seriously, a sizeable number of corrupt government officials."[82]

While the US State Department appeared to be pursuing stability in the region, private right-wing groups continued to aid Renamo. Prexy worked to expose these troubling interventions. The Conservative Caucus Foundation, the Coors Foundation, and the Heritage Foundation all accused the Reagan administration of being "soft on communism," and even "pro-Soviet" in urging improved US-Mozambique ties. James Blanchard III, a Louisiana businessperson, provided medical supplies, radios, and cash donations to Renamo. Support also came from a deceptively named group, Freedom Inc. whose director, Robert K. Mackenzie, fought in Vietnam and then served with Rhodesian and South African special forces. The religious right provided additional support. The "Frontline Fellowship, an organization considered by Mozambican government circles to be a major cover for mercenary activities throughout southern Africa, has led groups of 'missionaries' from the California-based Christian Emergency Relief Team (CERT) into Mozambique illegally," ostensibly to deliver bibles. Jimmy Swaggert Ministries was also said to be involved in this murky transnational network. "Americans may not have been killing the hundreds of thousands of Mozambicans who have died in the last eleven years," Prexy wrote. "But these people are as guilty as the Renamo killers; and they, too, must be stopped."[83]

The solidarity network in Chicago continued to organize material support for war-torn Mozambique. Proceeds from an annual anti-apartheid walkathon went to the Christian Council of Mozambique, which provided emergency supplies to people displaced by the war and resources to rebuild medical clinics and build schools, and to the Organization of Mozambican Women, which promoted maternal and child health programs, conducted literacy campaigns, and built temporary housing for displaced people.[84]

Prexy was a major proponent of "people-to-people" diplomacy and began bringing delegations to southern Africa as a solidarity activist and continued it for decades as an educator. A trip in 1990 led to the formation of the Mozambique United Methodist Health Care Foundation, which sent $300,000 worth of medical supplies and equipment to Mozambique's Chicuque and Reclatla hospitals.[85] In 1991 Prexy brought a group of pastors, educators, and activists to South Africa, Zimbabwe, and Mozambique to "observe political realities and to build solidarity." Back home, they called on "the U.S. government (to) take action to stop private organizations and individuals from funding the terrorization and brutalization of the Mozambican people."[86]

COOPERANTES, PART II

Two Chicago-based activists, both inspired by Prexy, went as cooperantes to Mozambique after years of war and a fitful shift toward a market economy. Rachel Rubin, a physician, first met Prexy when she was an undergraduate at the University of Illinois and he gave presentations on Black poetry as an artist-in-residence. They both later organized with the Coalition for Illinois Divestment from South Africa. She said "his intellect, his understanding of the situation . . . helped the rest of us. And certainly, he fostered my interest in Mozambique." She was drawn to Mozambique solidarity work because Frelimo was "building a society where there's economic equality and education and health care for everybody," and "they also talked about women's rights and racial equality." Rubin felt strongly that cooperantes should be fully prepared to perform professional duties, so she finished her residency and studied Portuguese before moving there in 1990. Rubin was pleased that even though she was paid a small salary by UNICEF and supported by the Mozambique Health Committee in Seattle, she was hired by the Ministry of Health and incorporated into their community, serving as a district medical chief in Manica Province.[87]

"They had a rule that you couldn't be there for more than one to two years on a particular project," Rubin recalled, because they were promoting indigenous development and self-sufficiency. "I really appreciated that I was integrated into the health system there. And that I was replaced by a Mozambican trained physician. When she came, we overlapped for about six months or so. I felt gratified to leave knowing that there was a Mozambican physician in my place." Rubin recalled that malaria, tuberculosis, and malnutrition were the major health threats. She usually had access to malaria and TB medication but rarely pain medicine. "I would go to Zimbabwe to buy medication at the pharmacies there and bring it back, because we didn't even have aspirin." During her second year there, she lost water in her house due to a drought. "We started to see malnutrition in adults. There was just no food." Rubin ended up getting hepatitis A.[88]

Rubin shared a house in Manica with her sister-in-law Anne Evens after Anne arrived to begin her own sojourn as a cooperante. A widowed Mozambican woman and her five children regularly stayed overnight with them in fear of Renamo attacks in the village. Being in a town was somewhat safer at night. "You would go down the main street in Manica," Rubin noted, "and it was covered with people sleeping on the ground, on the sidewalks or on the road. And then during the day, at dawn, they moved back to their homes and got their kids ready for school or did their work and opened the shops."[89]

Rubin lived in Mozambique during a time when Western aid was increasing but typically conditioned on liberalizing the economy. In contrast to the internationalist ethos of the post-independence era, this was a new era of NGOs. Rubin remembered that many NGO employees lived with many more material comforts than the average Mozambican and brought a kind of arrogance to the work. Rather than an ethic of mutuality or working together, the attitude among many was, "If you want our money, this is how you have to do it."[90]

As Rubin was leaving at the end of 1992, Mozambique accepted a deal with the IMF and World Bank aid, which "meant that they had to denationalize the health system and the educational system. They had to allow private practice." Even though, in Rubin's words, the private system "failed miserably, because there weren't enough people that had enough money to support a private medical system and to support a private hospital." For Rubin, the challenging question was, "How do you maintain a nation-state that is steeped in poverty? How do you build your country unless you latch onto the capitalist machinery? It's very hard." And yet, "my time in Mozambique was life transforming," Rubin reflects. "I mean, it's thirty years ago now and I still think about it all the time."[91]

Anne Evens first met Prexy when he came to speak at Cornell in the early 1980s. "He made me believe that I could do things that I myself couldn't imagine, which is probably part of the reason I wound up going to Mozambique when I was twenty-four." After college she plunged into solidarity work and got arrested around twenty-three times in the fight against apartheid, including at the South African consulate in Chicago. An engineer, Evens was a founding member of the MSN. She worked for Technical Aid for Nicaragua where the United States was funding a counterinsurgency against the elected socialist government. Mozambican Ambassador Ferrao invited her to Mozambique to investigate the feasibility of doing similar work there. Her three-month visit in 1989 coincided with Frelimo's Fifth Congress. From a departing British cooperante, she inherited the job of inputting the congress's materials into an early-stage word processor. She trained staff at the Ministry of Foreign Affairs in the use of computers; she set up a database system with Mozambique's Information Agency; and she trained staff at the Central Committee of Frelimo in desktop publishing. She accompanied Dr. George Povey, an early cooperante, who was building midwifery programs, to Manica to scope out projects in the North. After completing a master's degree back in the US, Evens moved to Manica as an employee of the Seattle-based Mozambique Health Committee, which "had gotten a grant from UNICEF to start building clinics outside of the city center." She explained, "I was hired to go to do that."[92]

Upon arrival, Nancy Anderson, a physician with UNICEF told her, "It's good that you have a little meat on your bones, because you're going to need that when you get malaria." And she did get malaria. "She and I are still good friends. She was married to a British cooperante, and they helped me get settled." Evens was a brave young woman. She shared a house with Ray McCardle, a UNICEF staffer. "Most of the cooperantes were based in Maputo, because of the safety situation, so there were very few of us outside. There was some safety in the Beira Corridor, so we were fairly safe as long as we didn't travel at night and did what we were told." But Evens did have a harrowing encounter. "Renamo came to kidnap Ray, but his dog attacked them, so he was fine. He didn't get kidnapped, but UNICEF made him leave. I stayed in the house, because I was not being targeted, and we got increased security, but that was only for a limited time."[93]

There were many rewards and challenges in her work as a rural building engineer. "The first project I was asked to build was in a village called Penhalonga up in the mountains." It was challenging just to assemble a construction crew. They consulted spiritual leaders for site selection. Thinking everything was set she awaited the delivery by villagers of local stones to build a foundation. None came. "It took several weeks for me to figure out that the site was not actually acceptable to the spiritual leader. We had to pick a different site and do a different ceremony in order to get that project started. As a pretty young person who didn't have a lot of experiences, it was really eye-opening to see that people communicate in different ways." The site was along the border with Zimbabwe, a Shona area. "They don't say 'No,' they just find other ways for things not to move forward."[94]

Another challenge was that "food was really scarce, and we were all living on food aid, mostly beans." The cement they were using was very valuable, and one day it disappeared. A worker was caught reselling it and was jailed. "The conditions in the jail were just horrific, he got no food whatsoever, so I used to come and bring him food." Navigating that was difficult "because the other members of the crew felt that he had betrayed them by selling supplies," but they didn't want him to die in prison. And another challenge was procuring materials: she often drove by herself to Zimbabwe under difficult conditions to buy cement.[95]

Having fallen in love with a Mozambican with whom she had a child, Evens lived there for eight years. She returned every year until her daughter was 16. "I'm happy that I was able to build real community there and not have this sheltered expat life; I was as much a part of the Mozambican community as I could be." She loved the music: "It lifts your soul up, and it's everywhere all the time." The traditions also

Figure 13. Anne Evens talking with Manica District medical director Domingo at a construction site for a health clinic in Manica Province, Mozambique, 1991. Courtesy of Anne Evens.

made an impression. "Every single project that we did began and ended with a ceremony. I never had that growing up, so it was beautiful to experience ceremony in community with others."[96]

Whenever Prexy brought a group to Mozambique, Evens provided Portuguese translation. "He definitely had access," she recalls, noting the top officials they'd get to see. "He designed tours to meet the interests of the people who were coming," but the tour would "certainly include Frelimo leadership." Prexy "had a lot of patience. Tours can be challenging when humans start being human. A number of people would lose it at some point, but he was really good at decreasing the anxiety."[97]

For Evens, "some of the most challenging and maybe even traumatic visits included going to the camps where the child soldiers were trying to heal and just hearing their stories. I can still feel it." Renamo destroyed two schools that she built, but as far as she knows the other structures have survived. The structural adjustment programs imposed by the IMF and others also inflicted damage. "To see the impact that it had on people was horrific. I think every single system, the health care system, the educational system, agricultural services, infrastructure, electricity, all of it suffered."[98]

She witnessed how newly arriving corporations put profits over people. Electricity and water were always being rationed, because funds were diverted to support private "economic development projects and startups." She witnessed "a lot of extraction. In the area I lived in, there was gold extraction, and they were using alluvial mining techniques, so they were literally shaving off mountains and running a lot of water through to pan out the gold. The environmental destruction was horrific."[99]

MAKING CONCESSIONS AND DEBATING
THE NATURE OF SOLIDARITY

Intermittent peace talks began in 1990. Presidents Daniel Arap Moi of Kenya, Robert Mugabe of Mozambique, and Kenneth Kaunda offered to broker peace if Renamo agreed to forego violence and embrace constitutional norms. Renamo brought James Blanchard and other right-wing Americans to their negotiating team—and reportedly their advice "added to the confusion and missteps that led to multiple delays."[100]

Devastated by war and with the fall of the communist bloc, Frelimo increasingly found itself pivoting toward the West and adjusting its policies to please donors. The culture of solidarity shifted to one of markets, dependency, and neoliberalism. According to the Mozambique Information Office, the introduction of structural adjustment measures by the IMF and the World Bank brought a massive deterioration of living conditions.[101] Food prices skyrocketed when subsidies vanished. In 1990 Chissano visited Washington to press for more aid. The Bush administration pledged to give more than the already promised $110 million and praised the Frelimo government for revising the constitution, liberalizing the economy, and committing to elections.[102]

During this difficult period, a debate arose among solidarity activists about how to relate to Mozambique as the dream of socialism rapidly receded. In November 1990 the MSN hosted a convening of activists, academics, government officials, and religious leaders. Pedro Comissario, Mozambique's ambassador to the United Nations, expressed concern about the view that his government was "giving in" to Renamo terrorism. He stressed that activists needed to consider Mozambican perspectives. A British advocate complained that international aid is given on the condition of privatization. "Bank loans are conditional on what they consider 'good governance.'" A University of Illinois professor active in solidarity work concurred that "Frelimo and Mozambique are caught in a trap as they enter into IMF and World Bank policies."[103]

Kevin Danaher of the MSN executive committee voiced a perspective that's been termed "critical solidarity." Prexy had first worked with Kevin years earlier at the IPS and largely shared his perspective. Danaher called aid a mixed bag. "There is some good and some bad, but it is part of a larger imperialist state apparatus. We should make clear our support for Frelimo yet remain critical." He made the point that "our job is to change US policy, not to take sides with Mozambique's political parties"; but certainly activists' ideological affinities had inspired their initial involvement. California activist Rachel Chapman echoed this perspective, "Our support must also remain progressive and with the workers in mind." At a solidarity event in Milwaukee later that month, former ambassador Valeriano Ferrao, acknowledged the "trade-offs" in accepting IMF loans but noted the great need for foreign assistance. He argued that Americans can best help Mozambique by pressuring the US government to increase aid.[104]

In a long open letter to mark the start of 1991, Prexy assessed the situation in Mozambique. It's clear he wanted to encourage greater humility, empathy, and understanding among his Western comrades. He had just returned from Mozambique and Zimbabwe and before that had attended the European Campaign Against South African Aggression Against Mozambique and Angola in Paris and the A Luta Continua conference on Angola and Mozambique in London. At this point, Prexy was truly a citizen of the activist world, and very influential—yet he always sought to model modesty. He wrote, "I met with long time Mozambican, Namibian, Zimbabwean and South African leaders and friends, long time Southern African solidarity workers ranging from missionaries and teachers to agronomists and engineers." He remarked on the amazing "humanity, warmth and hospitality" of the Mozambicans even though the crisis was staggering. Mozambique endured what Prexy termed "killer droughts" in 1990–1991. "What it all boils down to is that next year, Mozambique will need more than 1 million tons of food aid to avert mass starvation." Compounding matters, the Soviet Union was ending its oil concessions to Mozambique, meaning the oil and gas bills in Mozambique would jump from $0 to $140 million. "For me there is no alternative to supporting Mozambique and trying to increase the amount of political and material support that can be mobilized from the United States." And yet, "it is true that Mozambique has changed very much."

"The partial cease fire with Renamo, the new constitution, multipartyism, elections, the formal abandonment of scientific socialism and the adoption of democracy—all these events and developments mark a new and extremely difficult period for young Mozambique." Prexy emphasized important continuities as well. "Mozambique remains, it seems to me, a nation where the government, despite all the limitations, problems and new directions, fundamentally is committed to the people and the people to the government." Chissano continued to call socialism "a necessity" for Mozambique even though he had introduced market forces. Longtime cooperante Ruth Minter, told Prexy that people in Mozambique "find it hard to think long term about anything. They are weary of news of deaths and land mines, of kidnappings and rapes."

Prexy described the grassroots process of debating the new constitution at local meetings nationwide. Some had criticized it for dropping the word socialism, but in contrast, Prexy argued that it was much more progressive than many Western constitutions—guaranteeing health care and granting citizens' rights to use state-owned land. "It was debate and struggle at the Assembly, for instance, that forced the dropping of an original land use formulation calling for individual ownership of land." Prexy found a lot to be proud of in the document and the process, but he also felt that much more work needed to be done around race and gender issues to bridge proclamations with the reality of everyday life. "What must be instituted and deepened in this new historical period for Mozambique is mechanisms of actualizing into daily living the rhetorical stance of non-racialism. And, of course, this must be extended into an anti-sexism and homophobia-free way of living as well. Women remain subordinated and underrepresented in Mozambique."

Prexy struggled with what he saw as "Mozambique-bashing" by the Western Left. In his view, the American Left was "the last 'left' in the world which [had] any right to be involved in criticizing other people's revolutionary struggles." Moreover, and most importantly, "The future and its difficulties are not options for the Mozambican people," Prexy wrote in anguish. They "cannot decide that the situation is not revolutionary enough, not 'correct' enough and therefore abandon their country."

In Prexy's view "there has never been a moment when concrete support to Mozambique was more critical than right now. The gaping holes of aid, assistance and support left by Eastern European cooperantes and workers need to be filled. This is the time for us to be mobilizing concrete support for Mozambique, whether in the form of hard money or the two new ambulances Chicago City Council Member, Helen Shiller, is organizing or the steady flow of medical personnel which Seattle's Mozambique Health Committee keeps sending to work in Manica Province."[105]

Prexy closed by reminding his friends "that the elections and the period ahead for Mozambique will not be, as old folk in the U.S. South say, 'no crystal stair.' Rather, it is probably going to be one of the most perilous times conceivable for any nation." He underscored the outsized impact of South Africa. "For Mozambique, for all the Southern African countries, very, very much is riding on what kind of society emerges in the post-apartheid South Africa."[106] No truer words were spoken.

Compounding the challenge for Prexy and others was that the demobilization of the US anti-apartheid movement after the passage of sanctions and release of Mandela made it difficult to activate Americans against the aggression South Africa was unleashing in the region during apartheid's last years. South Africa continued to finance Renamo. A few MSN chapters continued to mobilize support, but the solidarity movement had lost its intensity.[107]

Prexy increased efforts to bring Americans to the beleaguered nation and see for themselves the great harms that were being inflicted and great needs Mozambicans had. He led two delegations across southern Africa in the summer of 1992, just as the government and Renamo were declaring a ceasefire. Twenty-three church and solidarity activists from Sweden visited Mozambique, and South Africa and a smaller contingent of US educators and activists from upstate New York visited Namibia, Zimbabwe, Mozambique, and South Africa. That trip marked Prexy's thirty-seventh visit to the region. Everywhere the visitors were confronted with a parched landscape and human suffering during one of the worst droughts of the century. Prexy made a detailed record. At a camp for dislocated people in Mozambique, "one mother, after being helped off the tractor-pulled wagon, tried desperately to get her infant to suckle off her fingers the special paste of oil, vitamin C and maize which had been given her. She began shaking her child when she realized it was not sucking. Camp workers gently but firmly took the dead child from her." Even before the drought, nearly half of Mozambique's population lived on "the edge of starvation."[108]

Educators Vera Michelson and Eileen C. Kawola of the Capital District Coalition Against Apartheid and Racism (CD-CAAR) in Albany joined the trip hoping to identify a material aid project. In Namibia they were honored to attend a wedding of someone who had previously visited them in New York. In Mozambique, they saw the consequences of seventeen years of war and conflict. "Mozambique had this wonderful socialist dream," says Kawola, "which got crushed by the South Africans." Witnessing the traumatic impact of a war waged on civilians, especially the conscription of children, shook them. "Our most chilling memory, the one that will never go away," Kawola said, was a meeting with six teenage boys who had been forced to serve with Renamo. "The atrocities these children had seen or even committed were told in their eyes—eyes so sad or devoid of feeling." The effects of the drought were exacerbated by Renamo's destruction of infrastructure and large swaths of the countryside. Once one of the most productive agricultural nations in Africa, Mozambique had become the poorest, most debt-ridden, and most foreign-aid-dependent country in the world. "One of the things we are pressing for now is forgiveness of debts," says Nesbitt.[109]

A letter of greeting addressed to the school children of Mozambique from the Albany Board of Education was presented to Graça Machel, who ran the National Organization of Children of Mozambique, an organization set up to address the devastation caused by the war. Mrs. Machel stressed the importance of placing orphans and reclaimed boy soldiers in village homes, using family and community support to help them heal. After visiting the Mocatini school for some six hundred dislocated children, the Albany delegation made a commitment to raise funds for the school. Kawola said it's "a school without walls, since Renamo would destroy it." On the plane leaving the country, "I just sat and quietly cried," says Kawola. "And we certainly did not see the worst of Mozambique."[110]

When Prexy returned home that summer he sought to dispel two prevalent ideas that circulated in US media: that Mozambique was consumed by "civil war" and that the violence in South Africa was "black on black"—"a kind of tribal violence that's really OK since it's them doing it to each other." Rather, the "systematic killing in Mozambique and the violence today in South Africa are essentially products of the same machinery," Prexy wrote, seeking to demystify the root causes of the conflict. "Far from being civil wars or mere tribal fighting," he insisted, drawing attention to US involvement, "the events and dynamics of Mozambique and South Africa are derived from over thirteen years of specific campaigns of destabilization and terror conducted by the South African government and its various allies, including US nationals like the Rev. Pat Robertson, and US Senators Jesse Helms and Dan Burton" who have tapped right-wing networks to send money and arms to Renamo.[111]

Prexy and his dear friend, the renowned South African scholar and ANC member Bernard Magubane, participated in a report back to the Albany community in November 1992. The twin themes of their talks reflected their insistence on a regional understanding of conditions and struggles in southern Africa. Magubane's talk was "South Africa: Stop the Violence" and Prexy's was "Mozambique: Promote the Peace."[112]

TOWARD PEACE, A NEW CONSTITUTION AND ELECTIONS

There's no question that Frelimo faced few good options during the peace talks. Mozambicans desperately needed peace and stability. As much as Renamo faced international pressure to cease fighting, Frelimo faced domestic pressure to make peace. Janice McLaughlin, a Maryknoll nun with two decades of experience in the region, observed that during the peace talks, "the mediators, and the observers as well, seemed to favor Renamo, forcing all the concessions from Frelimo." Moreover, she argued that Mozambique, as one of the poorest countries in the world, should be relieved of foreign debt and IMF imposed structural adjustment. "To me it's as if Mozambique is being triply wounded. We have a terrible drought which is causing great starvation.

Then we have the war. And on top of that we have structural adjustment which is causing tremendous inflation." She worried about demobilized soldiers on both sides, facing escalating prices and few job prospects.[113]

Mozambicans faced a dire situation in 1992, after years of war, and the worst drought in living memory. It's estimated that a million people, mostly civilians, had perished in the long assault by Renamo, with four to five million more displaced from their homes. "A staggering 8 million, out of a total population of 15.7 million, have faced severe food shortages and starvation. Cities, towns, and villages have been decimated and the national economy destroyed," one observer put it.[114]

Immensely frustrating to solidarity activists, and no doubt Frelimo, was that the peace talks reframed Renamo as a legitimate force of opposition rather than a violent proxy of foreign powers, but to relief all around, a peace accord was signed in Rome in October 1992. A year later, President Chissano attended a large gathering in Harlem organized by Roberta Washington. He began by assailing the notion that Mozambique had just been through a civil war. "We never had any 'civil wars', only colonial wars, wars of destabilization, by racist countries." The peace accord held, but he lamented that progress on reaching agreed upon steps had stalled, delaying the elections until 1994. Renamo had a stake in delaying elections as it needed time to cultivate a base as a newly emerging political party. Chissano urged friends to pressure the US government to step up aid to Mozambique. "Although the country is currently not in war, people's lives are still in a state of crisis."[115]

Prexy's employment as a consultant to Mozambique came to an end in 1992. Allen Isaacman had implored President Chissano to keep him, writing that "Prexy's skill, energy, ability to speak to diverse audiences and his willingness to travel anywhere have borne substantial fruits. His knowledge of Mozambique, his connection to the anti-apartheid movement, to the trade union movements, the progressive churches and to the African American community have enabled us to forge a broad-based network in support of Mozambique. There is no one else I know," he wrote, "who is as dedicated and committed to Mozambique as Prexy."[116] It was a valiant effort, but the country was broke. And peace was on the horizon.

The first multiparty elections for president and parliament were held in October 1994 with Frelimo winning both, maintaining its position as the governing party. Chissano won a new term. The results brought joy and relief to the nation, but its struggles continued. The wars in Mozambique and Angola had devastated the environment and landscape of both countries and of grave concern were the millions of unexploded landmines. UN Secretary-General Boutros Boutros-Ghali said, "Of all the tasks involved in setting a nation on a road to peace and prosperity, perhaps none has the immediate urgency of mine clearance. Landmines not only injure, but limit mobility and restrict economic opportunities, particularly in the rural areas where most people work in agriculture.[117]

As Prexy put it, landmines meant "you couldn't go back to your land. The landmines devastated people's relationship to their land. They were such a vicious methodology of warfare." Prexy had become a program officer at the MacArthur Foundation and was able to steer support to the International Committee to Ban Landmines, led by Jody Williams. Not long thereafter, Williams won the Nobel Peace Prize. MacArthur head and fellow Parker School alum Adele Simmons sent Prexy "a beautiful note thanking me for that work."[118] As the internationalist community knew, though, the only prospect for lasting peace and a genuine opportunity to rebuild Mozambique, hinged on the outcome of the anti-apartheid struggle and the parallel effort to win peace and freedom in South Africa.

5

INTERNATIONALIST CHICAGO AND THE END OF APARTHEID

‗‗

THIS CHAPTER DESCRIBES EFFORTS to keep the pressure on South Africa after the passage of sanctions; the joy and celebration after the release of Nelson Mandela; and the violent and anxious times before the first democratic elections in 1994. In the late 1980s, crises escalated in southern Africa. In 1986, South Africa declared a state of emergency and banned foreign reporters from covering the unrest. The United Democratic Front (UDF) aimed to make South Africa "ungovernable," while South African troops continued to illegally occupy Namibia, wage war against Angola, and train and finance Renamo in Mozambique. But South Africa's mad pursuit of regional plunder in the defense of white rule was turning out to be unsustainable. The defeat of the South African army by Cuban and Angolan forces in the Battle of Cuito Cuanavale in southern Angola dealt a blow to the morale of white South Africans who began to flee conscription and emigrate in higher numbers, ultimately pushing the government into secret talks to broker peace. At the same time, the devastating effects of international sanctions propelled business and political elites into secret talks with the ANC. But the outward story remained crackdown and repression. Security forces continued to jail and kill dissident forces. The winning of congressional sanctions had slowed down anti-apartheid protest, but in Chicago, a dedicated band of activists, with stronger support from organized labor, continued the work.

KEEPING THE PRESSURE ON

The fight for sanctions did not end in 1986: the act of congress was historic but full of loopholes. Many corporations claimed to have withdrawn from South Africa, but their engagement continued. "It is essential to distinguish between those corporations for which withdrawal means the termination of all economic ties to South Africa," the five major US anti-apartheid groups stated, "and those for which withdrawal merely indicates a restructuring of economic relations." They praised Eastman Kodak and others that had severed all ties. But "companies like General Motors, IBM, and Coca Cola have announced withdrawals," still they "continue to provide vital economic support to South Africa through ongoing licensing, distribution, marketing and service agreements. Such companies have not ended their links to apartheid." The groups created guidelines "to clarify what the national anti-apartheid movement means by economic disengagement from South Africa and Namibia."[1]

Many pushed for stronger sanctions. In Congress, Ron Dellums continued to introduce legislation and ultimately an important bill strengthening sanctions introduced by Harlem congressman Charles Rangel did pass. When Helen Shiller, member of the Chicago City Council, was in Zimbabwe in 1989, Prexy Nesbitt arranged for her to visit Mozambique. Shiller met and photographed many amputees who were victims of Renamo land mines. Deeply affected, she returned to Chicago and helped pass stronger municipal sanctions against South Africa.[2] And sanctions were working. In 1989, Secretary of State for Foreign Affairs Herman J. Cohen acknowledged that "sanctions have had a major impact on the thinking of the white community. There is no capital inflow. There is disinvestment. People worry about the future. They say to themselves 'this is preventing us from having the kind of economy that will maintain living standards for our children.'"[3]

Building a big tent of support was critical to many of the successes of the US anti-apartheid movement, but in this period, a committed core of leftists and labor radicals dominated the work. Prexy took the lead in creating the Chicago Committee in Solidarity with Southern Africa (CCISSA) to continue mobilizing support for struggles in southern Africa. Solidarity work extended to Angola, Namibia, Mozambique, and Zimbabwe, but South Africa remained key, especially because, on its last legs, the apartheid regime was spreading havoc domestically and across the region. "These were the years in which the apartheid government, mounting its total onslaught, was really giving hell to the states around them," Basil Clunie recalled. "There were constant attacks." As a result, "we upped the demonstrations" at the South African consulate.[4]

The significance of organized labor to the fight against apartheid can't be overemphasized. It broke from the AFL-CIO's long Cold War history of collaborating with the US government to promote anticommunist unionism in the global South. Inspired by a strike of three hundred thousand South African mine workers and the rising labor militancy in South Africa in general, union locals came together to form the Illinois Labor Network Against Apartheid in 1987. Kathy Devine, a white social justice activist, served as coordinator, and AFSCME's Rosetta Daylie and the UAW's Mike Elliott played leading roles. Prexy was a key source of advice and support.[5] The ILNAA stood with "South African unions as they [fought] the atrocities of the apartheid regime"

Figure 14. Cole Wright of the United Food and Commercial Workers Union, left; Michael Elliot of UAW Local 551, center; and Kathy Devine, co-chair of ILNAA, right, 1989. Courtesy of Mary Pat Hamilton.

and supported their calls "for total sanctions, for action on Shell, and for exposure of their government's brutality against the black majority."[6]

"We were supporting international workers' solidarity," Devine noted, such as when Ford closed a plant in South Africa and took part of the workers' pensions with them. The ILNAA organized UAW workers to protest. "They would stand up at meetings and ask 'Why are you doing this to the workers in Port Elizabeth? We asked you to divest. We didn't ask you to take their money from them.'" Other American unions hosted South African trade unionists who brought indispensable perspectives to US audiences.[7]

As South Africa killed, banned, and jailed thousands of protesters and imposed additional constraints on COSATU, the United Democratic Front, and others, the ILNAA and CCISSA teamed up to assail this violent state repression. They organized a rally in March 1988 to protest an "exclusive briefing" in Chicago by the South African Ambassador with select American leaders. Basil Clunie called it "totally immoral for the South African government to send officials to the Midwest to talk to American citizens about South Africa, while the South African government refuse[d] to talk to its own citizens."[8]

The ties that activists had built with the City Council during the divestment fight remained helpful in this next stage of struggle. The ILNAA and CCISSA organized the council to declare March 18 "A Day of Solidarity with South African Trade Unionists," and hundreds of union members rallied that day at Federal Plaza and marched to the South African Consulate. They demanded the release of jailed unionists, especially Moses Mayekiso, General Secretary of the National Union of Metalworkers of South Africa, the nation's largest union, and a founder of COSATU. A committed socialist, Mayekiso advocated for the following: "a workers' charter that will say clearly who will control the farms, the factories, the mines. There must be a change of the whole society . . . people are opposed to the idea that there will be two stages toward liberation. It's a waste of time, a waste of energy, and a waste of peoples' blood."[9] He was referring to the South African Communist Party (SACP) and the ANC's evolving stance that the fight for democratic elections was the first stage of liberation, with the push for socialism beginning after that. Mayekiso faced charges of high treason. Jack Parton of the United Steelworkers of America, and Bill Stewart of the UAW led a delegation to the consulate, where they delivered petitions signed by thousands demanding the release of political prisoners and staged a civil disobedience. Parton, Stewart, as well as Elcosie Gresham of the Amalgamated Transit Union; Rosetta Daylie of AFSCME; Rev. Michael Pfleger of St. Sabina Catholic Church; Richard Ziebell from the UAW; Johnnie Jackson from the Coalition of Labor Union Women; and Carole Travis, president of a UAW local were arrested for trespassing. That American union leaders would wage such a fight to free an avowed socialist unionist in the global South was a stunning departure from organized labor's long-standing anticommunism.[10]

Figure 15. Chicago demonstration on behalf of Moses Mayekiso, spring 1988. Courtesy of Mary Pat Hamilton.

While the charges were later dropped, the group spent close to twelve hours in jail. "I didn't plan on being arrested," Daylie recalled. AFSCME president William Lucy came to Chicago for the protest. "And he was the one who was supposed to be arrested, but something happened, and he had to leave town, and he assigned me to take his place." They expected to be jailed for a brief period and then released on their own recognizance, "but there was another group that was protesting something else in Chicago and they didn't want to be bailed out. So, we got confused with that group." As it happened, Daylie represented civilian workers at that precinct "and a lot of my members knew that I was in there. So, they made sure I had something to eat, and they came in checking on me. But it was kind of cold for them to close the cell door. To be locked in."[11] In 1989, after three years in prison, and following a massive domestic and international campaign, Mayekiso and his codefendants, including his brother, were acquitted.[12]

An anti-apartheid boycott of the Shell Oil Company drew important union support. Prexy spoke at a "Get the sHell Out of South Africa!" rally in Chicago alongside Richard Trumka, president of the United Mine Workers of America. "Without supplies from companies like Shell," Trumka declared, "the apartheid regime could not continue to send its forces into townships to terrorize black families. Without Shell, the apartheid government could not deploy its troops to shoot down protestors and detain strikers and political activists. Shell is the largest multinational corporation in the world—and despite the loud and clear demand of the black majority that foreign corporations get out of their country, Shell remains where it is not wanted." Trumka lauded the nationwide Shell boycott and praised labor's vigorous role in the movement. He assailed the conviction for treason, just the day before, of four Black anti-apartheid leaders in South Africa. "There is treason in South Africa. It's the treason to human rights committed by apartheid. It's the treason to human dignity committed by apartheid."[13]

Prexy was very active in the fight against the illegal South African occupation of Namibia, then known under its colonial name South West Africa. He came to be very close to Toivo ya Toivo, the extraordinary Namibian who co-founded SWAPO, and was incarcerated on terrorism charges for sixteen years on Robben Island. The solidarity movement in Chicago fully embraced the Namibian freedom struggle, frequently welcoming SWAPO leaders. In 1988 Chicago hosted SWAPO president Sam Nujoma who gave a speech at a rally at Jesse Jackson's Rainbow/PUSH headquarters, assailing apartheid as a crime against humanity. In a striking example of the breadth of internationalist connections in Chicago, Nangolo Ilonga, the General Secretary of Namibia's Public Workers Union also visited in 1988 and met with Prexy, Congressman Charlie Hayes, and leaders of TransAfrica and AFSCME. But he also met with a Black doctors' association, went to a Black Studies conference, and attended an Earth Day demonstration.[14]

As I have argued, the anti-apartheid movement and the solidarity efforts with national liberation struggles in southern Africa more generally tended to weaken anticommunist voices among US liberals and progressives (although certainly not in the government, as Ronald Reagan reinvigorated anticommunism.) The role played by US labor leaders is a good example of this shift. Whereas for much of the postwar era, unions were expected to eschew entanglements with leftists, foreign or domestic, and endorse US foreign policy, the rise of the anti-apartheid movement shifted the terrain. It opened a way for unions to engage in a progressive internationalist movement, as the righteousness of the anti-apartheid struggle helped imbue the work with a moral fervor.

This contrasted sharply with the AFL-CIO's long collaboration with the American government to undercut or prevent the rise of socialist or pro-communist unions in Europe and the global South.[15] A vehicle for this AFL-CIO work in Africa was the African American Labor Center (AALC) founded in 1964. In 1988 Prexy co-authored a scathing rebuke of the international policy of the AFL-CIO, which had "stepped up its efforts to coopt the revolutionary fervor" of workers and unions in South Africa by directing funds to more politically conservative labor groups. The AFL-CIO had the gall to tap an expelled Pan-Africanist Congress leader with no union experience (and who it was later revealed had been recruited by the CIA) to head a new Program of Action in Support of Black Trade Unions, in 1981. The international affairs department of the AFL-CIO, Prexy argued, was consumed with "a rabid anticommunism" that lead them to subvert progressive forces. The AALC also had ties with Unita in Angola and Renamo in Mozambique. In a telling move, in 1982 the AFL-CIO had given its George Meany Human Rights Award to Inkatha leader Gatsha Buthelezi, "the apartheid-government appointed chief of the Zulus," who many Black South Africans regarded as a collaborator. In Prexy's view, the independent flow of information in the internationalist movement enabled the UAW, ACTWU, and ILWU to challenge the AFL-CIO and expose and confront Buthelezi.[16] For Prexy, this was yet another example of the importance of international rather than simply national organizing against apartheid.

"REMEMBER CUITO CUANAVALE!"

In a major turning point for the whole region, in 1988 Pretoria agreed to free elections in Namibia and to end their support for Jonas Savimbi's brutal warfare against the government and people of Angola. President Reagan tried to credit his policy of "constructive engagement" for this turnabout, but it was an obscure battle at Cuito Cuanavale in southern Angola that pushed South Africa to more seriously engage in diplomacy and accede to international pressure to withdraw from Namibia. Cuban troops successfully defended Cuito Cuanavale from Unita/South African attacks, and they advanced toward the Namibian border. "Their prowess on the battlefield and their skill at the negotiating table reverberated beyond Namibia and Angola," according to one scholar. In the words of Nelson Mandela, the Cuban victory "destroyed the myth of the invincibility of the white oppressor . . . (and) inspired the fighting masses of South Africa . . . Cuito Cuanavale was the turning point for the liberation of our continent—and of my people—from the scourge of apartheid." SWAPO won elections a year later thwarting South African efforts to install a puppet regime.[17]

Prexy first learned of the importance of the defense of Cuito Cuanavale on a 1989 trip with foundation officials to the frontline states, where they had a long meeting with ANC leaders, including Thabo Mbeki. Mbeki stressed the importance of the South African defeat to Namibian independence. "We finally understood why South Africa had agreed to Namibian independence: it wasn't the triumph of moderates, but the defeat of the military." The ANC made them better understand how much a free Namibia boosted their own confidence in the coming of freedom to South Africa too.[18]

Crushingly, after the South African pull back, the US became the primary source of support for Unita. "US resentment about the defeat of their joint intervention into Angola with South Africa in 1975–76 fed into right-wing Cold War calculations in the Reagan period," Bill Minter observed.[19] Aid to Unita escalated, with the war ultimately producing "the highest per capita amputee rate in the world."[20] And yet, former Unita supporters began to reveal the extent of Savimbi's atrocities. According to one dissident, Savimbi burned opponents he had accused of being witches to death: "Savimbi watched it all. As a woman tried to escape the flames, he took out his gun to shoot her. There's a long list of Savimbi supporters who have disappeared or been killed." But this didn't reduce support for him by Republicans in Congress.[21] Tragically, US support for Savimbi's counterinsurgency continued into the 1990s.

WALKATHONS

While continuing efforts to influence US foreign policy, activists also undertook material aid projects. From 1987 to 1994, ILNAA, CCISA,

Wellington United Church of Christ, and Trinity United Church of Christ organized annual walkathons to commemorate the June 1976 Soweto uprising and murderous state response. The ten-kilometer walkathons helped to keep Americans informed about conditions in South Africa as they raised at least $10,000 each year for human needs organizations. As always, organizers strove to make connections between racial and economic struggles locally with those in southern Africa: "We're talking about a common enemy and a common fight," Harold Rogers declared at the 1989 walkathon rally, "just on different continents." That rally took place at the Charles Hayes Center on the South Side—Hayes, a longtime union leader, was a member of Congress who championed anti-apartheid protest—and showcased the internationalist sensibility that pervaded progressive political culture in Chicago because of the anti-apartheid and other solidarity movements.[22]

Also speaking at the rally, Rosetta Daylie, the AFSCME leader and ILNAA co-chair, declared "an injury to one is an injury to all," as she offered her union's solidarity with "our union brothers and sisters in South Africa." The ILNAA was deeply involved in trying to free jailed labor activists, and she celebrated the recent acquittal of Moses Mayekiso thanks in large measure to an international campaign. Speakers urged passage of Ron Dellums's stronger sanctions bill and pressed the ongoing boycott of Shell. Kathy Devine gave an update about South African workers efforts to get Mobil Oil to withdraw from South Africa in a way that protected workers. There were petitions to sign and politicians to call. Devine read a message of solidarity from the Chemical Workers Industrial Union, which she had just received via fax, and proclaimed: "We have great technology today!"[23]

Prexy's rousing speech closed out the rally. Future Congressman Danny Davis, then an alderman from the West Side, introduced him as one of "the most effective international advocates for democracy and freedom for the continent of Africa on the face of this universe." He had

Figure 16. Soweto Day Rally at the Charles Hayes Center in Chicago, June 1989: Charles Hayes, standing, and Basil Clunie, seated on the right. Courtesy of Mary Pat Hamilton and Basil Clunie.

so "immersed himself and his life into the movement" that he now worked for the government of Mozambique. And yet, Davis emphasized, Prexy was "a hard-working brother from the West Side of Chicago." There it was: Prexy's commitment to the global and the local summed up in an introduction. Prexy began by describing how he had enlisted friends and family to leaflet across the West Side in 1970 to publicize the local premiere of the documentary *A Luta Continua*. But only Prexy, his cousin and a nun who ran the venue braved the freezing temperature that night to see this groundbreaking film on Mozambique. The turnout of hundreds of people that day, raising $14,000, he declared, showed the progress in building solidarity with southern Africa. He called for tougher sanctions. "Why sanctions? Because the repression today in South Africa is reaching new heights. Why sanctions? Because today South Africa is the number one terrorist state." He described the "state sponsored killing" inside the country and the long history of gunning down ANC leaders abroad. To make the push for tougher sanctions hit home, he described his personal experiences with antiblackness in his travels across the country. Why Sanctions? Because "it was our contribution to freeing South Africa" and "our contribution to say no to the growth of racism in this country." Our solidarity, he insisted, was not just a moral position but propelled by self-interest too.[24]

The walkathons reveal a notable collaboration between progressive churches and the anti-imperialist movement, while the grant recipients show the broad focus of the Chicago solidarity movement. In 1990 Soweto Day funds were given to "victims of South Africa's war against neighboring Mozambique," while funds raised in the 1991 walkathon were donated to the Alexandra Civic Organization (ACO), as its residents confronted immense violence during the last years of apartheid.[25] Alexandra Township, an impoverished Black township nestled among posh white suburbs of Johannesburg, had a long history of resistance to apartheid. The vast majority of its 350,000 residents lived on one square kilometer of land in one room shacks with no plumbing, electricity, or

Figure 17. Soweto Day march, 1991. Courtesy of Joan Gerig.

regular sanitation services. Founded in 1982, the ACO led the town-ship's militant opposition to apartheid and as a result, its leaders were targeted by the state. Union leader Moses Mayekiso chaired the ACO and lived in a one-room shack with his wife, brother, and seven chil-dren. The ACO was part of the "civic" movement in South Africa: grassroots community-based organizations in Black townships, which after Mandela's release from prison, shifted their focus toward prepar-ing for development and governance in a post-apartheid future.[26]

In 1990 the Chicago City Council passed a resolution—organized by CCISSA and sponsored by Chuy Garcia, Danny Davis, and Bobby L. Rush, all future members of Congress—declaring Alexandra a Chi-cago sister-community and recognizing the ACO as the legitimate voice of the people of the township. The Chicago-Alexandra Sister-Community Project worked with the ACO to cultivate community-based leadership and advocate for better housing, education, and healthcare for the residents of the beleaguered township. In addition to material support, many trips back and forth between Alexandra and Chicago strengthened the work. Mayekiso forged close relationships with Chicagoans through both the ILNAA and the sister-community project. "The ACO represents one of the strongest efforts at self-governance in South Africa's townships," the CCISSA noted. "Our linkage with them places us in direct contact with grassroots, democratic organization that will be key to the future of South Africa."[27]

The ACO's Mary Ntingane and Mzwanele Mayekiso spent six weeks in Chicago before the 1991 walkathon, scouting out technical support, collaborations, and other ideas to advance development in Alexandra. Ntingane usually stayed at labor activist Rosetta Daylie's home on her visits to Chicago: "She really got to meet my family and my family just loved her." In turn, Ntingane took Daylie to see Alexandra when Daylie was in South Africa as an election observer in 1994.[28]

For Prexy, the sister-community project "continued the tradition of embracing each other's struggles in a very real way" and added to "the Chicago-Johannesburg connection," which the poetry and friendships of the South African poet Keorapetse Kgositsile were also a part of. Kgositsile, whom Prexy had first met in Tanzania in 1968, was married to Cheryl Harris, a lawyer in the Harold Washington administration and an activist alongside Prexy in CIDSA. Harris became a professor and legal scholar, author of the influential article "Whiteness as Property."[29]

INTERNATIONALIST CHICAGO

CCISSA and ILNAA anchored a vibrant left-internationalist activist culture in Chicago, which encompassed many struggles beyond the ones under consideration here. For example, CCISSA teamed up with the Committee in Solidarity with the People of El Salvador to host Get Up, Stand Up, a "music video dance night" in 1988, to raise funds for

Figure 18. Children listen intently to Nomonde Ngubo speaking in Chicago. Courtesy of Mary Pat Hamilton.

Central American and Southern African human rights projects. Sylvia Ewing, who worked with both CCISSA and the Mozambique Support Network, helped organize it. Musicians and artists from Billy Bragg, Artists United Against Apartheid, Tommy Boy Records, and Global Vision performed.[30]

In January 1990 ILNAA hosted a visit by Nomonde Ngubo, a South African woman who was a founding member of the National Union of Mineworkers. Prexy had barnstormed with Ngubo across Kansas in 1986 to galvanize support for sanctions. Ngubo updated ILNAA leaders on the momentous Conference for a Democratic Future recently held in South Africa with over two thousand anti-apartheid organizations. She urged a redoubled effort on the part of unions and anti-apartheid organizations to counter the widespread disinformation in the US media regarding southern Africa issues. At a rally, Ngubo sang South African and US labor songs, just as she had done in Kansas. She also performed a Zulu dance, "accompanied by Ron Bowden of AFSCME and Mike Elliott of UAW with AFSCME's Alan Schwartz on guitar."[31]

The major media largely ignored events in southern Africa, as well as local events aimed at raising awareness among Americans. CCISSA planned a rally at the South African consulate after a walkathon one year, so Basil Clunie reached out to the *Chicago Tribune*. "Are you going to break any windows? Are you going to get arrested?" they asked. "Well, not necessarily," he replied. Well, then "it's not news," the *Tribune* replied to justify its failure to cover local organizing. "An important weapon in South Africa's war has been its public relations campaign in Western countries, especially in the United States," Prexy wrote, in a scathing analysis of the US media's accommodation to, even complicity with, apartheid. "South Africa spends millions of dollars in the West, to project the image of itself as the great reform government and peacemaker for the region. The near total silence of the US press in the face of such South African brutalities both within South Africa proper and extending to the frontline states has to be understood as another 'weapon' of the apartheid system. Indeed, one can easily build a case that the US media, given its silence, has become a collaborator with apartheid's genocidal schemes." Indeed, a 2016 publication corroborated Prexy's contemporaneous understanding and documented the hundreds of millions of dollars Pretoria spent during the height of the struggle to produce propaganda to mislead and conceal the true nature of conditions in southern Africa.[32]

As a result, the movement developed their own media, which alongside the Black press, were critical sources of news and analyses. CCISSA and other groups issued their own newsletters and lobbied WTTW, the local PBS station, to carry the extraordinary New York–produced thirty-minute weekly show *South Africa Now*. Initially WTTW refused to air it, but activists pressured the station's donors, and they gave in. Created in April 1988 by activist-journalist Danny Schechter, who had worked for *20/20*, and hosted and led by African journalists in the US and on the continent, *South Africa Now* was extraordinarily important in teaching American audiences about the politics and culture of southern Africa. The show was created in response to the apartheid regime's harsh censorship, which had kept much of the resistance movement's story hidden from global media. "When the South African government began imposing severe restrictions on the media," Schechter observed, "the networks almost seemed to be collaborating; certainly, none of the networks was challenging the South African government." With funding from the UN, foundations, and celebrities, the show aired on 109 outlets around the world. According to Schechter, they trained "black South Africans so that they (could) tell their own story and bring their own sensibility to the news." Sylvia Ewing was the Midwest liaison for *South Africa Now*. "Prexy was totally instrumental," she recalled, "because if someone was coming to town, he could help us get those few minutes to get a recording of them." In 1990 the Right began attacking the show as "ANC propaganda," and it ended production a year later for lack of funding.[33]

THE RELEASE OF NELSON MANDELA

By early 1990, many began to anticipate Nelson Mandela's release from prison. Lindiwe Mabuza, the ANC's representative in Washington, DC, visited Chicago to thank anti-apartheid activists for contributing to the international economic pressure that had brought South Africa to a crossroads. She speculated that Mandela would soon be released, but she decried the credit given to South African president De Klerk for making reforms. No, she said, "the ANC has been 'unbanned' by the people who have been displaying ANC flags and logos for many months. Petty apartheid laws have become unenforceable." Nelson Mandela, she said, is dictating the conditions of his own release.[34]

Already in possession of negotiating skills due to his training as a lawyer and childhood exposure to the consensus character of tribal decision-making, Mandela sharpened these skills during his long incarceration. In 1985 he decided on his own, against ANC strictures, to reach out to the government. "We thought he was selling out," Cyril Ramaphosa, then-president of the National Union of Mineworkers, recalled. "He took a massive risk." But Ramaphosa came to see the wisdom in his act. "He's a historical man. He was thinking way ahead of us." Mandela held dozens of meetings with a committee led by the head of security in South Africa, most of which happened after he was transferred to a prison outside of Cape Town in 1988. Through his attorney George Bizos, Mandela kept ANC leaders informed, especially Oliver Tambo. He was not making deals but, in his words, acting as a "facilitator." Negotiations to forge a democratic government commenced with a wider group after Mandela's release from prison.[35]

On February 11, 1990, after twenty-seven years of incarceration, Mandela walked out of prison alongside his wife Winnie Mandela. No one knew what he'd look like: the regime had banned his image and voice hoping he'd be forgotten, but instead this had turned him into a global icon and symbol of a free future South Africa. Chicago activists hosted a celebration—"an extraordinary event," Basil Clunie recalled—at Malcolm X College. Anne Evens was in Mozambique and celebrated with ANC members in exile: "I was there when Nelson Mandela was freed, and being in the streets with my friends who were South African was amazing."[36]

Prexy was at a radio station in Madison "when somebody phoned in and said Mandela had been released." Prexy immediately called his friend Father Michael Weeder in Cape Town to get an update. "There was a great desire to have Madiba speak," Prexy learned, invoking a family name for Mandela, widely used as a term of endearment and respect, "but tremendous concern about protecting him." Another pressing concern was arranging for Mandela to meet with the scattered ANC leadership. "Part of it's in London, part of it's in Lusaka, Zambia, part of it's in Angola, part of it's in Dar es Salaam, and part of it is in South Africa, and part of those in South Africa are also underground."[37]

A month later, the first president of independent Namibia was inaugurated. SWAPO invited Prexy to the ceremony, which is when he first saw Mandela in person, if at a distance. "I couldn't find anywhere to stay, so I slept for three nights on a chair in the Kalahari Sands Hotel. But I was privileged to be at one of the most extraordinary moments, probably of my whole career." Prexy watched as the flag was raised for a free Namibia. "I was teary-eyed and had goose bumps," he recalled. The crowd cheered the President, Sam Nujoma. "But when Mandela was brought up a few minutes later, they went bananas—they just went berserk," Prexy observed. "And that was one of the first indications that I had of the power and the appeal, the love, that existed around this man. I had seen this with other leaders, I'd seen it with Rev. King, and I'd seen it with Samora Machel."[38]

Prexy first met Mandela in New York in June. "I called him Madiba, which pleased him because at that point, not a lot of African Americans knew this nickname. And he gave me one of those smiles, and said, 'I know your name.'" Mandela could have heard about Prexy and the Chicago movement from any number of ANC leaders, including Barbara Masekela, sister of Hugh Masekela and a South African exile in Ohio. Prexy had known her for years, and she had become an aide and speech writer for Mandela.[39]

Nelson Mandela traveled the world to thank activists and strategize for the end of apartheid. His first stops were to Tanzania, Zambia, and Angola, frontline states that had provided indispensable support to the ANC. Their support was Pan-Africanism in action. Mandela then traveled to Scandinavia and to Cuba, which inspired the wrath of American conservatives. But the visit was an important acknowledgement of Cuba's essential role in helping to end apartheid. "If I've learned anything from all my years of involvement," Prexy said, "the critical role played by Cuba is never emphasized enough in this country."[40]

The Mandelas visited eight American cities in June, arriving to much fanfare in New York City, where hundreds of thousands lined Broadway for a ticker-tape parade. Everywhere Mandela emphasized the need to continue sanctions and press for democratic elections.[41] The ANC and ACOA convened a National Activist Briefing; Prexy was the lone person on the steering committee who didn't represent an organization, such as the Washington Office on Africa, the UAW, the AFSC, or TransAfrica. In contrast, Prexy was described as "a key individual involved in the anti-apartheid movement for the last twenty years." Over 150 activists conferred with ANC and COSATU leaders. Joining Prexy from Chicago were Basil Clunie for the CCISSA, UAW leader Carole Travis for the ILNAA, Lisa January for the Mozambique Support Network, and a TransAfrica representative. Prexy offered opening remarks. Jennifer Davis spoke and assailed the Bush administration's push to end sanctions, insisting that they continue until free elections were held. At that juncture, "26 states, 19 counties and 83 cities [had] taken action against companies that [did] business in South Africa." A year later the total rose to twenty-eight states, twenty-four counties, and ninety-two cities.[42]

South Africans at the briefing stressed the dire conditions on the ground. Sister Bernard Ncube, of the Federation of Transvaal Women, reported, "the pillars of apartheid are crumbling. The prospect of a black, ANC-led South Africa is scaring whites and stirring the growth of the radical right-wing." She also noted that "with the unbanning of the ANC, women need to get educated and mobilize." Thomas Nkobi, the secretary-general of the ANC said "Police brutality is increasing. Massacres are on the increase in Natal. Children are running away from home in fear. Thousands have run to Lusaka, Tanzania and Botswana. ANC supporters must not be lulled by the fact that Nelson Mandela is out of jail." He, like others, pressed the point that the international struggle must continue.[43]

The Americans asked Chris Dlamini, vice president of COSATU, about the role of the Pan-Africanist Congress. The PAC wants to continue armed struggle, he reported, but it has no army. "The PAC wants land handed over to the blacks," he shared, "but the ANC thinks that this should come out of discussion." Dlamini's words foreshadowed the compromises that would come. When asked about worker support for nationalization of private firms, he offered that its appeal comes from the hardship of workers in certain industries: Black miners for example made one-eighth of the income of white miners. But ultimately, he said, the decision as to the "final type of socio-economic order will come from all sectors of South Africa." And in a striking capitulation to efforts to discredit COSATU's commitment to economic justice, he pointed as cause for his moderation to the fact that Pretoria "paints COSATU as terrorists and communists."[44]

Soon after Mandela's release and signals from De Klerk that apartheid would end, many Western governments began to ease sanctions. Continuing the push for economic isolation was the main weapon the movement still had to shape the outcome in South Africa. Jennifer Davis summed up the task for US activists: "The anti-apartheid movement is entering new and dangerous times. If we are not careful, the US will throw its weight behind some complicated constitution that falls short of 'one person, one vote' in a unified South Africa." And economic questions must remain at the fore, since, as Davis put it, "South Africa is a capitalist system of the grossest inequality."[45]

Nelson Mandela arrived shortly before the National Activist Briefing came to an end. "After a rousing 'keep the pressure on' and standing ovation from participants," he described the immediate needs of the ANC. Basil Clunie wrote that Mandela "reminded us that the greatest difficulties lay directly ahead," because "seeds of confusion and discord continue to be sowed in an effort to blunt the efforts of anti-apartheid work."[46] During his visit to the US, Mandela also appeared before a live audience on *Nightline*, a popular late-night news show hosted by Ted Koppel. When asked about racism in the United States, Mandela replied that "it would not be proper for me to delve into the controversial issues which are tearing the society apart," a rather stunning statement because that's exactly what the global anti-apartheid movement had been doing. Taken aback, Harry Lennix, a student activist at Northwestern who had become a professional actor, said to himself, "I wish I could take that time back. I would have devoted that time to the domestic issues of Black Americans." In some respects, this was a sign of the changed political landscape as Mandela negotiated for elections and contemplated an assumption of state power.[47]

Heeten Kalan, the South African student activist at Dartmouth, was surprised to get an invitation to meet Mandela during his second visit in 1990. "I'm sure Prexy had something to do with that. I'm thinking of the two hundred people invited, Why me? So, I got to be in this tiny room with Mandela thanking people for their work." Kalan noted that Prexy was never a gatekeeper but was, rather, someone who opened doors.[48]

NEGOTIATIONS AND VIOLENCE, 1990–1994

Two developments constrained the ambitions and confidence of the ANC as it began to engage the government in negotiations to end apartheid. One was an aggressive full-court press by South African, American, and global capital elites to stanch the ANC's pursuit of socialist or other redistributionary policies. The second was the apartheid regime's brutal deployment of lethal violence within the nation and the region as an additional intimidation tactic. These two factors help explain the ANC's decision to focus on securing political freedom in the form of democratic elections, rather than foregrounding its commitment to economic justice.

Many in the international anti-apartheid movement hoped that the end of apartheid would lead, if not to socialism, then to some significant land redistribution or redress for the many economic injuries of apartheid. Negotiations on South Africa's future, known as the CODESA talks, focused on achieving a democratic political system but unfortunately avoided the harder economic questions. ANC policy had long called for transferring the nation's immense wealth to the people, but when leaders, like Jay Naidoo from COSATU, and others sought to make structural change part of the negotiations, they lost. At that juncture, Mandela was reportedly "being cultivated by influential top business leaders in South Africa and overseas." It turns out that Harry Oppenheimer, the CEO of the largest gold and diamond conglomerate in the world, began having weekly luncheons with Mandela as soon as he left prison.[49]

But the signals were often conflicting. In a 1990 interview from Lusaka, ANC and Communist Party leader Joe Slovo was still touting socialism: "The South African model of capitalism has been at the very foundation of racism," he said. "You don't have to be a Marxist to see this." Even though 80 to 90 percent of Africa is run in a capitalist way, "the misery of the majority remains in place in the context of market economics and a capitalist orientation," Slovo said. He too would shortly be on a negotiating team making major compromises.[50] With such public statements, it's perhaps understandable that many people in South Africa and abroad missed the cues about where the post-apartheid economy was headed.

Appreciating the political context of the early 1990s is crucial to understanding the political choices of ANC leadership. The Berlin Wall fell in 1989, and the USSR collapsed in 1991. The communist bloc, an important source of support for the ANC, was in shatters, and neoliberalism was ascendant globally. An aggressive form of capitalism, neoliberalism idolizes the free market and castigates unions and government regulation and taxes as roadblocks to economic freedom. Both US political parties drank from the well of neoliberalism, including George H. W. Bush and Bill Clinton, the two Americans in the White House as South Africa shifted away from legal apartheid.

Mandela heard the neoliberal message everywhere. The Freedom Charter's promise to nationalize key industries was suddenly deemed foolhardy. According to Danny Schechter, "when Mandela visited the World Economic Forum in 1991, he was advised—not just by capitalists but by leaders of socialist countries like Vietnam as well—to promote a mixed economy. His original speech was promptly modified to appease that sentiment." Moreover, Mandela told his ghostwriter that the US was putting tremendous pressure on him not to nationalize industries and to preserve private property rights in a new constitution. Mandela feared a post-apartheid flight of capital and made many compromises as a result.[51]

The US continued its efforts to constrain the ambitions of the ANC. In July 1991, during the presidency of George H. W. Bush, the United States ended sanctions against South Africa, claiming that progress toward the defeat of apartheid had been made. Mandela assailed the move, saying it undermined the power of the ANC in negotiations. And in 1992 it was leaked that State Department officials were pushing hard for a capitalist economy. "We are starting the process of educating the ANC," one official said, with typical American arrogance. "The ANC remains fuzzyheaded about economics, unaffected by the lessons of Eastern Europe."[52]

There were views and groups to the left of the ANC/Congress Alliance. For example, the 1983 Azanian Manifesto pledged to overthrow racial capitalism and stressed the critical importance of Black working-class leadership in the struggle. Many of these ideas were deeply embraced by many ANC supporters too, but the ANC was a big tent. By the release of Mandela, most activists in the international arena took direction chiefly from the ANC. According to Prexy, for most activists in the United States, "there was no other option"—although he does recall that activists in California and Washington, DC, had greater contact with ANC dissidents. The ANC encompassed a range of opinions, even as it inspired incredible unity and discipline. Prexy recalls that after Johnny Makatini left his ANC position in New York in the mid-1980s, "the ANC ceased to carry the banner of the Left." And other contradictions surfaced. Prexy became aware of instances of sexual assault by ANC men against US women activists, and in one instance, he confronted the man.[53]

The four years between Mandela's release from prison and the first democratic elections in South Africa saw an escalation of violence against both ordinary people and leading activists. As a historian of the era has argued, "soon after Mandela's release, media reports turned to the growing threat of 'black-on-black violence.' In a diabolical attempt at agenda setting, the South African government shifted the focus from apartheid to 'tribal animosities' by orchestrating massacres to provoke violence between the United Democratic Front and the Inkatha Freedom Party." And as the South African Truth Commission has shown, "the government orchestrated a campaign to discredit Mandela and the ANC and hold the township violence as a trump card in negotiations over power sharing and sanctions."[54] In other words, one purpose of the violence was to undercut the unity and confidence that would be required to forcefully push the nation into a new direction.

While negotiations in South Africa continued, activists in the United States intensified efforts to expose the culpability of the regime in fomenting violence. Africans across the region blamed South Africa for the violence—even when it was outsourced to various professional death squads—but the American media still tended to characterize it as "tribal."[55]

Beginning in the mid-1980s the Inkatha Freedom Party (IFP), led by Mangosuthu Gatsha Buthelezi, chief minister of the KwaZulu Bantustan, instigated violence against members of the United Democratic Front, killing thousands. In the early 1990s Inkatha-led violence intensified against UDF, ANC, and COSATU partisans. But the violence went both ways, as each group saw itself in a struggle for power in a changing South Africa. In a content analysis of major US networks, newsmagazines, and newspapers stories on South Africa in 1990, Chicago historian and anti-apartheid activist Lisa Brock found a depoliticized analysis in favor of a "Black-on-Black" or "senseless violence" framing. The outlets ignored evidence that Inkatha forces received military training and money from the apartheid state. "Buthelezi has taken important political positions markedly different than those of the ANC. He has been willing to work within the apartheid Bantustan system as chief of KwaZulu. He has lobbied widely against sanctions in the international arena. He asserts that he and his organization stand against armed struggle, uphold a free enterprise system, and he has been quoted as saying that he believes in some form of ethnically constructed future South Africa," Brock wrote, drawing attention to the political differences at stake in the conflict.

On the other hand, "the ANC, the UDF, and COSATU have advocated the right of armed struggle against apartheid, have encouraged sanctions and nationalization of certain aspects of the economy, and strive for an integrated and nonracial South Africa. Inkatha's disputes with the ANC, UDF, and COSATU are clearly more ideological and political than they are ethnic." Nor had the media linked violence to poverty or the systems created by apartheid: "Migrant labor, the core of apartheid, has torn families apart and left large segments of the South African population in poverty. Unemployed and undereducated youths are often left to their own psychological and physical defenses. These social conditions often breed gangs and persons who may engage in misdirected violence."

Brock and others argued that Buthelezi feared losing power if the ANC should set the direction for a post-apartheid South Africa. As a result, "violent conflict may be one way for him to secure a place at the negotiating table." Brock argued that the National Party gained from the media story of "tribal" violence as it would tap into long-standing colonialist ideas of Black incapacity for self-government.[56]

Solidarity activists worried that the violence would undermine the ANC's negotiating stance and weaken their commitment to economic redistribution. "The escalating violence by the South African police and military, together with lnkatha vigilantes, has reached crisis proportions," declared the ILNAA, "directly undermining democratic organizations and potentially derailing national negotiations to end apartheid." They endorsed COSATU's call for the prosecution of those responsible for the violence and for the dismantling of both the Bantustan system and the KwaZulu police. They further called upon the United States to condemn Inkatha and pressure South Africa to end the violence.[57]

South Africa and the Bush administration both sent millions of dollars to the IFP. Chicagoans were especially upset by those funds financing attacks on residents of Alexandra, Chicago's sister community. Hit squads targeted ACO leader Mayekiso, and IFP partisans stole money and goods, harassed residents, and in some cases, forcibly conscripted them into Inkatha. The CCISSA stressed that, contrary to US press portrayals, none of this violence was "tribal;" it was "orchestrated political attacks designed to destabilize the anti-apartheid movement and to terrorize all South Africans in order to slow or stop negotiations for majority rule."[58]

Buthelezi visited the United States in 1991, and for some reason— perhaps the fact that he was included in the negotiations to end apartheid—Jesse Jackson invited him to speak at Rainbow/PUSH. But Chicago's solidarity community quickly mobilized calls and telegrams from leaders across the country, and they withdrew the invitation.[59] Prexy spoke at PUSH the following day, and *South Africa Now* aired a portion of his remarks. As was his style, Prexy found a local analogy for what was happening abroad. "As with the killing of Black Panther Party leader Fred Hampton in Chicago in 1969, when Black functionaries played such a decisive role, what has emerged in South Africa today is a situation where the governing apartheid regime has subcontracted the dirty business of killing apartheid's enemies to surrogate forces— most of them Black." The primary source of the violence domestically and in the region, Prexy declared, "is the South African government and its various security structures ranging from the army, police and constables to vigilantes and surrogate armed gangs."

Prexy reminded listeners that while "the ANC is in dialogue with the Inkatha (as it is in dialogue with the government) this is not the time for anti-apartheid groups to emulate such dialogue—unless requested to do so by the national liberation movement. We Chicago-based organizations, while maintaining our organizational autonomy and integrity, have also always coordinated our decisions with the ANC and its political allies and have never attempted to preempt them."[60]

The American Committee on Africa, a leading anti-apartheid group, reinforced this message: The apartheid regime has "worked to incite blacks to fight each other. It created and continues to finance ten tribally based homelands, including the KwaZulu homeland operated by Gatsha Buthelezi." While the killings are dismissed as incidents of "Black on Black violence," "Inkatha in fact is a tool of the Government."[61]

Meanwhile, in South Africa, the Goldstone Commission, "an unprecedented public inquiry," investigated allegations that a "Third Force" within the South African security forces was behind much of the violence that had claimed about ten thousand Black lives since the mid-1980s. Mbongeni Khumalo, a former IFP official, testified that he had worked with the South African Defense Forces to train hit squads to kill members of the ANC. The five-person commission, which had two Black jurists, had the support of both the government and ANC, but top military and police brass destroyed evidence. Still, it found that twenty-five senior members of the South African police and military had worked with the Inkatha Freedom Party in orchestrating township violence with the goal of undermining the ANC. As a result, President de Klerk fired twenty-three top army officers for their covert role in provoking violence.[62] Historians have documented at least three secret military units that engaged in assassinations and promoted violence in Natal. "The South African police systematically aided and armed Inkatha fighters in the Natal violence," according to one account.[63]

As always, Prexy regularly visited the region, sometimes bringing Americans, who would return and share their knowledge. In July 1992 he accompanied Vera Michelson and Eileen C. Kawola, activists with the Capital District Coalition against Apartheid and Racism in Albany, on a month-long trip to Mozambique, Namibia, and South Africa. They bore witness to the violence across the region. "We're talking about the violence in South Africa that is sponsored by apartheid," Michelson said, "and the violence apartheid has organized across its borders." They met with Albertina Sisulu, the courageous ANC activist whose husband, Walter, was incarcerated on Robben Island. They visited a squatter camp in Durban where "water is a concern every day. They saw several hundred families using a single outhouse. They saw one water tap for 3,000 families, and it was turned off each weekday at 5 PM. 'People spend hours getting to work,' Kawola says, then they have to come home and find water."[64]

Back home, Michelson and Kawola presented a slide show to 150 people. Violence had "disrupted the negotiating process," and they worried that "the eye of the international community is not on South Africa anymore." Material support typically followed these tours. This trip culminated in supporting a school in Mozambique; two years earlier the Albany group had donated money to SWAPO, and on the 1992 trip, Vera Michelson learned that the money had helped purchase a computer SWAPO used in the 1990 elections. Another financial contribution to the ANC was used to set up a rural radio network in South Africa.[65]

The prominent South African historian Bernard Magubane joined Prexy in Albany for a discussion of ways to stem the violence in the region and promote peace. It's worth pausing to note Dr. Magubane's extraordinary contributions, first as a scholar-activist in exile in Zambia, California, and Connecticut, and then, after the fall of apartheid, as the lead author of a multivolume history of the global anti-apartheid struggle commissioned by the ANC. Prexy and Ben first met in late 1968 at the airport in Dar es Salaam. Thinking Prexy was the driver sent by the ANC to pick him up, Magubane approached him speaking Zulu. "We always laughed about that," Prexy fondly recalled. Magubane stayed in

Prexy's Chicago home many times and got to know Prexy's father. "Ben's intellectual and political perspective was unalterably rooted in a rejection of imperialist tenets and the forthright assertion of an anti-capitalist, class struggle analysis," Prexy wrote after his close friend's death. Magubane's *The Political Economy of Race and Class in South Africa*, was indispensable to the global anti-apartheid movement, and his later *The Ties That Bind: African American Consciousness of Africa* "contributed significantly to groups developing theories and strategies for their work."[66]

As negotiations stalled, COSATU launched a general strike and called on its allies to support the demand for elections and the ouster of De Klerk. "One more day of apartheid is one more day too long," COSATU declared. In response, many Chicago union leaders, CCISSA, and other anti-apartheid groups launched a series of actions, including pressuring American officials to exert greater pressure on De Klerk to step down.[67]

1993 was a year of sorrow and anxiety. CCISSA opened the year with a sobering assessment: "The failure of the Reagan/Bush policy in southern Africa is obvious: US brokered elections in Angola have been violated by the US backed UNITA forces; Mozambique has been devastated, brought to its knees by South Africa's war of destabilization; and in the 3 years since Mandela's release, thousands have been killed in township violence while the racist regime stalls plans for an interim government and constituent elections." And yet, "1993 promises to be a watershed year," as the ANC continued to push for elections, and many were hopeful that the new president Bill Clinton would pivot US foreign policy in a more positive, less lethal direction.[68]

Sadly, the extraordinary Oliver Tambo passed away before getting to witness the fall of apartheid; and then two white gunmen assassinated the highly regarded Chris Hani, a leader in the South African Communist Party and head of MK, the ANC's armed wing. It was a crushing blow. Hani's assassination put the nation on the brink of all-out warfare. Nelson Mandela went on television and urged Black South Africans not to seek vengeance. "So many saw the moment Mandela spoke on television—both his wooden remarks on the night of the killing and the more moving speech three days later—as a watershed moment in South African history, when the balance of power and authority passed from De Klerk to Mandela."[69] Hani's murder removed a forceful advocate for economic redistribution in a new South Africa. As one observer noted of ANC dynamics that year, "The most serious potential fissure is between the ANC's negotiators who accept the interim power-sharing formula and a major role for free markets, and its more militant wing, which favors mass action and greater government economic intervention. Hani, though often in the latter group, could have served as a bridge."[70]

In 1993 Chicago activists welcomed Moses Mayekiso and finally got to host Nelson Mandela. As it happened, these two pillars were pursuing different paths for a post-apartheid South Africa. Mayekiso came in the spring to strengthen ties with Chicago internationalists and deepen his understanding of "community-controlled development." Prexy arranged for him to meet with bank and foundation representatives, and CCISSA and ILNAA hosted Mayekiso at a "solidarity reception" at Malcolm X College. The money raised in that June's Soweto Day walkathon—dedicated to Tambo and Hani—was dispatched to Alexandra for voter education projects.[71]

Later that year, CCISSA sent Wanda White, director of a Chicago grassroots economic development organization to Alexandra "to assist in the creation of an economic development strategy for the township." Anticipating the shifting terrain in South Africa, she also shared with the ACO "her experience in the Harold Washington administration where community activists came to work for the city government and found themselves on the other side of the table from their former allies."[72] The ACO envisioned alternative development strategies including a land trust, a cooperative housing program, and a People's Bank. Mayekiso wanted to pressure South African banks to target lending toward the townships and away from the apartheid-structured homelands. His organizations imagined the use of "organized with-drawals" and "nonviolent occupations." Allies in Chicago contemplated a grassroots campaign against US banks tied to these South African banks, but "mixed signals" from the ANC put the effort on hold.[73]

For his part, Nelson Mandela embarked on a fundraising tour of the United States in July that was sponsored in part by Coca-Cola and other companies. "The ANC's main message to supporters was the pressing need for practical help and expertise in building a post-apartheid soci-ety." Some in the solidarity community, however, expressed concern "about the way in which the movement is seeking consultations with establishment political figures and US corporations about future invest-ment opportunities."[74]

TransAfrica hosted a reception for Mandela in Washington with an array of Black leaders who had championed the anti-apartheid move-ment, including Ron Dellums, Charles Rangel, Maxine Waters, Gay McDougall, Sylvia Hill, and William Lucy. According to host Randall Robinson, five minutes before the meeting was to end Barbara Masekela announced that they were fundraising among American elites, including J. Wayne Fredericks, an influential diplomat and staunch opponent of sanctions, who had spent the 1980s directing inter-national affairs for the Ford Motor Company and Chase Manhattan Bank. Robinson had butted heads with him in Washington many times. While Robinson understood the ANC's financial needs, he was appalled at not having been consulted in advance. Longtime activist Sylvia Hill recollected Masekela words: "look, it's time for us to move on. We have to make allies with other groups of people." Hill heard this as the ANC "saying that you no longer need citizens as allies because corporate and government political forces are your allies." For Hill, this was "a strategic mistake of the highest order for the people of South Africa and all of Africa." Prexy also vividly recalls that Randall Robinson felt that the ANC did not give him and TransAfrica enough credit for their role in liberating South Africa.[75]

Figure 19. Nelson Mandela receiving the Oliver Tambo portrait from Basil Clunie at Plumbers Hall in Chicago, 1993. Courtesy of Carol Thompson and Basil Clunie.

Mandela spent two days in Chicago during this 1993 trip, and met with business, professional, and labor groups. Basil Clunie presented him with a portrait of Oliver Tambo, taken during Tambo's visit to the city. Prexy was working as a program officer at the MacArthur Foundation in Chicago, where he steered funds to southern African solidarity work and other antiracist work, including to CCISSA and the Coalition of Black Trade Unionists (CBTU). Prexy's three years at MacArthur overlapped with the elections in South Africa and Mandela's visit to Chicago. He was able to direct MacArthur funds to support both. Kennette Benedict had hired Prexy at MacArthur on her father's recommendation. Legendary in Chicago, Don Benedict was imprisoned as a young seminarian for protesting the class bias of the military draft. He was the longtime head of the Community Renewal Society and launched the publication of the *Chicago Reporter*. MacArthur was another instance in Prexy's life when the dense web of influential graduates of the Francis Parker School came to the fore. Adele Simmons, the head of MacArthur, was a Parker grad, and Prexy's close friend and high school football coach, Bill Lowry, was then head of human relations at MacArthur. Prexy took advantage of the custom that MacArthur would (more than) match employee donations to organizations—even political or activist ones deemed ineligible for foundation grants. Prexy organized an informal caucus of Black staff there and worked to spread this form of grant-making.[76]

In 1993, CCISSA initiated an Illinois "Southern Africa Response Network" to better lobby Washington "to pressure the South African regime to curb township violence [and] halt land transfers and other moves designed to cripple a future democratic government." The network also aimed to support the struggle by Alexandra Township residents for decent housing, medical care, and education. The network mobilized members to urge Secretary of State Warren Christopher to recognize the government of Angola, and not long after, President Clinton did.[77]

In October, anti-apartheid organizations joined with the DuSable Museum of African American History to host "Amandla! South Africa at the Crossroads," a weekend of poetry, performance, and political updates. Lindiwe Mabuza, the ANC's representative to the United States, delivered the keynote, and alongside Prexy, speakers included veteran Chicago activists Cheryl Harris, Lisa Brock, Cheryl Johnson-Odim, Basil Clunie, Harold Rogers, and an historian new to Chicago, Barbara Ransby, who had first met Prexy as a student leader and would become a close friend and comrade of Prexy's over the ensuing decades. The event included the photographic exhibit "Why Are They Weeping? South Africans under Apartheid," which documented the brutal violence.[78] Mabuza would later remark of her comrades in Chicago: "They dedicated themselves to our struggle as if they were experiencing the pain and the hurt of the people of South Africa."[79]

As it turns out, democracy would indeed come to South Africa, but with major strings attached. In a September 1993 address at the United Nations, Nelson Mandela called for the end of sanctions and the return of international lending and investment in South Africa. "We hope that the cities and states that were the firm backbone of the anti-apartheid movement in the US will commit themselves to actively supporting reinvestment in the South African economy in a socially responsible manner." The internal violence, pressure from international financial institutions, and high rates of unemployment had convinced ANC leaders to seek foreign capital.[80]

The ANC and the National Party, as the Transition Executive Council, had just reached a deal with the International Monetary Fund, which locked South Africa into a future of neoliberalism before the first elections were even held. In exchange for an $850 million loan, South Africa committed itself to fiscal austerity and privatization. Twenty years later, Ronnie Kasrils, once an MK commander, would call this "our Faustian moment."[81] Writer Naomi Klein argues that the ANC, with its understandable focus on winning majority rule, was outmaneuvered in negotiations about the future shape of the economy. They accepted, for example, a proposal to make the central bank independent of state control, to inherit the extraordinary debt of the apartheid state, and to pay considerable pensions for retired white civil servants ultimately at the expense of effecting any economic redress for the harms of apartheid state policies.[82]

At an AFSCME gathering in Washington, Mandela acknowledged the concern over not having briefed the large activist sector in the United States about the decision to call for an end to sanctions at the UN address. "We called a meeting of some leaders of the anti-apartheid movement . . . and they gave us their backing. We would have preferred to have a conference, but events have moved so quickly," he implored. "We are faced with grave problems of unemployment, high crime, disease and poverty," and "in this light we had to lift sanctions."

The ANC began to push hard for foreign investment, a pivot that American activists found difficult to navigate. Mandela met later that same day with corporate executives at the Institutional Investment in a Post-Apartheid South Africa conference. One observer noted it was jarring to watch corporate executives who had long shunned the ANC now wooing ANC officials "like old buddies." They noted the challenge of listening to discussions of everyday needs such as housing "without even attempting to address the issue of land redistribution."[83]

TOWARD ELECTIONS

The Reverend Frank Chikane, the General Secretary of the South African Council of Churches, visited Chicago in October 1993 and voiced a growing concern over whether the military would ultimately allow free and fair elections. He urged the international church community to send observers. He also lamented that the status of whites had loomed so large in the negotiations. "We're negotiating the freedom of the whites, who ask what we will do with their wealth and their pensions," Chikane said. "They are asking us, who have no wealth and no pensions, to protect theirs."[84] After a trip to southern Africa where he witnessed the struggles of ordinary people firsthand, Prexy echoed the worry that there "appears to be a growing sense among South Africans that national negotiations are far removed from the fear and desperation of people's daily lives."[85]

Dumisani Kumalo of the ACOA worried about obstacles to a truly free and fair election, including the fact that a quarter of the electorate resided in apartheid-created homelands, such as Inkatha's KwaZulu, where the ANC was barred from campaigning. How could voters learn about their platform? Moreover, the same forces that had been terrorizing people during the last few years—the police—will be patrolling polling places. Hardly a welcoming group to the Black majority.[86]

Since major media coverage of southern Africa was both minimal and untrustworthy, travelers to the region provided important feedback.

CCISSA's Toni Moore visited South Africa in late 1992 and reported that "everything is in transition." She felt that "the ANC and other progressive forces are almost a shadow government. They are consulted by the World Bank, businessmen, and others regularly because everyone is preparing for the near future." She described schisms between younger activists in the UDF and older cadre who had spent many years or decades in exile or prison, as well as debates over the use of violence as a defensive weapon. She also found differences of opinion about the future economy. Will it be market-based, mixed, or socialist? She reported "a high level of respect and deference to the leaders" but said "people express their opinions, consistent with leadership or not, freely." She found "a hotly debated and constantly brewing struggle about women's rights." Many clamored for quotas to ensure the representation of women in both the negotiations and the new government, but a greater number opposed to quotas urged greater sensitivity to women's inclusion.

She shared the grave concern that the state was "transferring land to homelands with the obvious hope of gaining new allies and making it more difficult for the next government to resolve the vital land issues that will face them." Most land was given to KwaZulu. "While we were in South Africa, Buthelezi announced a 'unilateral declaration of autonomy,' declaring that KwaZulu would have a new constitution regardless of what happened in future negotiations with the central government."[87]

The Bantustans, which were ostensibly independent of South Africa, were led by autocratic figures, widely seen as puppets of Pretoria, who resisted allowing their citizens to vote in the upcoming elections. But in early 1994 ordinary people rose up and overthrew the chief of the Bophutatswana Homeland, sending a signal that induced the IFP to jettison their plan. "The people of Bophutatswana wanted to be incorporated back into South Africa and allowed to vote in the first democratic election," an observer wrote, "and nothing was going to stop them." Shortly before the first free elections the Inkatha Freedom Party announced that it would participate, and this somewhat reduced the fear over election day violence.[88]

These formidable challenges, divisions, fears, and anxieties made many people appreciative of Nelson Mandela's leadership and immense popularity. Prexy saw him as a unifying figure. "The exile community made up largely of people in the ANC and the SACP had not been as in touch with the situation inside the country as the United Democratic Front. Now, spanning all these different formations, the exile politics, the international community, and those inside the country," Prexy noted, "is the giant footstep of Mandela. Other people had tremendous followings too, but nobody could match Mandela's capacity to span these groups."[89] In a visit to the Transvaal a month before the elections, the ACOA's Kumalo was moved by the popularity of Madiba. To see "Mandela surrounded by crowds of up to 50,000 people, young and old, excited, enthused and charged with hope was unforgettable." And "seeing the 75-year-old Mandela so energized by the support of his people is something I will never forget."[90]

A HISTORIC ELECTION

Chicago played an important role in ensuring that the historic election days in late April 1994 would be free and fair. The Chicago Committee for Fair Elections in South Africa, led by Basil Clunie and Harold Rogers, channeled financial and material support. In a fundraising visit to Chicago, ANC leader Jeff Radebe spoke at a CCISSA rally at a West Side Black church. Prexy also spoke, and joining them was Elkin Sithole, a South African scholar who specialized in the music of the African Diaspora and had taught for many years at the Center for Inner City Studies on Chicago's South Side. He was close friends with fellow Zulu-speaking scholar Ben Magubane and a strong supporter of the ANC. Prexy recalled him as a regular presence at events over the years and marveled at his ability to work with the staunch Black Nationalists at the center, many of whom supported the PAC rather than the ANC. Sithole arranged for performances of South African songs whenever South Africans visited the city. Reportedly, he was the first in line at the South African consulate to cast his ballot on April 27. Tragically, he died in a plane crash in Indiana in November 1994.[91]

Many groups—such as the Democratic Party and the Lawyers' Committee for Civil Rights—organized election support for the first free election in South Africa in April 1994. Jesse Jackson headed the US observers on behalf of the Clinton administration, and over five hundred Americans were among the thousands of observers from around the world.[92] Many Chicagoans were part of this extraordinary global affirmation of democracy. Rosetta Daylie, the AFSCME activist in the ILNAA, observed elections in Cape Town. "To see people so happy to be standing in line to vote," she said, "and not be shoved aside because they were Black, but to be treated like human beings. That brought tears to my eyes." She observed balloting in hospitals and prisons, where political prisoners had the right to vote. "That was the most touching part for me." She also had an education in the material ramifications of South Africa's fictive racial schemas in her encounters with the large "Coloured" population. "Several of the Coloureds would say I would like to vote for Nelson Mandela. But if I do, I will no longer have the special arrangements I have." They likely worried about losing such things as their access to running water or electricity, which many Africans did not have. "So, they were afraid that if Nelson won, they would lose that. And to hear them say it was just amazing. I wanted to say, honey you're just as Black as I am." The ANC lost in Cape Town.[93]

Basil Clunie supervised a team of twelve election monitors for three towns in the eastern Cape. "It was an extraordinary trip," Clunie said. What he particularly cherished was the fact that "two-thirds of the people who came from the United States were African American. It gladdened my heart because very few of them were people of means." Clunie himself had borrowed money from his credit union and had a version of "a rent party" to finance the trip. The ANC had secured the right to vote for most incarcerated people, arguing that many were indeed political prisoners. Clunie's group visited a prison filled exclusively with Khoikhoi men and women—an ethnic group who were the main source of labor for the surrounding white owned farms. For Clunie, guessing that many had been jailed for some sort of labor resistance or noncompliance, it "showed you in a microcosm how that particular economy worked." He also remembered a very elderly illiterate man who was brought to the polling place on a stretcher. "He looked at us with steely eyes and pointed to Mandela's face and said, 'Mandela.' To me that was the essence of what was going on. People were finally having a chance to participate in their own self-determination."[94]

Heeten Kalan traveled back to his hometown in the northern Transvaal for the election. Recalling all the racial slurs, slights, and threats of his childhood, he found his conservative town emblazoned with posters for Mandela. "The past few weeks have been exhilarating, electrifying, busy, angst-ridden, momentous, joyous, sad, and eye-opening," he declared. Yet, when he arrived at the polling station as a registered agent of the ANC on the first day of voting for the elderly and disabled, he found no ballots, ink, or pencils. The exhausted voters left but returned the next day when "hundreds lined up at the polling station to cast their votes." Kalan recounts: "I stood in utter awe as I watched Indians, Africans, and whites stand patiently together in line to cast their votes—many for the first time in their lives."[95]

"Because of all the election mess-up," Kalan later wrote, "the 28th was declared a public holiday to allow people to vote. Our polling station was swamped because some of the stations in the nearby Black areas still had not received ballots. The lines were longer and the sun hotter, but the people's patience was unchanged. People had waited decades, and a few more hours of waiting would not hurt." Despite these obstacles, at 93%, the Northern Transvaal recorded the highest vote for the ANC."[96]

The Inkatha Freedom Party decision to participate in the election did not stop the reign of terror in KwaZulu/Natal. Days before the election, seven youths circulating electoral information were tortured and killed, and two ANC canvassers were shot dead. The IFP took over many polling stations in the region, and international observers witnessed vote tampering and voter intimidation.[97] Prexy was assigned to Natal. A Canadian volunteer described events on the special voting day set aside for the elderly and infirm: "I had the privilege of setting off with Prexy Nesbitt, a longtime anti-apartheid activist from Chicago. Our emotions were close to the surface. Nothing had prepared us for the sight of hundreds of people, old, often infirm, sitting patiently in the hot sun to vote. Most had arrived at the site at about 6:30 a.m." Like others, she already saw the tentacles of neoliberal dictates constraining the promise of a new South Africa: "The patience and determination of the voters bodes well for positive change in the country. But will the international community allow Mandela to begin the necessary economic equity work or will structural adjustment win out?"[98]

Despite many reports of irregularities, the Independent Electoral Commission called the election "substantially fair and free." Canadian scholar-activist John Saul described it this way: "Sprawling, loose-limbed, often chaotic, the drama of the event as a 'liberation election' stood out above all else. A personal case in point: on one occasion we fulfilled one of our duties by monitoring a presiding officer as she asked a certain aged and illiterate voter where he wanted his 'x' to be placed. I expect that as long as I live my ears will harbour the echo of his fervent, almost whispered, response: 'Mandela.'"[99] The ANC won handily, showing itself to be the only national party. But Buthelezi's maneuvering ensured his survival as the leader of the second most populous province, even as homelands officially became a thing of the past.[100]

Chicago attorney Tim Wright served as an election observer but had to leave before the victory celebration. On his way out of the hotel he ran into ANC leader Thabo Mbeki who invited him to say goodbye to

Nelson Mandela. Wright walked in the suite and saw Coretta Scott King seated next to Mandela. "He got up and hugged and thanked me, and I said hello to Mrs. King." He will never forget that image. "It was just an incredible confirmation of all that I have thought in terms of understanding the relationship between the two peoples and the two places and the two movements and the oneness of all that struggle." That image "brought it home."[101] At the victory celebration in the Johannesburg hotel ballroom, Mandela told the exuberant crowd, "I stand here before you filled with deep pride and joy. Pride in the ordinary, humble people of this country—you have shown such a calm, patient determination to reclaim this country as your own. And joy that we can loudly proclaim from the rooftops: free at last!"[102]

Longtime activists savored the moment. John Saul said, "in a lifetime of accompanying the ups and downs of African politics, I had never experienced anything quite like it. We danced and laughed, all of us, embraced, and danced again. My memory drifted back thirty years, to the ANC's dusty offices in Dar es Salaam, where I had first met, as exiles from their own country, many of the people now dancing in the Carlton ballroom."[103] Heteen Kalan said the scene at the airport after the election was like a reunion: "Activists young and old had travelled to observe the elections. We recognized most of them, yelled out each other's names, hugged, introduced to others, and waved a celebratory goodbye as we all departed for our various destinations. These were people who had supported the democratic forces for decades, they were dedicated, hopeful, and proud to be here for this joyous occasion."[104]

Right after the election Prexy and Kalan went to Maputo "for a quick reconnaissance trip" because the first multiparty elections in Mozambique were coming up. Kalan was able to help Frelimo connect with his South African friends, who had produced effective outreach materials to publicize the South African elections. Kalan recalls their dinner at Graça Machel's house: "She spent a lot of time talking to us about Madiba and Madiba's kids," and indeed, not long after, they learned the pair had become a couple. "It was one of those cool evenings," Kalan recalled.[105]

At the victory celebration in Chicago, longtime activist Lisa Brock's moving speech captured the joy of the moment. On election day, she had gone to the South African consulate in Chicago where over nine hundred South Africans living across the region voted. "I was ecstatic at being at that damn Consulate for something good." She approached "with weak knees and a thumping in my chest." She continued, "I felt tears coming from my eyes. The flood was so intense that I had to stop and simply cry. I think I cried for about 15 minutes and then I danced, and toyi-toyied and hugged." A South African dance of protest, toyi-toyi meant stomping your feet and chanting. In her speech Brock balanced this joy with the lessons that activists had learned from other struggles. "The leaders of South Africa must be able to control the economic destiny of their country," she told the crowd. "The Western elite have financed war in Angola and Mozambique, blockaded social revolutions in Cuba, Nicaragua, and Vietnam, propped up dictatorships in Haiti, Chile, El Salvador, and Zaire and invaded progressive countries such as Grenada. So, we cannot be romantic about the future." Brock recounted the key contributions of Chicagoans to the international anti-apartheid struggle, including Prexy, Linda Murray, Harold Rogers, and her husband Otis Cunningham's production of the important *Africa Agenda* twenty years earlier; the work of CIDSA; the Free South Africa Movement; the Illinois Labor Network Against Apartheid; and many other leading figures and campaigns.[106] Chicago produced an extraordinarily wide and deep base of support for multiple struggles in southern Africa, and Prexy's leadership and connections played an important role in making that happen.

WHICH WAY AHEAD?

The election results were a clear mandate for the ANC, but would they be able to deliver on the expectations of the millions of poor South

Africans who had cast ballots, and the millions around the world who were looking to them for inspiration? Had the ANC traded too much away at the negotiating table? Progressive critics had immediate concerns about the nature of the settlement. The National Party had succeeded in warding off demands for economic redistribution "symbolized by the retention of the finance minister of the old regime." A South African journalist noted that "the ANC's efforts to achieve an inclusive and peaceful transition read like a catalogue of magnanimity," though he guessed there must have been an intense struggle inside the ANC. The "ANC has maintained an uncanny degree of unity, despite the fact that it enfolds a range of ideologies, interests and social classes." But most concerning was that the settlement may have hamstrung the new government at a time of dire need: "South Africa remains trapped in a knee buckling crisis. In the past 20 years, the poorest 40% of blacks have seen their incomes decline by 42%. Hardest hit are the rural poor, almost a third of the population, locked out on the fringes of perception and geography."[107]

Many applauded the ANC's ambitious Reconstruction and Development Program and its promise to shift resources toward the poor, but as a journalist noted, "given its acquiescence to IMF insistence on austerity, how will this happen?"[108] Sadly he proved correct, as the new government scuttled the RDP two years later.

In 1994, shortly after Mandela's inauguration, Prexy wrote about the magnitude of the challenges facing the new government. "In general, the mood amongst thirty-year friends and colleagues that I talked to when I was there for those days, while jubilant, also contained a measure of grim acknowledgement that ahead are the most difficult portions of the journey. It's all part of waking up in the new South Africa."[109] Everyone was deeply aware of the immense challenges and obstacles that stood before the new government. Tragically, apartheid's devastating tentacles were vast and far-reaching and would reverberate for years to come.

6

A LUTA CONTINUA

Reflections on Solidarity in a Neoliberal Age

THE RISE TO STATE POWER of the African National Congress capped decades of a global struggle to end apartheid—and several decades of Prexy's life. From the 1960s to the 1990s, Prexy built concentric circles of comrades across the United States, Canada, Europe, and southern Africa, while continuously trying to interrelate local and global concerns, center antiracism, and emphasize the importance of Black leadership and voices in the movement while simultaneously forging a multiracial attack on colonialism, imperialism and white supremacy in southern Africa and, indeed, the United States. Prexy built lasting comradeships and friendships with scores of leaders in Frelimo, SWAPO, and the ANC, among other national liberation organizations, plus a very long list of fellow internationalists in the United States, Europe, and Canada in particular. Prexy played a major role in educating Americans about events in southern Africa and their own government's deeds and misdeeds. Through his organizing and advocacy, he influenced local, state, and federal policy-making in the United States; raised money and material aid for African liberation; and succeeded in infusing the broad solidarity movement with a progressive political perspective and pushing it in a progressive direction. Prexy was also a movement analyst and intellectual—regularly penning articles on various dimensions of African liberation, US and global organizing, and corporate and state policy. He spoke at hundreds of rallies, events, meetings, picket lines, and conferences, becoming an extremely well-known figure in the movement worldwide. Prexy occasionally appeared in the media, but at the same time, he was not a person who jumped in front of the camera or longed to be in the public eye. He rarely sought the limelight. He was a movement builder, and crucially, a mobilizer, who consistently encouraged and empowered others to educate themselves, get involved, and act and speak out.

Prexy and his orbit of organizers built an extraordinarily effective and cohesive anti-apartheid movement that powered change in scores of states and cities over many years. What accounts for this organizing success in the aftermath of the racial fracture of Black Power and on behalf of a society on the other side of the world? For one, while apartheid was far away, it was also close to home, and activists regularly stressed its parallel to racial conditions in the United States. While movement leaders were politically conscious, left leaning, and deeply informed, many ordinary participants were likely motivated out of a sense of moral concern rather than ideological conviction. In addition, there were many pathways into the fight against apartheid—from churches to unions to campuses—and one did not need to be a member of a particular organization. This created multiple accessible ways into the movement, without an ideological litmus test, that enabled mass participation.

Building trust and coordination between US internationalists and national liberation struggles had unique challenges, just as it did when those groups came to power. Co-strugglers included individuals, organizations, national liberation groups, and nation-states. The inequality in power, authority, position, and status in the orbit of internationalism was baked in and hard to structurally surmount. Solidarity activists watched with great disappointment and grave concern as socialist dreams gave way to capitalist maneuvers. And yet, even though their organizing for freedom in southern Africa may not have given rise to nation-states that went in directions they always admired, they struggled with principle and conviction over many decades to expand the reach of anti-imperialism and socialist aspiration in the world. Moreover, their internationalism and dedication to African liberation informed the trajectories of their continuing activist work.

SOUTH AFRICA

Perspectives among activists on post-apartheid South Africa have evolved, gradually moving away from celebration and optimism toward a more sober engagement with the difficulties of achieving major reforms under global capitalism or to stronger critiques shaped by feelings of disappointment and frustration over widening inequality and unkept promises—even betrayal—especially over revelations of state corruption. In 1996 the government scuttled the progressive Reconstruction and Development Program in favor of a neoliberal Growth and Development Plan. In the run-up to the 1994 election, the ANC and SACP embraced a "two stage" approach to change in South Africa—the achievement first of electoral democracy followed ideally by a push for socialism. Yet even in the first stage, the SACP insisted on the need for land redistribution and nationalizing of key industries, a direction hopefully portended by the RDP. But this never happened. Neville Alexander, former Robben Island political prisoner and a prominent voice to the left of the ANC, insisted that in South Africa, a nonracial capitalism was impossible. Informed by observations of decolonization on the continent and theorists such as Frantz Fanon,

Alexander long doubted that the now ruling ANC, whose big tent included many aspiring capitalists, would press a socialist path.[1]

Prexy was also critical of the Growth and Development Plan's emphasis on market forces, privatization, and deregulation. Shortly after Mandela's victory, he offered an assessment of the profound tasks ahead for the new government. Apartheid had affected every aspect of life, so truly moving away from it would entail monumental change. Economic arrangements were on everyone's mind. Unfortunately, in Prexy's view, the United States promoted development "motored by a market economy awash with McDonald's and Coke bottles."[2] ("At one point South Africa was opening more McDonalds than any other country in the world," Trevor Noah quipped. "With Mandela came freedom, and with freedom came McDonald's.")[3] For decades, the US government had obsessed over the potential for socialism under an ANC-led government. But now, Prexy noted, "there is little doubt. What has emerged is a South African government wrapped in a passionate embrace with capitalism."[4]

In retrospect, Prexy wonders if the Nkomati Accord, which had ejected the ANC from Mozambique, undercut the potential for a more radical organization. The two countries shared a border. The accord mandated that the ANC abandon military and clandestine operations from Mozambique. These operations could have enabled the entry into South Africa, through various covert means, of ANC cadre who could have seeded greater internal mass action. In Prexy's view, this greater internal ANC presence and its pivot toward armed struggle to get there might have put the ANC in a stronger position internally when Mandela was released.[5]

John Saul, the influential Canadian internationalist scholar-activist, shared Prexy's disappointment. Saul was initially hopeful "that the ANC's Reconstruction and Development Program provided some openings to advance structural transformation of the economy," but when the government shifted gears, Saul became a vocal critic of the

ANC's neoliberal turn.[6] It was difficult "and very sad" for Prexy when Saul and Ben Magubane, two of his longtime friends and comrades, parted ways ideologically and personally. Magubane remained a staunch ANC supporter, and Prexy recalls as well that Saul's arrogance about his own stance could be off-putting. "John and Ben could not be in the same room together," Prexy remembered.[7] Naomi Klein sees the post-apartheid settlement as a case study of "disaster capitalism," when powerful forces intervene to take advantage of a nation in transition, aggressively promoting the notion that the only route to internal growth or prosperity is obedience to the dictates of international capital markets. Sadly, as she points out, this obedience rarely leads to growth or prosperity; in South Africa, international institutions continued to discipline and punish the ANC, while the new government carried the burden of inherited debt and ballooning pensions to white retirees. The "ANC government," she contends, "carried the costs of two governments—its own, and a shadow white government that was out of power."[8]

People tend to see race and gender identities and arrangements as naturally occurring phenomena. The system of apartheid engineered a complex regulation of race and labor that threw traditional family life into a free-for-all. "A system of social relations forged almost wholly within a racially based, socially engineered modality of super exploitation, must be turned into a non-racist society. How can such a society be attained?" Prexy asked. "Neither the party nor the government," he noted two years after the fall of apartheid, "have yet articulated detailed and specific plans for eliminating the racism and racial privilege and ethnic chauvinism that abounds throughout South Africa." While apartheid had distributed differing privileges and penalties to legally codified racial groups, the new paradigm was just emerging. So far, post-apartheid whites had succeeded in maintaining their wealth, however, many in the officially designated Coloured population worried about losing privileges in a nonracial democracy, and this intensified antiblackness among some in the Coloured community. The apartheid state had encouraged division and distrust between Zulus and Xhosa as a strategy of rule, and these dynamics took root—we saw the lethal ramifications of this in the early 1990s. Prexy suggested that "ethnicity" was the new reality, rendering "non-racialism" and "an undifferentiated Africanness" as no longer adequate. Prexy argued that the subordination of women demanded redress in the post-apartheid reckoning. "Today, the reality often totally contradicts the rhetoric of a non-racist, non-sexist, non-homophobic society. Women are abused, objectified, exploited and brutalized in all aspects of their lives. The level of violence against women, specifically rape and spousal abuse, cannot be matched anywhere else in the world."[9]

Despite these considerable shortcomings, the ANC's commitment to offering Black South Africans access to better housing, jobs, and education bore some fruit during its first years in power. "This democratic dividend persisted for at least the first 15 years of South Africa's post-apartheid history when economic growth was strong, international market conditions were favorable and state management was competent," according to one account. "The turning point came in 2009—the year [Jacob] Zuma took power and a year after the global financial crisis. What followed was a comprehensive backsliding in life chances, political expectations and economic prospects."[10]

As corruption grew, and even the ANC's more modest promises remained unfulfilled, many began to reappraise the vaunted settlement ending apartheid. ANC leader Ronnie Kasrils came to feel that "in the early 1990s, we in the leadership of the ANC made a serious error. Our people are still paying the price." Prexy shares Kasrils's point that the ANC should have put more disciplined, political people in government posts rather than the cadre "who wanted a piece of the pie, a part of the action."[11] Similarly, Danny Schecter finds that the "lack of focus and clarity on economic issues" helps explain why the ANC became "dominated by the corporate sector."[12]

"What I call our Faustian moment came when we took an IMF loan on the eve of our first democratic election," Kasrils wrote in his 2013 autobiography. The ANC considered the loan "a necessary evil" even as it came with provisions foreclosing substantive economic change. "Doubt had come to reign supreme: we believed, wrongly, there was no other option, that we had to be cautious, since by 1991 our once powerful ally the Soviet Union had collapsed. Inexcusably we had lost faith in the ability of our own revolutionary masses to overcome all obstacles. Whatever the threats to isolate a radicalizing South Africa, the world could not have done without our vast reserves of minerals."[13]

Chicago scholar-activist Lisa Brock shared this view. "I thought that Mandela had moral capital that he didn't spend," Brock reflected. "I thought that he could have pushed for more." She wonders why the ANC didn't nationalize De Beers or at least make it a parastatal to secure a lucrative source of revenue for economic redistribution. "Because there was money," Brock noted. "It was a wealthy country. You didn't need to rely upon money from the Soviet Union."[14] Prexy has wondered about this too and suspects that "they were scared. They were very scared of what the capitalist world would do to them if they took those steps. They didn't want to be Cuba. They didn't want to be isolated." And the devastation of the long wars in the frontline states and "the huge numbers of lives lost, certainly made an impression on them."[15]

The failure or insufficiency of economic redistribution—especially around access to land ownership—is by far the biggest disappointment for solidarity activists. Cheryl Johnson-Odim felt "a terrible disappointment that whites still own much of the land, and so much of the economy. Black South Africans haven't experienced that change."[16] Tim Wright, the attorney for Harold Washington echoed this feeling. "It's one thing to have fought for regime change and to have fought for empowerment and the right to lead yourselves," Wright reflected, "but the fight is not yet won. The fight has to be won economically . . . that's the next stage that we have to get to."[17]

To be sure, many internationalists who hoped to see broad social and economic transformation in South Africa also insisted on the need for change in the United States and Europe. In a prescient 1992 talk to an American audience, South African church leader Frank Chikane said just as South Africa will need to create a new economic order, so will the world: "We need to talk about something that is not just capitalism, not just what the Eastern bloc was trying to do. We need to create a new order. But we cannot do that in South Africa alone. . . . We are hoping that you, United States citizens, will participate in the struggle to produce an economic order, internationally, that will produce peace rather than debate profit and interest."[18] Prexy emphasized this theme constantly—that activists in the West could not just project their desires for socialist transformation onto the global South—they needed, we need, to wage the fight here too.

The revelations of public and private corruption in ANC circles created tremendous disillusion. "You wonder what has happened," Prexy asked. "Tokyo Sexwale was a man who wept when his comrade Chris Hani was shot down in front of him, but today he's this multibillionaire . . . what has happened to his old values?"[19] Prexy was reacting to an unsettling interview with Sexwale on the American television show 60 Minutes in 2004. Certainly, mainstream American journalists have their own biases, but Sexwale seemed unaware of how his self-representation might affect viewers globally. The segment's title, "Comrade Capitalist" captures Sexwale's journey from poor Soweto youth to political prisoner on Robben Island to billionaire. Correspondent Bob Simon called him "one of a handful of Black leaders and former political prisoners who've gotten really rich by converting their political capital into, well, capital." White business leaders had curried favor with ANC elites, protecting their own survival under the banner of Black empowerment. Sexwale founded a bank that gave him an "open checkbook" to put together deals. With investments in mining, banking, and hotels, Sexwale's company was worth $500 million in 2004. Seemingly oblivious to how his story might come off, Sexwale expressed pride in his achievements.[20]

In 2016, Prexy told longtime Africa advocate and radio host Walter Turner that "the ANC as we've known it, is maybe at an end." He called the very low level of Black land ownership "a standing assault on all those who gave their lives to make change in that part of the world," and he assailed "systematized, generational patterns of corruption." A few years earlier Danny Schechter had sent Prexy a letter saying more or less, "we have a responsibility to face truths and talk about things that are going wrong in South Africa." Prexy wishes he had heeded his friend's advice sooner.[21]

On the thirtieth anniversary of democratic elections, the *New York Times* offered these measures of worsening economic inequality: "At the end of apartheid, when almost all of South Africa's agricultural land was white-owned, Mr. Mandela's government pledged in 1994 to transfer 30 percent of it into Black hands within a few years, by encouraging white landowners to sell. The government failed to meet its goal, and it stretched the deadline to 2030. So far, about 25 percent of white-owned farmland has been transferred to Black ownership."[22]

According to the World Bank, South Africa is "the most unequal country in the world:" ten percent of the people possess 71 percent of the wealth, while the bottom 60 percent own 7 percent. "To a large extent, the wealth disparities have kept millions of Black South Africans relegated to some of the most deplorable conditions. White South Africans make up roughly 7 percent of the population, but white-owned farms still cover about half of the country's entire surface area." Black unemployment is dramatically higher than white unemployment and has risen since the end of apartheid.[23]

And yet, after the 2024 election when the ANC was compelled to form a government with a white dominated party to its right, one journalist stressed the recency of the post-apartheid nation. "The ecstatic moment of freedom's birth in South Africa 30 years ago was a beginning, not an end," they wrote. "We call birth a miracle not because we know how it's going to turn out, but because of the limitless possibility that it contains. The birth of a nation is no different. The new South Africa is still at the beginning of its story."[24]

MOZAMBIQUE

Frelimo's quest to build an independent Mozambique responsive to human needs has been decimated by South African aggression. "The cost quantified, here, in human and economic terms," said a UN task force examining the frontline states, "must be calculated through the prism of lost development, lost education and job opportunities, national defence and foreign debt."[25] Prexy personally experienced the rise and fall of Frelimo's freedom dreams. He witnessed their acute vulnerability to external pressure. While he acknowledged mistakes made by Frelimo, he stood shoulder to shoulder with his longtime Mozambican friends in pressing for peace and the opportunity to heal and rebuild. In contrast to so many activists, who felt that the combination of global capital and Renamo's decimation of the country had shattered the hopes and dreams articulated at its founding, Prexy held faith in the Mozambicans he had known and cherished for so long. "I do not for one minute believe that all the Marxists, socialists, democratic socialists and revolutionaries are gone from either Frelimo, the party, or Mozambique, the country. If, in fact, being a socialist and revolutionary is in large measure about the basic values one holds vis-à-vis race, gender, sexuality, organization of society, what's good in life, what's just—then I believe that Mozambique is still about the things that we hold dear like peace, health care, education, loving children, and deeply esteeming elderly people."[26]

Prexy felt that his life experiences had prepared him to balance "the perspective of the achievable and the unachievable," and to help him understand "that many of the goals that these liberation movements wanted to achieve couldn't be achieved because the dominant, world superpower has to change." He always recalled the advice of Amilcar Cabral and Marcelino dos Santos to make change in the United States. "We can't fight on both fronts, and we need you to develop a real front of struggle in the United States," they urged.[27]

Like South Africa, postcolonial Mozambique was derailed by the allure of luxury and wealth, which seduced elected officials. Prexy lamented the path taken by Armando Guebuza, a former guerrilla who became a wealthy businessman after the privatization of state companies. "The guy who had been the political commissar of Frelimo becomes president, and plunges Mozambique into a debt that it still has to this day." During Guebuza's administration, Prexy, Anne Evens and so many others were devastated by the brazen murder of their good friend, the prominent investigative journalist Carlos Cardoso. Not long before his death, Cardoso had stayed with Prexy on a trip to the US "and in a late-night conversation shared his fear that he could be killed."[28] After Mozambique's first multiparty elections in 1994, "the economy began to score stunning growth rates." As of 2001, "Mozambique had one of the fastest growing economies in the world," according to one account, and it became "a poster child for the IMF and the World Bank, which attribute Mozambique's economic success to structural adjustment programs." But Cardoso was "skeptical that Mozambique's capitalist revolution was actually helping the country's impoverished people." He began to investigate reports of widespread corruption and abuses of power, and before long, Cardoso and others "began to charge that the size of the legal economy . . . could not account for Maputo's banking and real estate boom; they suspected money laundering, drug trafficking, and other illegal pursuits."[29]

In 2000, the US Drug Enforcement Administration "reported that Mozambique was one of the main ports of entry for illegal drugs coming into the region from Southeast Asia." The international drug trade began to hit Africa hard in the early 1980s, especially countries on the coast with active ports, like Mozambique. Prexy recalled seeing it firsthand. "And it's related to the wars, because there's the new problem of what to do with soldiers who are demobilized or disabled. You don't have an economy able to train them and to give them jobs. All of that hit Mozambique. It set up a difficulty that was just unimaginable."[30]

Cardoso was active in the municipal council. "One week before his death, Cardoso stood up at a council meeting and verbally attacked what he described as the 'gangster faction' within Frelimo." At the time he was reporting on money-laundering.[31] In 2006 Anibal Antonio dos Santos Junior was convicted and sentenced to thirty years for his role in the murder but the question of who ordered the killing remained unresolved.[32] In 2022 Guebuza's son was sentenced to twelve years in prison for his part in "a corruption scandal in which the government sought to conceal huge debts, triggering financial havoc.[33]

Historian Allen Isaacman has remained close to many Frelimo leaders. "Some remain faithful to the principles of the revolution" in a changing world, but many others don't. "As a result of the new orientation of Mozambique, and also the need to support their families and get a good education for their kids," many others "became very pragmatic, and some of them now are the most prosperous or some of the most prosperous people in Mozambique. And some use their party ties to gain access to scarce resources."[34]

"Mozambique was always kind of revered," South African born activist Heeten Kalan recalls. "If you came out of the anti-apartheid movement, you were just blown away that these countries, who were deprived on so many levels, were sacrificing themselves even more for South Africa." He felt very grateful for what Angola, Zimbabwe, Mozambique, Lesotho, and Namibia did for the anti-apartheid movement. But "one of the saddest things for me is that South Africans have kind of abandoned the region."[35] But of course, this does not relieve Portugal and the US and others of their much greater responsibility for redressing the many harms and injuries of colonialism and the long wars waged to preserve it. Apartheid's enablers owe reparations to the peoples of southern Africa.

Despite the many challenges and disappointments, leading activists in the Mozambique Support Network continued to rally solidarity and material aid in future years in response to the twin plagues of debt and disaster. A devastating flood in the spring of 2000 induced Prexy, Heeten Kalan, and Jenny Dahlstein to create the Chicago-Mozambique Flood Relief Fund to channel donations to the Africa Fund in New York.[36] In another initiative, Andy Epstein—who had been a cooperante with her husband Paul Epstein—and Loretta Williams, a leader of the Boston MSN chapter, used the flooding crisis to assail the imperial stranglehold over Mozambican finances. They praised the recent debt cancellation by the UK. "The United States should do no less. It must join in total debt cancellation and encourage all creditors, including the International Monetary Fund and World Bank, to stop taking payments." Indeed, the call to cancel debt became a rallying cry of the southern Africa solidarity movement at the turn of the twenty-first century.[37]

ANGOLA

As in Mozambique, an externally funded counterinsurgency wreaked havoc and derailed postcolonial development plans in Angola. As an Angolan diplomat said to Prexy: "Diamonds and fuel were used to buy arms to defend ourselves, so we couldn't use them to boost our own economy. We have plans to have a strong economy in the future, but first we need peace."[38] That peace was extremely hard to come by. The United States bears considerable blame for the senseless death and destruction in Angola. Scholar-activist Elizabeth Schmidt assailed US complicity in decades of war making, which as in Vietnam, turned out to be about saving face rather than advancing honest foreign policy objectives. Prexy had mentored Schmidt decades earlier when they worked together at the Institute for Policy Studies. It was Prexy, she said, who "launched me into 'Africa work' back in the 1970s. He encouraged me, gave me faith in myself, and urged me on—as he has for generations of activists and scholars."[39]

Schmidt penned an impassioned indictment of US policy. "As so many regions of Africa descend into economic and political chaos," she wrote, "American opinion-makers often decry Africans' seeming inability to govern themselves." But they fail to acknowledge Western culpability for this calamity. In Angola, "we are witnessing the destruction of a nation and a people. The destroyer, guerrilla leader Jonas Savimbi . . . has long been the darling of the American right wing and the CIA. Billed as an anti-communist freedom fighter during the height of the Cold War, Savimbi is, in fact, no more than a power-hungry opportunist who changes his colors to suit the tastes of his current financial backers." For sixteen years, Savimbi's US-funded forces fought the Angolan government, which was recognized by every country in the world except South Africa and the United States. "More than 500,000 Angolans—in a population of 10 million—have died as a result of this senseless war. Millions more have been made homeless . . . . The country's economy is in a shambles, and the maimed and terrorized population has one of the highest amputee rates in the world."[40] With the end of the Cold War, a ceasefire agreement was reached, and in 1992 elections were held. With ninety percent of the voters turning out, Savimbi lost.

Savimbi refused to acknowledge his loss and plunged the country back into war, dramatically escalating deaths and displacements. Schmidt noted the hypocrisy at the American financing of so-called freedom fighters. "Having long championed the Unita rebels as proponents of freedom and democracy," she wrote, "the United States looked the other way when the ugly truth emerged. In the face of Savimbi's flagrant disregard for free and fair elections, the United States did nothing. When Savimbi recommenced the war with US-made weapons, the US made no move to stop him. After footing the bill for a devastating war that has cost more than half a million lives, the United States bears a unique responsibility to the Angolan people."[41]

It wasn't until Savimbi's death in 2002, that the long war finally came to an end. It's important to include Angola in a much-needed international accounting of the cost of apartheid and the cost of the Cold War on the global South; by refusing to acknowledge their mistakes and failures the Americans brought even greater death and destruction. "Four days after Savimbi's death, in February 2002," Schmidt wrote, "President George Bush received President dos Santos at the White House. Bush expressed America's goodwill toward Angola and urged dos Santos to reach out to all Angolans and bring peace to his devastated country." But as Schmidt notes, "instead of lecturing dos Santos, Bush should have asked for his forgiveness for the crimes perpetrated by the United States against the people of Angola."[42]

ASSESSMENTS OF THE MOVEMENT

Like all American social movements, the Africa solidarity movement was shaped by the racial and gender dynamics of the broader society— even as it sometimes fought to change those dynamics. Women played leading roles in the solidarity movement but didn't always get credit or recognition. Still, there is no doubt that the women's liberation movement influenced the anti-apartheid and other internationalist movements of the 1970s and 1980s, lessening the more blatant chauvinism of movements in the 1950s and 1960s. Nevertheless, Prexy criticized "the failure of my generation of activists to achieve real equality between the sexes in the struggle." Another weakness, in Prexy's view, was the racially divided character of organizing on the American left, which he thinks has blunted its power. "1968 had the potential of being a moment of structurally transcending and changing these mechanisms of power in the United States. It was a revolutionary moment really. And I think we never realized fully—some people did—how incredibly close we were." He blames the "failure to understand who the enemy was. We got caught up in race again and again . . . . And we are still paying that price."[43]

In Prexy's view, racial divisions and friction weakened the US anti-apartheid movement. "I believe more and more firmly that the US anti-apartheid movement would have been more effective and achieved more political goals," he wrote, "were it not for the strains and difficulties of major national and regional *Black* and *white* and racially mixed organizations working together (or failing to even communicate with one another). In Bill Minter and Sylvia Hill's language, we could have gone faster from "'the margins to the mainstream' had we been able to overcome the paralyzing dimensions of multiracial progressive work—an ongoing challenge in the U.S.A. to this day."[44]

Prexy felt that southern Africans were adept at offering models and lessons to overcome these divides, but that their example was often misunderstood or unevenly felt. "The southern Africans knew the history and tradition of African American identification and solidarity with Africa, and this helped generate a consciousness of responsibility," Prexy noted. He recalls that Jennifer Davis, a white South African who replaced George Houser as leader of the American Committee on Africa, inspired African Americans to feel part of a tradition of Black internationalism.[45]

Prexy even contends that race has shaped the historiography of the movement in a way that at first glance seems empowering to African Americans but that has had the effect of producing a liberal narrative, dislodging the US story from the global left that Prexy lived and breathed. "What made the Anti-Apartheid Movement in the USA effective, as was the case with anti-apartheid movements worldwide," Prexy contends, "was the fact that thousands of individuals and hundreds of organizations nationwide, moved by righteous anger, took steps to oppose the apartheid government. From Amsterdam and Accra to Tokyo and San Francisco thousands of ordinary people took action against a glaring and intransient case of racial injustice. The recent revisionism in US coverage has included a pattern of situating anti-apartheid work solely within the province of Black American political activity. It is a tendency that, along with other recent developments, is only serving to isolate the Black American struggle from the remainder of the world's progressive forces and movements."

Prexy suggests a different narrative. "I wish to assert that the US Anti-Apartheid Movement never belonged to only one grouping of peoples or one region. Part of its uniqueness in the annals of social change movements was that the US Anti-Apartheid Movement was multi-racial, trans-class, and national (including Alaska, Hawaii and Puerto Rico) in its scope." He proposes a multiracial account of the anti-apartheid movement, one that champions Black perspectives and leadership in the long struggle. "Despite how pervasive and paralyzing they were, at times, these class, race and gender challenges within the US anti-apartheid struggle provided and yet provide (in the long term) a rich bedrock for discussion and strategizing toward social change in America." Prexy balanced this aspiration with a clear acknowledgement of the outsized role of Black leadership. "My perspective is not intended in any way to misestimate the particular and historic contribution of the US Black American community to the African continent's liberation struggle(s)," he wrote. "There is no doubt that various Black Americans—individuals and organizations—have made the leading, if not 'critical' contributions to many arenas of social change in the USA, including but not limited to the Anti-Apartheid Movement and solidarity work with Africa."

And yet the movement was global and global linkages were critical to its success. Prexy highlighted a Swedish finding that "between 1969 and the 1994 elections in South Africa, the Swedish government gave 4 billion Swedish Kronor (approx. $521,640,000) of humanitarian assistance to Southern Africa, 40% of which went directly to six liberation movements. At that point it was only Sweden and India in the western capitalist world whose governments gave direct support to African liberation movements." But the most important source of support to the ANC, which Nelson Mandela recognized and honored in his first visits abroad, were the frontline states. In this sense, the ANC was truly Pan-Africanist, relying to a tremendous degree on support from Tanzania, Zambia, Mozambique, Zimbabwe, and Angola. Prexy acknowledged this crucial source of support: "We, in the West and elsewhere, were awed and inspired by the extraordinary solidarity that the Front-Line States gave to the struggle to defeat apartheid. Our efforts paled in comparison to the millions of ordinary people throughout the region who died or were made homeless." Other nations played critical roles, too. "We recognized the tremendous sacrifice that came from countries like Cuba and India," Prexy wrote. They "modeled for us in the West what solidarity was all about."[46]

To advance movement building, Prexy emphasizes what has been the major lesson for him: building and maintaining relationships. "I believe the motor of effective organizing is building trusting relationships. It is a long and painstaking effort for which there are few shortcuts. It entails building bonds of confidence and trust. This we did, with a few shaky moments, during the anti-apartheid struggle. This kind of organizing entails reciprocity."[47]

JOURNEYS, LEGACIES, AND TIES

The Africa solidarity movement shaped the course of the lives of many of the activists in this study. The Chicagoans stayed close to each other, and Prexy has remained a close friend and comrade to many. Jenny Dahlstein and Heeten Kalan, the young publishers of *Baobab Notes*, decided to wed in South Africa in 2000. "Way more people came from the US, other countries, and Sweden than we thought would be able to. We ended up having a traditional Hindu wedding in Heeten's hometown, which is a small town in the north," Jenny recalled. "It was a classic Hindu wedding that lasted for days and days. And after that, we drove in a caravan of twenty-one cars to the Kruger National Park where we had another ceremony, at which Prexy officiated."[48]

For Sylvia Ewing, Chicago's internationalist community was rich with connections that guided the rest of her life. She credits Prexy for opening doors and introducing her to people like Danny Schecter and Jennifer Davis in New York and the CCISSA and MSN people in Chicago, who would be lifelong friends and comrades. "Prexy opened a portal that lasted." She later co-hosted Reverend Jesse Jackson's radio show and produced his daughter Santita Jackson's television show. "All those things really came through that anti-apartheid work, working with Prexy and the doors that he opened in my mind as well as in my space. He and that whole Chicago group had a hand in shaping a political perspective and a solidarity that I took into disability rights, housing rights, and reproductive rights." She credits the Africa advocacy work with infusing her approach to social change with a humanism that emphasizes arts, culture, and bringing people together. Interestingly one of the solidarity movement's great triumphs made her pivot to work closer to home. "In that shining moment of Mandela coming out and living up to everybody's hopes and dreams," Ewing thought, "why can't we do more for our young people? Why aren't we doing more uplifting? Why isn't that closer to home?" She noted that she "did this work for places far away and loved it and valued it, but what about here? So that was my shift into youth activism, wanting to raise young people's voices. Everything I did with Young Chicago Authors was all a through line of wanting to bring closer to home the power of advocacy and activism."[49]

Cheryl Johnson-Odim has had a distinguished career as an influential historian and leader in higher education. The election of Donald Trump brought her back to the streets. She played a prominent role in planning the Women's March in Chicago in 2017. "We embraced it when the DC people did a new manifesto after they got people of color in charge," she said, noting that white women had problematically dominated the organizing effort. Cheryl helped ensure that the Chicago planning group and roster of speakers included many women of color, but it took assertiveness and intentionality to break the default whiteness that many white feminists failed to confront. At a press conference, "they were about to parade all these white women out front, I was like, 'What the hell are you doing?' The whole leadership of the DC March had changed based around that critical issue, and I'm like, 'Are you deaf? You can't do that.'" She had reached out to other Black feminists in Chicago but encountered disinterest among some who likely imagined having to play this kind of role. But Cheryl "felt we just couldn't afford," to stand back, and she's proud that the turnout vastly exceeded their expectations.[50]

As the public health medical officer for the Cook County Department of Public Health, Rachel Rubin was deeply involved in crafting mitigation strategies during the COVID-19 pandemic, and she also provided regular updates on Chicago public television. Tragically Rubin lost both of her parents—within two weeks of each other—to the virus. Born in Jerusalem, Rubin's mother was a staunch civil rights advocate. Rachel remains an activist and internationalist, most recently fighting for an end to the Israeli military assault on the people of Gaza through the Arab-Jewish Partnership for Peace and Justice in the Middle East.[51]

Anne Evens runs the non-profit, Chicago-based Elevate, which "seeks to create a just and equitable world in which everyone has clean and affordable heat, power, and water in their homes and communities—no matter who they are or where they live." The bonds between this generation of activists remain tight. In 2023 Anne Evens and Sylvia Ewing worked with others to support the production of an award-winning podcast on the life of Hazel Johnson, a Black woman environmental justice activist and "founder of People for Community Recovery, a 40-year-old organization that fights to address the toxic industrial pollution that has been killing the members of her community."[52] In 2024 Evens hosted several Mozambicans who traveled to Chicago to see her daughter graduate from the University of Illinois Chicago.[53]

Keorapetse Kgositsile, the great South African poet known as Bra Willie, lived many years in exile in the US helping to shape the Black Arts Movement. He was a dear friend of Prexy's and a committed socialist and poet of the people. Returning in 1991, Kgositsile was "profoundly disillusioned by the dialogue of negotiation and decided to return to the United States." For him, "the decades-long revolution that sent him into exile was not progressing to its logical conclusion." He also became a critic of the post-apartheid government, which, he felt, "had forgotten the important roles that art and artists played in the struggle against apartheid and their roles in voicing the hopes of a new, democratic country."[54] Kgositsile married the legal scholar Cheryl Harris, who had been very active in the Chicago anti-apartheid movement mostly through CIDSA. Their son Thebe Neruda Kgositsile became a successful hip-hop star known as Earl Sweatshirt. His middle name, after the acclaimed Chilean poet Pablo Neruda, reflected Kgositsile's own identification as a revolutionary poet. He "aligned his work with the poet of Mozambican revolution Jorge Rebelo as well as with poet-president of the Popular Movement for the Liberation of Angola, Agostinho Neto." Kgositsile returned to live in South Africa in 2001 and in 2006 was named the national poet laureate.[55]

Moses Mayekiso, the trade unionist and Alexandra Civic Organization leader, who was active in both the ANC and South African Communist Party, also experienced disappointment with the direction of the ANC government. Elected to Parliament after the fall of apartheid, Mayekiso resigned after complaining of the government's disconnection from grassroots needs. Prexy's friend the Rev. Michael Weeder married Bonita Bennett, founding director of the District 6 Museum in Cape Town, which uses storytelling to remember the vibrant multiracial neighborhood that the apartheid government destroyed and then designated as whites-only. For Prexy, Weeder and Bennett personify the enduring social justice values and commitments of the anti-apartheid movement. The poetry of southern African liberation leaders has been a touchstone in Prexy's life, and Weeder, like many other leaders, is a poet. Father Weeder, who retired in 2024, was also an outspoken advocate for Palestinian rights, in keeping with the ANC's long tradition of solidarity with Palestinians.[56]

Lisa Brock, a historian of the African diaspora, taught for many years at Columbia College in Chicago, including co-teaching a class for eight years with Prexy. Brock recalls Prexy's teaching style: "He has a very personable way with students, and so they loved him. They liked his informality, his openness and friendliness. He was not formal, he was more of a Socratic teacher, talking to students and asking questions, and having them ask questions back." Brock was instrumental in creating an archival collection on the Chicago anti-apartheid movement at Columbia, which included scores of indispensable oral histories. She and her husband Otis Cunningham, who produced the *African Agenda* with Prexy in the 1970s, have been deeply involved in forging ties with Cuban scholars, artists, and activists over many years. In the early 2000s, Lisa Brock was in London and heard that Lindiwe Mabuza, her comrade from the anti-apartheid movement, was the South African high commissioner to Great Britain. She went to the High Commission and asked the receptionist if this was true. "Oh yes," she replied. "Well, tell her Lisa from Chicago is here and she slept on my couch many times." Lisa remembered the scene: "The workers all came out. They were laughing. Then came Lindiwe. 'You could have let me know you were coming,' she said to her old friend." Lisa was struck by "having been involved in something that actually succeeded, where the people who fought and suffered . . . were now in key positions."[57]

Some longtime connections remained fractious. In the 1970s Prexy had argued for divestment over an emphasis on shareholder activism, which was propounded by Tim Smith of the Interfaith Center on Corporate Responsibility. They had sharp disagreements. "Years later, I had a fight with Tim Smith at a Shared Interest board meeting," Prexy recalled. "The board had just awarded a prize to Coca-Cola as a leading anti-apartheid force. And Coca-Cola had given them a big bunch of money." In response, Prexy announced he was leaving the board. When Tim Smith asked why, Prexy explained that "Coca-Cola has been involved in killing union organizers in Guatemala. And Tim Smith said, 'I doubt that's the case. They never would do that.' And I said, 'What is your source?' He said, 'Coca-Cola executives.' We almost came to blows over this. And he and I never have talked, and I left the board at that point."[58]

A 2012 celebration of the centennial of the ANC gave Prexy an opportunity to reunite with old comrades and walk down memory lane. As part of a weekend of festivities, President Jacob Zuma hosted an outdoor dinner with more than 1,700 guests. "The dinner began at 4:00 p.m. and was still going on at my departure around 1:00 a.m.," Prexy noted. Cyril Ramaphosa, the former head of the National Union of Mineworkers, then a businessperson, and later president of South Africa, was an emcee. "Despite its length and the extensive agenda, the dinner was for me a highlight," Prexy wrote. Speakers included the presidents of Ethiopia, Tanzania, Botswana, Mozambique, Namibia, Zambia, Malawi, Uganda, and Rwanda. Kenneth Kaunda, the former president of Zambia, "received a standing ovation as he walked to the speaker's stage singing. Most present knew and were recognizing the tremendous contribution that Zambia and the Zambian people had made in the struggle to end apartheid. Another person who magnetized the audience with his presence was Ahmed Kathrada, the former Robben Island cellmate and close friend to Nelson Mandela. As it developed 'Kathy', as he is affectionately known, was the closest to any presence of Mandela at the Centenary festivities." Mandela wasn't feeling well and was sorely missed. The highlight of the event was "someone who is totally unknown to most non-ANC people and little known to even some of the most ardent South Africa watchers." Ruth Mompati became a leading figure in the ANC but began her involvement as a typist in the law office of Mandela and Oliver Tambo in the 1950s. When she reached the stage, she revealed that she had just been invited to speak—what Prexy guessed was "one of those faux pas moments when an organizer realizes that the whole speaker's platform does not have a woman." He remembers that "Ruth's words were spare, clear, and from her heart. She basically said we must become the ANC we once were and stop the fighting and corruption. Her eloquence and her message resulted in a standing ovation."[59]

The esteemed Cuban leader, Jorge Risquet also received a standing ovation before even reaching the podium. "The applause was an unequivocal statement of gratitude for Cuba's contribution to the southern African liberation movements and to ending apartheid, a contribution that includes the thousands of Cuban men and women combatants who died fighting apartheid forces in Angola and Namibia." It seems the South Africans, as much as or more than the Angolans, commemorate the contribution of Cuba to their liberation. In Pretoria's Freedom Park, "the Wall of Names commemorates those who 'paid the ultimate price' for South Africa's freedom. The names of the Cubans who died in Angola are inscribed on the Wall. No other foreign country is represented." As one scholar put it, "There is no other instance in modern history in which a small, underdeveloped country has shaped the course of events in a distant region—humiliating one superpower and repeatedly defying the other."[60]

Prexy relished running into old friends, and the list is too long to recount here. "Every time I turned around there was another friend, another comrade, another person who has been my teacher." This included the poet Kgositsile, whom Prexy first met in Dar es Salaam in 1968; Toivo ya Toivo, the Namibian leader and former Robben Island prisoner who served with Mandela, and his American-born lawyer wife, Vicki ya Toivo. "These three have been like family to me all these years." Marcelino dos Santos, vice president of Frelimo and one of its founders, made the long trip by train from Maputo. "I turn to greet him and saw Josiah Jele, first ANC Representative to the United Nations whom my oldest son is named after. Josiah and I used to discuss jazz together from time to time and munch on samosas in Dar es Salaam cafes. I turned back to Marcelino but bumped instead into Rev. Frank Chikane and Rev. Molefe Tsele, prominent United Democratic Front (UDF) activists, who in the late 1990s, left the church ranks and joined the administration of President Thabo Mbeki, who succeeded Nelson Mandela."[61]

Prexy brought his son Samora to Mozambique for a special naming ceremony—a similarly heartfelt moment that illustrated just how much Prexy had become part of an extended African internationalist family. Prexy and Janet MacLean had named their son after Samora Machel. "I was told to bring Samora." Graça hosted "a big feast" with members of her late husband's family, including three of Samora's brothers. "And they each gave me over a $100. This was the Mozambican way of bringing in a child named after some great figure. It was just fantastic." Then they traveled to Graça's home village. She had recently purchased cattle to replace cattle that President Nyerere had given to Samora when Frelimo was based in Tanzania and that had been killed by Renamo. "The trucks from South Africa arrived while we were visiting. So, Graça asked me, Janet, and Samora to help shoo these cattle as they came off the trucks." Samora "started out being really brave," Prexy remembered. But "as the cows got bigger and bigger," Samora ran to his father and got up on his shoulders and "did the work from there. It was just a wonderful, wonderful experience."[62]

Prexy's two sons also met Nelson Mandela. Prexy always had a warm relationship with Madiba whom he greatly admired, even as he became critical of other ANC leaders in later years. He cherishes one of Mandela's books that he had autographed "to comarada Prexy." Graça Machel honored Prexy another time on one of his many trips to

Figure 20. Nelson Mandela with Prexy's sons, Samora Nesbitt and Josiah Jele Magdalena. Courtesy of Prexy Nesbitt, Samora Nesbitt, and Jele Magdalena.

Maputo. She offered welcoming remarks to a group of American and Mozambican students. He was taken aback to hear her describe his contributions to the solidarity struggles not just there but in the whole region. "Hearing her cite all of those things in the context of a broader southern Africa struggle" deeply moved Nesbitt and made him realize that he was a well-known ally across the region, someone people talked about and relied upon. Machel mentioned the details of so many struggles. "And she knew all of that and she was so proud of me."[63]

Prexy has made close to one hundred trips to the African continent and has led around forty political and educational tours to southern Africa. He's brought American groups of students, judges, lawyers, clergy, educators, and philanthropists; Swedes, Canadians, World Council of Churches folk, and others. These tours began during the peak years of the solidarity struggle, but most took place after the fall of apartheid and as such are beyond the scope of this study. Cheryl

Johnson-Odim joined one. "It was just really amazing to go with him," she said, "because when you go to South Africa with Prexy you just have a whole other experience. We went to South Africa and Namibia, and it was just different than when you go with normal people because he knows everybody. In Namibia, at the airport we were picked up by the president's cars, it was crazy."[64]

Bernardine Dohrn, a leader of the anti-imperialist militant group the Weather Underground in the 1960s, who later founded the Children and Family Justice Center at Northwestern University School of Law, first met Prexy at his family's church when she volunteered to offer legal support for Martin Luther King's Chicago campaign. Years later, Dohrn brought her son Malik on one of Prexy's trips, and she savored the memory of his getting to meet Walter Sisulu. The Chicago activist legal community—notably Dohrn and Susan Gzesh, who had represented exiled South African poet Dennis Brutus at a deportation trial—had strong ties with many in South Africa, most notably constitutional court judge Albie Sachs. When activists were fighting to end the death penalty in Illinois in the 1990s, Bernardine was tasked with using her ties to ask Nelson Mandela to reach out to Illinois Republican governor George Ryan. Sure enough, Mandela phoned the governor while he was dining at Lou Mitchell's, an iconic Chicago eatery, and shortly before leaving office, Ryan commuted the death sentences of 167 men on death row, leading the way to the abolition of the death penalty in Illinois.[65]

In 2016 Prexy brought two delegations to southern Africa: one, deemed Unfinished Agendas: Liberation History and Today's Struggles, was comprised of activists from the Black Lives Matter, LGBTQ, Palestinian, and economic justice movements and another from the National Lawyers Guild. "In three Southern African countries, we visited with our counterparts from today's progressive movements in Africa ranging from #Feesmustfall and #ZumaMustFall to community, labor, and church bodies," Prexy noted in his account of the trip.

"We met young and emerging leaders in Maputo, journalists such as Khadija Patel at the Daily Vox Johannesburg and leaders of the student #FeesMustFall campaign in both Johannesburg and Cape Town. We also met with seasoned leaders from Southern Africa's former liberation struggles such as Terezinha da Silva, Murphy Morobe, Albie Sachs, Ronnie Kasrils, Roshan Dadoo, Stephanie Kemp, Bonita Bennett, Mandy Sanger, and Keoraptse Kgositsile."[66]

While Prexy's extraordinary life commitment to advocacy and connection in southern Africa is not something most people can emulate, his impassioned engagement with both international and local activism and robust willingness to question and challenge US foreign policy is something we would all do well to embrace. The movement he helped to guide and forge cut against the provincialism and insularity that continues to define so much of American political life. The United States is a global superpower operating nearly eight hundred military bases around the world and deploying troops in scores of countries year in and year out.[67] But in a major contradiction that likely helps sustain global imperial commitments over potential peacetime dividends, most Americans know little of the world and little of the details of their government's foreign policy. Prexy's life story urges us to rethink this and act.

Acknowledgments

I began this book in 2020, during the first summer of the COVID-19 pandemic when we were in lockdown, George Floyd was murdered, and we anxiously awaited signs of hope. My husband had died of cancer that January. Born in Zimbabwe, James Thindwa immersed himself in social justice organizing, championing, in particular, labor rights, racial justice, and international solidarity. James and I both knew Prexy Nesbitt before we knew each other. Writing this book helped me stay close to James and to more fully appreciate an important part of his activist world. This book is in tribute to and in memory of him.

Of course, I couldn't have written this book without Prexy Nesbitt's incredible generosity in sharing himself with the world. Thank you Prexy for making this book possible. As I hope you'll agree, his life overflows with rich lessons and insights. Prexy also opened his community to me, and they too, are a fundamental part of this book. I have tremendous gratitude for all the people who shared stories of their extraordinary lives and struggles. I hope I have gotten it right.

I first became friends with Prexy when I moved to Chicago over twenty-five years ago. We met through mutual friend Barbara Ransby, a leading Black feminist scholar-activist and longtime comrade of Prexy's, who has worked to extend the Chicago tradition of internationalist solidarity organizing into the twenty-first century. Thank you, Barbara, and Peter Sporn, for the deep web of connections you have built over many years.

I offer tremendous thanks to the many library workers and archivists whose labor in digitizing a wide array of primary sources enabled me to conduct significant research from home during the pandemic.

I presented chapters of the book manuscript at workshops at Princeton, Northwestern, and the University of Chicago and greatly benefitted from colleagues' comments and advice. A fellowship year at the Warren Center for Studies in American History at Harvard, generously augmented by Northwestern University, enabled me to complete the book. I am grateful for the leadership of Jarvis Givens, Brandon Terry, and Lisa McGuir. As director of the Warren Center, Lisa brought wisdom and calm to the enterprise, and Black Power seminar co-leaders Jarvis and Brandon each brought intellectual dazzle, warm laughter, and probing insights.

The entire Warren Center community was lovely and supportive, and I thank Monnikue McCall and Fatima Amjad for making that possible. For their wonderful insights, conversation, and comradery, I thank Jasmin Young, Robyn Spencer, Traci Parker, Charisse Burden-Stelly, Jacqueline Wang, Magana Kabugi, J. T. Roane, Sam Klug, Sage Goodwin, Soham Patel, Winnie Williams, and Christian Walkes. A special shout-out to the oyster fans among us who gathered many Thursdays to laugh, indulge, and appreciate our community.

Living in Cambridge gave me the opportunity to reconnect with old friends. I thank Tommie Shelby for always engaging conversation. It was fantastic to share many evenings of food and laughter with the wonderful and warm Cyrus Veeser and Lilian Bobea. I was able to catch up with Manisha Sinha and to see Annelise Orleck's wondrous Vermont with dear friend Lynette Jackson.

It was a special treat to spend time that year with my hockey-playing, opera-loving sister, Jane, and her family and wonderful circle of friends.

I want to acknowledge the many Harvard faculty and students who fell victim to concerted right-wing attacks for their expressions of support for free speech, Palestinian freedom, and racial justice during my time in Cambridge. It was stunning and heartbreaking to see the intrusion of wealthy donors and governmental pressure into the realms of academic freedom and campus life. And sadly, it has only gotten worse in 2025.

I thank my wonderful friends and colleagues in Chicago and New York for their comradery and support during the creation of this book. Thanks, especially, to dear friends Bill Ayers and Bernardine Dohrn for always urging me on. Mary Pattillo is peerless in her support and leadership, and I am very grateful for her friendship. And boundless thanks to all my Northwestern friends and colleagues!

I'm grateful to Elaine Charnov and Bruce Stutz for modeling how an urban life of conviviality, culture, and social engagement is possible in new places.

I thank Niels Hooper, Nora Becker, Stephanie Summerhays, Artemis Brod, and everyone at the University of California Press for their excellent work. And special praise to Jill Marr at the Sandra Dykstra Literary Agency.

Finally, I cherish memories of my beloved mother and father who each passed away while I was writing this book. Both cheered my life choices and would have been thrilled to see this book's publication. I am eternally grateful for their steadfast support.

Notes

INTRODUCTION

1. See Penny Von Eschen, *Race Against Empire: Black Americans and Anticolonialism, 1937–1957* (Cornell University Press, 1997).

2. See Kevin K. Gaines, *American Africans in Ghana: Black Expatriates and the Civil Rights Era* (University of North Carolina Press, 2006) and Seth Markle, *A Motorcycle on Hell Run: Tanzania, Black Power and the Uncertain Future of Pan-Africanism* (Michigan State University Press, 2017).

3. Scholars have written extensively about apartheid and the anti-apartheid movement. Helpful to this study have been William Minter and Sylvia Hill, "Anti-Apartheid Solidarity in United States-South Africa Relations: From the Margins to the Mainstream," in *The Road to Democracy in South Africa, Volume 3, International Solidarity, Part II*, ed. South African Democracy Education Trust (UNISA Press, 2008); Francis N. Nesbitt, *Race for Sanctions: African Americans Against Apartheid, 1946–1994* (Indiana University Press, 2004); and Robert Zebulun Larson, "The Transnational and Local Dimensions of the U.S. Anti-apartheid Movement," PhD diss. (Ohio State University, 2019).

4. Of the many works on Mozambique, particularly helpful to this study have been Allen and Barbara Isaacman's *Mozambique: From Colonialism to Revolution, 1900–1982* (Westview Press, 1983) and their *Mozambique's Samora Machel: A Life Cut Short* (Ohio University Press, 2020) as well as two dissertations, Elizabeth Banks, "Socialist Internationalism Between the Soviet Union and Mozambique," PhD diss. (New York University, 2019) and Carla Stephens, "The People Mobilized: The Mozambican Liberation Movement and American Activism, 1960–1975," PhD diss. (Temple University, 2011).

5. Erin McCarthy, "Interview with Prexy Nesbitt," Spring 2009, Oral Histories, Chicago Anti-Apartheid Collection, College Archives and Special Collections, Columbia College Chicago, http://digitalcommons.colum.edu/cadc_caam_oralhistories/2.

1. FROM THE WEST SIDE TO DAR ES SALAAM

1. In contrast to many accounts of the Black middle class, which portray their aspirations as antithetical to the working class, my scholarship on midcentury Black urban life discovers a pro-union story. See Biondi, *To Stand and Fight: The Struggle for Civil Rights in Postwar New York City* (Havard, 2003).

2. Prexy Nesbitt interview with author, September 4, 2020.

3. George B. Nesbitt, *Being Somebody and Black Besides: An Untold Memoir of Midcentury Black Life*, ed. Prexy Nesbitt and Zeb Larson (University of Chicago Press, 2021), 51–53.

4. Prexy Nesbitt interview with author, September 4, 2020.

5. Erin McCarthy, "Interview with Prexy Nesbitt," Spring 2009, Oral Histories, Chicago Anti-Apartheid Collection, College Archives and Special Collections, Columbia College Chicago. http://digitalcommons.colum.edu/cadc_caam_oralhistories/2.

6. Prexy Nesbitt interview with author, September 4, 2020.

7. Prexy Nesbitt interview with author, September 4, 2020.

8. Prexy Nesbitt interview with author, September 4, 2020. See also Biondi, *To Stand and Fight.*

9. McCarthy, "Interview with Prexy Nesbitt," and Prexy Nesbitt interview with author, September 4, 2020; author conversation with Prexy Nesbitt, August 14, 2024.

10. Prexy Nesbitt interview with author, September 4, 2020.

11. McCarthy, "Interview with Prexy Nesbitt."

12. In another family baseball connection, Prexy's maternal uncle, John Crain, a professional ballplayer in an east coast Negro League, was close friends with Brooklyn Dodger Roy Campanella, and when Prexy was doing an Antioch work-study experience at Rusk Rehabilitation Institute in NYC in 1962, Crain arranged for him to care for Campanella, who had been in a devastating automobile accident. Author conversation with Prexy Nesbitt, August 14, 2024.

13. McCarthy, "Interview with Prexy Nesbitt."

14. Prexy Nesbitt interview with author, September 4, 2020.

15. Author conversation with Prexy Nesbitt, August 14, 2024.

16. Dr. Eduardo Mondlane, "The Future of the Portuguese Territories in Southern Africa," a speech at the Royal Institute of International Affairs, Chatham House, London, March 7, 1968, https://www.chathamhouse.org/sites/default/files/images/events/8-3177%20Mondlane-The%20future%20of%20Portuguese%20territories.pdf.

17. Allen and Barbara Isaacman, *Mozambique: From Colonialism to Revolution, 1900–1982* (Westview Press, 1983); and see Eduardo Mondlane, *The Struggle for Mozambique* (Zed Press, 1983).

18. Carla Stephens, "The People Mobilized: The Mozambican Liberation Movement and American Activism, 1960–1975," PhD diss. (Temple University, 2011), 264; William Minter, "The United States in the 1950s," unpublished essay in author's possession.

19. Carla Stephens, "The People Mobilized," xxvi.

20. William Minter, "The United States in the 1950s."

21. Carla Stephens, "The People Mobilized," 36–39.

22. Mondlane, "The Future of the Portuguese Territories in Southern Africa," a speech at the Royal Institute of International Affairs, Chatham House, London, March 7, 1968; and see Mondlane, *The Struggle for Mozambique*.

23. Amilcar Cabral, "Connecting the Struggles: An Informal Talk with Black Americans," in *Return to the Source: Selected Speeches of Amilcar Cabral*, ed. African Information Service (Monthly Review Press, 1973), 81.

24. Mondlane, "The Future of the Portuguese Territories in Southern Africa."

25. Prexy Nesbitt interview with author, September 30, 2020.

26. Prexy Nesbitt interview with author, September 30, 2020.

27. Prexy Nesbitt, "Reminiscences," draft, in author possession.

28. Prexy Nesbitt interview with author, September 4, 2020.

29. McCarthy, "Interview with Prexy Nesbitt."

30. McCarthy, "Interview with Prexy Nesbitt."

31. Prexy Nesbitt interview with author, September 4, 2020.

32. McCarthy, "Interview with Prexy Nesbitt."

33. William Minter and Sylvia Hill, "Anti-Apartheid Solidarity in United States-South Africa Relations: From the Margins to the Mainstream," in *The Road to Democracy in South Africa, Volume 3, International Solidarity, Part II*, ed. South African Democracy Education Trust (UNISA Press, 2008), 749–750.

34. Trevor Noah, *Born a Crime: Stories from a South African Childhood* (One World, 2016).

35. McCarthy, "Interview with Prexy Nesbitt."

36. Prexy Nesbitt interview with author, September 30, 2020.

37. Prexy Nesbitt interview with author, September 30, 2020.

38. Prexy Nesbitt interview with author, September 30, 2020.

39. McCarthy, "Interview with Prexy Nesbitt."

40. McCarthy, "Interview with Prexy Nesbitt."

41. Prexy Nesbitt, guest lecture for Eve Sandberg at Oberlin College, Zoom, April 13, 2021.

42. Leo Zeilig, *A Revolutionary for Our Time: The Walter Rodney Story* (Haymarket Books, 2022), 38–43; 112.

43. Prexy Nesbitt interview with author, September 4, 2020; John S. Saul, *Revolutionary Traveller: Freeze-Frames from a Life* (Arbeiter Ring Publishing, 2009), 27.

44. Prexy Nesbitt interview with author, September 4, 2020.

45. Zeilig, *A Revolutionary for Our Time*, 46–47.

46. Prexy Nesbitt interview with author, September 4, 2020.

47. Prexy Nesbitt interview with author, September 4, 2020.

48. Prexy Nesbitt interview with author, September 4, 2020.

49. Prexy Nesbitt, "A Perspective on Teaching Africa," n.d., essay in author's possession.

50. Prexy Nesbitt interview with author, September 4, 2020.

51. Prexy Nesbitt, "On Eduardo Chivambo Mondlane," a talk at Howard University, October 3, 2014, in author's possession.

52. Prexy Nesbitt interview with author, September 4, 2020.

53. Prexy Nesbitt interview with author, September 4, 2020; "King Protector Paves Road for Others," *Medill Reports*, Fall 2018, https://news.medill.northwestern.edu/chicago/mlk-protector-paves-road-for-others-to-accomplish-more.

54. Don Terry, "Northern Exposure," *Chicago Tribune*, January 15, 2006.

55. Prexy Nesbitt interview with author, September 4, 2020. Prexy would later work with Brutus in Chicago, as the poet joined the faculty at Northwestern University in Evanston, Illinois.

56. Prexy Nesbitt interview with author, September 4, 2020.

57. See Martha Biondi, *The Black Revolution on Campus* (University of California Press, 2012).

58. Wright taught at Columbia from 1966 until 2008. I took her History of South Africa class while an undergraduate at Barnard.

59. Prexy Nesbitt interview with author, September 4, 2020.

60. Prexy Nesbitt interview with author, September 4, 2020.

2. THE TILT TOWARD INTERNATIONALISM

1. Prexy Nesbitt interview with author, September 10, 2020.

2. Scholars of Black American solidarity with African decolonization have tended to focus either on the 1930s through 1960s or on the anti-apartheid movement, but attention to other struggles on the continent in the 1970s and 1980s is increasing. See Seth Markle, *A Motorcycle on Hell Run: Tanzania, Black Power, and the Uncertain Future of Pan-Africanism, 1964–1974* (Michigan State University Press, 2017).

3. Herman Cohen, National Security Council Director for Africa, quoted in *Cuba: An African Odyssey*, directed by Jihan El-Tahir (Arte Vidéo, 2007).

4. "African leaders understood that the key to achieving majority rule in southern Africa was first supporting independence in Mozambique and Angola. This strategy was formalized at a summit conference of fourteen East and Central African states in Lusaka, Zambia in April 1969." Carla Stephens, "The People Mobilized: The Mozambican Liberation Movement and American Activism, 1960–1975," PhD diss. (Temple University, 2011), xxiii.

5. See William Minter and Sylvia Hill, "Anti-Apartheid Solidarity in United States-South Africa Relations: From the Margins to the Mainstream," in *The*

Road to Democracy in South Africa, Volume 3, International Solidarity, Part II, ed. South African Democracy Education Trust (UNISA Press, 2008), 770.

6. Samora Machel, "Establishing People's Power," printed speech (1976), 15; see Fanon Che Wilkins, "In the Belly of the Beast: Black Power, Anti-Imperialism, and the African Liberation Support Committee, 1968–1975," PhD diss. (New York University, 2001).

7. Sarah LeFanu, *S is for Samora: A Lexical Biography of Samora Machel and the Mozambican Dream* (Hurst, 2012), 142–143.

8. William Minter, "Propaganda and Reality in Mozambique," *Africa Today* 16, no.2 (April-May 1969).

9. LeFanu, *S is for Samora,* 143.

10. Prexy Nesbitt interview with author, January 8, 2021.

11. Allen and Barbara Isaacman, *Mozambique: From Colonialism to Revolution, 1900–1982* (Westview Press, 1983), 105; see also Elizabeth Banks, "Socialist Internationalism Between the Soviet Union and Mozambique," PhD diss. (New York University, 2019), 75–76.

12. Sarah LeFanu, *S is for Samora,* 143–144; Isaacman and Isaacman, *Mozambique: From Colonialism to Revolution,* 103. "By '68, '69, these ad hoc African-Americans—nobody really knew who they were—they'd see me walking around and they'd get friendly with me. Frelimo finally said to me, it was a message from Chissano, who was the security person and Samora, 'No more, Prexy. Do not interact with them.'" Prexy Nesbitt interview with author, January 8, 2021; Allen and Barbara Isaacman, *Mozambique's Samora Machel: A Life Cut Short* (Ohio University Press, 2020), 81.

13. The Portuguese "Africanized the colonial army." By the early 1970s, ten to twenty thousand Africans were fighting to defend colonial rule, including an elite brigade of four thousand paratroopers. Isaacman and Isaacman, *Mozambique's Samora Machel,* 116

14. "I was fortunate to get to know these personalities in all these struggles. Because of my links to Frelimo and ANC, I just didn't enter this as a cold, unknown entity. These brothers and sisters knew me. So, it made it different for me right away." Prexy Nesbitt interview with author, September 4 and September 30, 2020.

15. Prexy Nesbitt interview with author, December 19, 2021.

16. En route to Tanzania, Prexy's funders—the Church World Service and World Council of Churches—assigned him to assist with famine relief in the northern frontier of Kenya. Prexy reported that a provincial official was siphoning off relief aid, and as a result, the government expelled him and designated him a "prohibited immigrant." Julie Frederikse, "Interview with Prexy Nesbitt," October 12, 2004, Durban, South Africa, www.africanactivist.msu.edu. Nesbitt's candor in this report foreshadowed frank appraisals that would stir controversy when he worked for the World Council of Churches and much later, the AFL-CIO.

17. Carla Stephens, "The People Mobilized," 232. For more on the struggle inside Frelimo after Mondlane's assassination, see LeFanu, *S is for Samora*. Uriah Simango criticized Mondlane's marriage to a white woman in a conversation with Prexy. Prexy informed Frelimo leaders "about the lies Simango was spreading about Janet Mondlane and white people in general." Prexy Nesbitt interview with author, September 20, 2020.

18. LeFanu, *S is for Samora*, 157.

19. Prexy Nesbitt interview with author, September 20, 2020. According to John Saul, "the fact that Mondlane's assassination was probably facilitated as much by enemies within his movement as by the Portuguese provides some index of just how inevitable an eventual all-out confrontation would be." John Saul, foreward to *The Struggle for Mozambique*, ed. Eduardo Mondlane (Zed Press, 1983), vi. Prexy Nesbitt, "Eduardo Chivambo Mondlane," c. 2020, in author's possession.

20. Prexy Nesbitt, "On Eduardo Chivambo Mondlane," a talk at Howard University, October 3, 2014, in author's possession. Emphasis in original.

21. LeFanu, *S is for Samora*, 258–261.

22. Prexy Nesbitt interview with author, September 20, 2020.

23. Prexy Nesbitt to author via text, January 18, 2024.

24. "African Liberation Movement Militants Speak at Malcolm X," leaflet, July 28, 1970, https://africanactivist.msu.edu/record/210-849-28117/

25. Carla Stephens, "The People Mobilized," 272.

26. Prexy Nesbitt interview with author, October 30, 2020.

27. "Westside Teacher Arrested in Protest," *Chicago Defender*, June 27, 1970.

28. On Prexy's recommendation, Kermit Coleman was invited to be one of the few American international observers at a trial of mercenaries that was

held in Angola. Prexy described it as an incredible global event, "because these mercenaries had never been tried before, and here they are being tried and given full legal protections." Erin McCarthy, "Interview with Prexy Nesbitt," Spring 2009, Chicago Anti-Apartheid Collection, College Archives and Special Collections, Columbia College Chicago. http://digitalcommons.colum.edu /cadc_caam_oralhistories/2

29. "Westside Teacher Arrested in Protest," *Chicago Defender*, June 27, 1970

30. Prexy Nesbitt interview with author, September 20, 2020.

31. Banks, "Socialist Internationalism," 24.

32. Stephens, "The People Mobilized," 271.

33. McCarthy, "Interview with Prexy Nesbitt."

34. Prexy Nesbitt interview with author, September 25, 2020. James Garrett, of the Center for Black Education in Washington, DC, and formerly of CORE and SNCC, was drawn to Cabral's keen sense of organizing, which reminded him of Bob Moses. James Garrett interview with author, April 22, 2022.

35. Prexy Nesbitt interview with author, September 20, 2020. African Information Service, ed., *Return to the Source: Selected Speeches of Amilcar Cabral* (Monthly Review Press, 1973).

36. Amilcar Cabral, "Connecting the Struggles: An Informal Talk with Black Americans," in *Return to the Source: Selected Speeches of Amilcar Cabral*, ed. African Information Service (Monthly Review Press, 1973), 75–78.

37. Prexy Nesbitt interview with author, September 20, 2020; Wilkins, "In the Belly of the Beast."

38. *Cuba: An African Odyssey*; see also, Firoze Manji and Bill Fletcher Jr., eds., *Claim No Easy Victories: The Legacy of Amilcar Cabral* (CODESRIA and Daraja Press, 2013).

39. Robert Van Lierop, "Robert Van Lierop: *A Luta Continua*," in *No Easy Victories: African Liberation and American Activists over Half a Century, 1950–2000*, ed. William Minter, Gail Hovey, and Charles Cobb Jr. (Africa World Press, 2008), 142–143.

40. Carla Stephens, "The People Mobilized," 255; R. Joseph Parrott, "*A Luta Continua:* Radical Filmmaking, Pan-African Liberation and Communal Empowerment," *Race and Class* 57, no.1 (2015): 16, 5, https://www.youtube.com /watch?v = NUdeF2KNeCg&t = 9s

41. CCLAMG, "Southern Africa Solidarity Day," PN Madison, Box 7; Fred Melcher, "Liberating Mozambique, Angola and Bissau," *Chicago Express*, December 6–12, 1972, PN Madison, Box 7.

42. Parrott, *"A Luta Continua,"* 22, 27

43. Prexy Nesbitt interview with author, October 15, 2020.

44. Angela Davis conversation with author, September 22, 2024.

45. William Minter, "An Unfinished Journey," in *No Easy Victories*, ed. Minter, Hovey, and Cobb Jr., 31. Van Lierop made a second documentary to publicize the need for continued support of Mozambicans after independence. Like *A Luta Continua, O Povo Organizado* was used to raise awareness among Americans and build solidarity with struggles in southern Africa.

46. Daniel Schechter, "From a Closed Filing Cabinet: The Life and Times of The Africa Research Group," *Issues: A Quarterly Journal of Africanist Opinion* 6, no. 2/3 (Summer/Fall 1976): 41.

47. Writing in 1976, Schechter argued that recent revelations of "massive, covert US involvement in Angola" vindicated ARG's claims. Schechter, "From a Closed Filing Cabinet," 42.

48. Schechter, 42; Prexy Nesbitt interview with author, April 24, 2022; Nesbitt email to author April 28, 2022.

49. Schechter, 42. Schechter had an enormous impact as a solidarity activist for decades, mostly in creating or producing news shows about southern Africa, including the indispensable *South Africa Now*. Prexy Nesbitt interview with author, April 24, 2022.

50. Robert Van Lierop interview with William Minter, April 16, 2004, http://noeasyvictories.org/interviews/int07_vanlierop.php; Prexy Nesbitt interview with author, September 10, 2020.

51. Prexy Nesbitt interview with author, September 10, 2020. I have copies of the *African Agenda*, courtesy of Otis Cunningham.

52. Prexy Nesbitt interview with author, September 10, 2020; Otis Cunningham interview with author, April 13, 2022.

53. Otis Cunningham interview with author, April 13, 2022.

54. Danny Fenster, "Interview with Otis Cunningham," Fall 2009, Oral Histories, Chicago Anti-Apartheid Collection, College Archives and Special Collections, Columbia College Chicago, http://digitalcommons.colum.edu/cadc_caam_oralhistories/3

55. Nesbitt, "Eduardo Chivambo Mondlane."

56. Prexy Nesbitt interview with author, September 30, 2020.

57. Prexy Nesbitt interview with author, September 30, 2020.

58. Mimi Edmunds interview with author, December 12, 2020.

59. Chicago Committee for the Liberation of Angola, Mozambique and Guinea-Bissau, "Statement of Philosophy and Principles of Work," n.d., PN Madison, Box 7.

60. Eileen Hansen, "Testimony to the Committee of 24 of the United Nations," n.d., PN Madison, Box 7; Prexy Nesbitt interview with author, September 30, 2020.

61. Prexy Nesbitt interview with author, September 30, 2020.

62. Corporate Information Center, "A CIC Brief for Information and Action: Gulf Oil—Portuguese Ally in Angola," March 1972, PN Madison, Additions, Box 1.

63. Sheila D. Collins, *Ubuntu: George M. Houser and the Struggle for Peace and Freedom on Two Continents* (Ohio University Press, 2020), 3; Carla Stephens, "The People Mobilized," xxvii.

64. Prexy Nesbitt interview with author, September 10, 2020.

65. Collins, *Ubuntu*, 202–203; Stephens, "The People Mobilized," 246–248.

66. William Minter, "An Unfinished Journey," in *No Easy Victories*, ed. Minter, Hovey, and Cobb Jr., 31; see also Ronald W. Walters, *Pan Africanism in the African Diaspora: An Analysis of Modern Afrocentric Political Movements* (Wayne State University Press, 1993); Wilkins, "In the Belly of the Beast"; and Edward O. Erhagbe, "The African American Contribution to the Liberation Struggle in Southern Africa: The Case of the African Liberation Support Committee, 1972–1979," *Journal of Pan African Studies* 4, no.5 (2011): 26–56. Prexy Nesbitt, "Breakin' the Kneecaps of 'Baaskap': A Brief Discussion of the International Anti-Apartheid Movement and African Solidarity Work, Then, and Now," speech in Durban, South Africa, in author's possession.

67. Former CIA agent John Stockwell writes about organizing Black support for Unita. John Stockwell, *In Search of Enemies: A CIA Story* (Norton, 1978).

68. Prexy Nesbitt interview with author, September 20, 2020.

69. Prexy Nesbitt interview with author, September 25, 2020; Prexy Nesbitt interview with author, April 24, 2022.

70. Prexy Nesbitt interview with author, September 10, 2020. "Activist Talks Here," *Chicago Defender*, April 22, 1975.

71. James Garrett interview with author, April 22, 2022.

72. James Garrett interview with author, April 22, 2022; see also See Matthew Rothwell, "The Road is Torturous: The Chinese Revolution and the End of the Global Sixties," *Revista Izquierdas* 49 (April 2020): 2486 and Robeson Taj Frazier, *The East is Black: Cold War China in the Black Radical Imagination* (Duke University Press, 2015).

73. Manning Marable finds that "by early 1973, tendencies within the Pan-Africanist movement had begun to crystallize into firm and antagonistic political lines. The old division that had split the movement in California in the late 1960s, between Karenga's cultural nationalists and the Black Panther Party, resurfaced in a new form. In their writings and political activities, the cultural nationalists became more explicitly anti-Marxist. . . . White people on the left were untrustworthy allies because they were unable to overcome their psychological and even genetic hatred for blacks." *Blackwater: Historical Studies in Race, Class Consciousness, and Revolution* (University Press of Colorado, 1993), 109.

74. James Garrett interview with author, April 22, 2022.

75. Prexy Nesbitt interview with author, September 20, 2020.

76. "The delegation from the United States was . . . the most divided and disorganized of all . . . Many rightist nationalists were shocked by the appearance of 'white' delegates, including Arabs and Cubans. . . . A debate ensued between the leftists, who supported the MPLA (backed by the Cubans and Soviets) in the Angolan liberation struggle, and the rightists who endorsed Jonas Savimbi's UNITA, which was backed by the US, China, and South Africa." Marable, *Blackwater*, 111. See also La TaSha Levy, "Remembering Sixth-PAC: Interviews with Sylvia Hill and Judy Claude, Organizers of the Sixth Pan-African Congress," *The Black Scholar* 37, no. 4 (Winter 2008): 39–47 and Ashley Farmer, *Remaking Black Power: How Black Women Transformed an Era* (University of North Carolina Press, 2017).

77. E. M. Austin, "Reflections of the 6th Pan African Congress," *Sun Reporter*, Aug 3, 1974, p. 14, https://www.proquest.com/newspapers.

78. Markle, *A Motorcycle on Hell Run*, 155–160.

79. Lerone Bennett Jr., "Pan-Africanism at the Crossroads: Dreams and Realities Clash as Delegates Debate Class and Color at Historic Congress in Tanzania," *Ebony Magazine*, August 1974, 148–160.

80. Prexy Nesbitt interview with author, October 15, 2020.

81. Geri Augusto interview with Charles Cobb Jr., January 6, 2005, http://www.noeasyvictories.org/interviews/int10_augusto.php.

82. Geri Augusto interview with Charles Cobb Jr., January 6, 2005.

83. Geri Augusto interview with Charles Cobb Jr., January 6, 2005.

84. Max Elbaum, *Revolution in the Air: Sixties Radicals Turn to Lenin, Mao and Che* (Verso, 2002), 218–219.

85. Piero Gleijeses, *Visions of Freedom: Havana, Washington, Pretoria, and the Struggle for Southern Africa, 1976–1991* (University of North Carolina Press, 2013), 10, 25–36. China in short order severed its support for the FNLA.

86. "Angola: The Struggle Continues," *Southern Africa* 9, no. 4 (April 1976): 4.

87. Herman Cohen, quoted in *Cuba: An African Odyssey*; Gleijeses, *Visions of Freedom*, 15.

88. Walter Rodney, "The Lessons of Angola," April 22, 1976, PN Madison, Box 7.

89. "CORE Chief Cancels A Speech On Coast After A Black Protest," *New York Times*, February 13, 1976.

90. Florence L. Tate and Jake-Ann Jones, *Sometimes Farmgirls Become Revolutionaries: Notes on Black Power, Politics, Depression and the FBI* (Black Classic Press, 2021), 200–207.

91. James Garrett interview with author, April 22, 2022; James Garrett, "The Lessons from Angola, An Eyewitness Report," *Black Scholar* (June 1976): 42–59.

92. Prexy Nesbitt, "A Report on the 1976 Angola Seminar," *Southern Africa* 9, no. 4 (April 1976): 6, 7.

93. *The Angolan Struggle: Produce and Resist*, a booklet published by the Angola Support Conference, Chicago, IL, 1976, www.africanactivist.msu.edu

94. Marjorie Boehm, Women's International League of Peace and Freedom, "Report of Angolan Seminar Held in Havana, February 26-March 1," Jerry Herman Collection, Michigan State University, www.africanactivist.msu.edu.

95. "1,000 Here March Against a U.S. Role in War in Angola," *New York Times*, January 18, 1976; "200 Protest Angola Role," *Chicago Daily Defender*, January 12, 1976.

96. Prexy housed them at the home of his godmother, educator Bernice Brunson. He had asked a radical labor group from Detroit to provide security

for the MPLA and when they showed up at "Aunt Bunny's" house armed, she voiced her great displeasure to Prexy.

97. "Prexy Nesbitt to All Persons Who Attended the Angolan Support Conference," July 8, 1976, private collection of Richard Knight, www.africanactivist .msu.edu

98. McCarthy, "Interview with Prexy Nesbitt."

99. John Stockwell, *In Search of Enemies.*

100. Prexy Nesbitt, National Interim Steering Committee Coordinator to Members, September 30, 1976, https://africanactivist.msu.edu/recordFiles/210– 849–21114/african_activist_archive-a0a7j5-b_12419.pdf

101. Prexy Nesbitt, "Angola is Part of All of Us," *Black Scholar* (May-June 1980), 53.

3. THE GLOBAL AND LOCAL DIMENSIONS OF THE ANTI-APARTHEID STRUGGLE

1. Penny Von Eschen, *Race Against Empire: Black Americans and Anti-Colonialism* (Cornell University Press, 1997).

2. E.S. Reddy interview with Lisa Brock, July 20, 2020, http://www .noeasyvictories.org/interviews/int03_reddy.php

3. In 1977 Prexy met Don Will, a scholar of South African and Palestinian struggles, who organized social justice seminars for the Methodist Woman's Center at the UN. Like Prexy, Will was very influenced by Eqbal Ahmad. Prexy later presided over Will's marriage to the South African Ndathu (Leonora) Mbatha. Prexy Nesbitt interview with author, October 15, 2020; conversation with author August 14, 2024. To understand the importance invested in and expected of the UN, see Adom Getachew, *Worldmaking After Empire: The Rise and Fall of Self-Determination* (Princeton University Press, 2019).

4. African National Congress National Executive Committee Secretariat Lusaka to ANC Missions Representatives, "Obituary," June 12, 1988. Prexy Nesbitt Papers, Box 7, Wisconsin Historical Society, Madison, WI. Hereafter PN Madison.

5. Prexy Nesbitt interview with author, September 20, 2020.

6. Jennifer Davis, "U.S.-South Africa Foreign Policy," *Foreign Policy in Focus* 2, no. 22, January 1977.

7. Richard Knight, "Documenting the U.S. Solidarity Movement—With Reflections on the Sanctions and Divestment Campaigns," A Decade of Freedom: Celebrating the Role of the International Anti-Apartheid Movement, Durban, South Africa, October 2004, https://africanactivist.msu.edu/recordFiles/210-849-27846/AAAPpamresizedopt.pdf

8. "The Future of South Africa: The ANC View," Chatham House Meetings and Speeches, October 29, 1985, transcript, PN Madison, Box 8.

9. American Committee on Africa, *Annual Report*, 1977, https://africanactivist.msu.edu/record/210-849-29374/

10. George Houser, "Ending Bank Loans to South Africa," Statement Before UN Special Committee Against Apartheid, June 6, 1979, https://africanactivist.msu.edu/record/210-849-29796/

11. Kumbula, "US Banks Target of Apartheid Critics," *Los Angeles Times*, September 30, 1977.

12. Richard Knight, "Documenting the U.S. Solidarity Movement."

13. It "helped end the Vietnam War, pardon draft resistors, and stop the B-1 bomber," in "Clergy Concerned Concert to Benefit S. Africa," *Amsterdam News*, September 24, 1977.

14. American Friends Service Committee, *Southern Africa News*, October 1977, PN Madison, Box 5.

15. Michael G. Looney, "Banks, Firms Blamed in Death of Biko," *Oakland Tribune*, October 16, 1977, PN Madison, Box 1.

16. PBS, "Interview with Rev. Michael Weeder," *People's Century*, https://www.pbs.org/wgbh/peoplescentury/episodes/skindeep/weedertranscript.html.

17. Kumbula, "US Banks Target of Apartheid Critics," *Los Angeles Times*, September 30, 1977. By the end of 1977, several unions and the United Methodist Church, the Episcopalian Church, and the United Church of Christ had withdrawn $30 million from offending banks. ACOA, *Annual Report* (1977), https://michiganintheworld.history.lsa.umich.edu/antiapartheid/items/show/348.

18. Prexy Nesbitt interview with author, September 10, 2020; ACOA Executive Board Meeting, Minutes, June 14, 1978, https://africanactivist.msu.edu/recordFiles/210-849-24863/PWACOAEB6-14-78opt.pdf; "National Conference in Support of the African National Congress and Other Democratic Forces in South Africa," program, November 13–15, 1992, Riverside Church, New York, PN Madison, Box 6.

19. Prexy Nesbitt interviews with author, October 30, 2020 and May 7, 2024.

20. Prexy Nesbitt interview with author, October 30, 2020.

21. Labor Committee Against Apartheid, "Summary U.S. Trade Union Actions Against Apartheid," c. 1981, PN Madison, Box 7.

22. Peter Cole, "No Justice, No Ships Get Loaded: Political Boycotts on the San Francisco Bay and Durban Waterfronts," *International Review of Social History*, 58 (2013): 185–217; Prexy Nesbitt interview with author, May 7, 2024.

23. Corporate Data Exchange Handbook, *US Bank Loans to South Africa*, 1978, PN Madison, Box 2; Prexy Nesbitt interview with author, September 30, 2020.

24. Prexy Nesbitt, "Outrage into Action," International Conference on a Decade of Freedom, Durban, South Africa, January 13, 2004, Nesbitt Collection, Columbia College; Prexy Nesbitt interview with author, September 10, 2020.

25. Committee to Oppose Bank Loans to South Africa, "Press Release," n.d., PN Madison, Box 6.

26. CIDSA, Press Release, June 20, 1985, PN Madison, Box 6.

27. Press Announcement, "stop Banking on Apartheid," November 17, 1978, PN Madison, Box 6, https://livinghistory.as.ucsb.edu/2019/10/09/bofa/; Prexy Nesbitt interview with author, September 10, 2020

28. "U.S. Film Premier. South Africa: A Rising Tide," flyer, n.d., PN Madison, Box 6; Prexy Nesbitt telephone interview with author, May 7, 2024. In another example, at a different Bay Area event, Paul Isaacs, a Namibian student and member of SWAPO, and Prexy Nesbitt discussed events in Namibia in an international context. Miloanne Hecathorn, "Greetings," August 17, 1977, PN Madison, Box 6.

29. Ron Nixon, *Selling Apartheid: South Africa's Global Propaganda War* (Pluto Press, 2016), viii-ix.

30. Southern Africa Collective, "Proposal for a Southern Africa Coalition-Bay Area," August 26, 1978, PN Madison, Box 6.

31. Southern Africa Collective, "Proposal for a Southern Africa Coalition-Bay Area."

32. Prexy Nesbitt interview with author, September 10, 2020; "South Africa Loans Barred by Citibank," *New York Times*, March 11, 1978. It wouldn't be until the peak of the anti-apartheid movement that major US banks would withdraw their financial support of South Africa.

33. Prexy Nesbitt, "New Strategies for International Action Against Transnational Corporate Collaboration with Apartheid," *Notes and Documents*, November 1979, PN Madison, Box 6.

34. Nesbitt to ACOA Executive Board, "A Report on Trip to Southern Africa," June 11, 1978, PN Madison, Box 6.

35. Prexy Nesbitt interview with author, September 20, 2020.

36. Robert Baade and Jonathan Galloway, "Economic Sanctions Against the Union of South Africa: Policy Options," *Alternatives* 4, no. 4 (March 1979): 487–505.

37. Prexy Nesbitt, "Breakin' the Kneecaps of 'Baaskap': A Brief Discussion of the International Anti-Apartheid Movement and African Solidarity Work, Then, and Now," speech in Durban South Africa, in author's possession; see also Nixon, *Selling Apartheid*, 128.

38. Prexy Nesbitt conversation with author September 13, 2023.

39. Prexy Nesbitt interview with author, October 8, 2020.

40. William Minter and Sylvia Hill, "Anti-Apartheid Solidarity in United States-South Africa Relations: From the Margins to the Mainstream," in *The Road to Democracy in South Africa, Volume 3, International Solidarity, Part II*, ed. South African Democracy Education Trust (UNISA Press, 2008), 771. Nesbitt noted the irony in his helping to elevate Robinson's profile. He came to have many criticisms of Robinson's organizing style, even as he respected his savvy in escalating the anti-apartheid movement. Erin McCarthy, "Interview with Prexy Nesbitt," Spring 2009, Chicago Anti-Apartheid Collection, Columbia College Chicago, http://digitalcommons.colum.edu/cadc_caam_oralhistories/2

41. McCarthy, "Interview with Prexy Nesbitt."

42. World Council of Churches, "Draft Press Release," September 15, 1981, PN Madison, Box 2; Beate Klein, "Report on the Application of Executive Committee Banking Criteria to WCC Banks Doing Business in South Africa," July 1981, PN Madison, Box 2; McCarthy, "Interview with Prexy Nesbitt." Prexy founded and edited *PCR Notes*, circulated to church people worldwide; it covered liberation movements in southern Africa, spotlighting ways to help.

43. Prexy Nesbitt to Philip Potter, "Current Situation in the South African Struggle," August 8, 1980, PN Madison, Box 1; P. Nesbitt to Dr. P. Potter, "South African Liberation Movements—A Further Note," August 19, 1980, PN Madison,

Box 1; "Many times I wished that they put all that energy into seriously engaging the apartheid regime." Prexy Nesbitt to "all my relatives, friends, comrades . . ." March 1983, PN Madison, Box 1. McCarthy, "Interview with Prexy Nesbitt."

44. McCarthy, "Interview with Prexy Nesbitt." See also "Operation Daisy: An Agent Surfaces," *Southern Africa*, March 1980.

45. McCarthy, "Interview with Prexy Nesbitt." The IRA would lean on its relationship with the ANC underground during its own peace negotiations.

46. McCarthy, "Interview with Prexy Nesbitt."

47. Prexy Nesbitt interview with author, September 20, 2020.

48. Prexy Nesbitt telephone interview with author, May 7, 2024.

49. In a letter alerting First to his forthcoming travel to Maputo, Prexy also inquired about the possibility of returning to live there. "Any ideas about someone like me working at something there in Mozambique? Fighting Reagan beckons me strongly back to Babylon, but Mozambique surges strongly in my system these days." Prexy Nesbitt to Ruth First, October 5, 1981, PN Madison, Box 7.

50. Prexy was also close to ANC activist Dulcie September, who was gunned down in Paris where she was investigating covert weapon sales from France to South Africa. "On March 29, 1988, Dulcie was shot in the back at close range with a 22-caliber silenced rifle as she entered the ANC Paris office early in the morning." Prexy Nesbitt, "One of the Movement's Most Principled People," March 7, 2017, author's copy.

51. Stephanie Urdang, "South Africa: Questions and Answers on Divestment," American Committee on Africa, December 1984, PN Madison, Box 6.

52. Knight, "Documenting the U.S. Solidarity Movement."

53. Francis N. Nesbitt, *Race for Sanctions: African Americans Against Apartheid, 1946–1994* (Indiana University Press, 2004), 115, 119–120.

54. Cheryl Johnson-Odim interview with author, April 14, 2021.

55. Johnson-Odim was also active in the largely unsuccessful effort to pressure Northwestern to divest. Cheryl Johnson-Odim interview with author, April 14, 2021; Carrie Armbruster, "Interview with Cheryl Johnson-Odim," Fall 2009, Chicago Anti-Apartheid Collection, Columbia College Chicago. http://digitalcommons.colum.edu/cadc_caam_oralhistories/9

56. Marcia Monaco, "Interview with Carol Thompson," Spring 2009, Chicago Anti-Apartheid Collection, Columbia College Chicago, http://digitalcommons.colum.edu/cadc_caam_oralhistories/5

57. Juston Ori, "Interview with Basil Clunie," Spring 2009, Chicago Anti-Apartheid Collection, Columbia College Chicago, http://digitalcommons.colum.edu/cadc_caam_oralhistories/7

58. CIDSA Pamphlet, "Stop Illinois Money From Being Invested in Racist South Africa," 1984, PN Madison, Box 1.

59. Basil Clunie interview with Richard Knight, November 17, 2008, https://africanactivist.msu.edu/record/210–849–19616/

60. *CIDSA Update*, July/August 1985, PN Madison, Box 6; "Divestment Demonstration Planned May 6 at New State Building," press release, May 3, 1985, PN Madison, Box 6.

61. *CIDSA Update*, June 1985; "Final Report of the Coalition for Illinois Divestment from South Africa," December 1987, PN Madison, Box 6.

62. *CIDSA Update*, October 1984, https://africanactivist.msu.edu/record-Files/210–849–28178/african_activist_archive-a0b2g7-a_12419.pdf.

63. In February 1988, the United Democratic Front was banned and COSATU, the UDF's largest affiliate, was prohibited from conducting any political activity. Rachel Rubin, "Defiance Campaign Takes Anti-Apartheid Action to New Level," *CCISSA Briefing*, Fall 1989, https://africanactivist.msu.edu/record/210–849–27871/.

64. Basil Clunie interview with Richard Knight, November 17, 2008, https://africanactivist.msu.edu/record/210–849–19616/.

65. Carol Thompson to the editor, *Chicago Tribune*, April 13, 1984.

66. Danny Davis, Editorial Reply, WBBM NewsRadio, October 15, 1985, PN Madison, Box 6.

67. "Final Report of the Coalition for Illinois Divestment from South Africa," December 1987, and *CIDSA Update* January/February 1986, PN Madison, Box 6.

68. Association of Concerned Africa Scholars, "New Resources in Print," *Bulletin* 21, Fall 1987, PN Madison, Box 6.

69. Jordan Heller, "'It's a Racial Thing, Don't Kid Yourself': An Oral History of Chicago's 1983 Mayoral Race," *Intelligencer*, April 2, 2019.

70. Carol Thompson, testimony in favor of IL House Bill 0569, September 18, 1983, Peoria, PN Madison, Box 6.

71. Kathy Devine interview with Columbia College; Kevin Klose, "ANC Leader Welcomed to Chicago," *Washington Post*, January 25, 1987.

72. *CIDSA Update*, Winter 1987, PN Madison, Box 6; McCarthy interview with Nesbitt.

73. Jonathen Vogel, "Interview with Tim Wright," Fall 2009, Chicago Anti-Apartheid Collection, Columbia College Chicago, http://digitalcommons.colum.edu/cadc_caam_oralhistories/29

74. McCarthy, "Interview with Prexy Nesbitt."

75. Nesbitt, *Race for Sanctions*, 124.

76. Armbruster, "Interview with Cheryl Johnson-Odim."

77. Carruthers quoted in *Mandela in Chicago*, directed by Ava Thompson-Greenwell.

78. Armbruster, "Interview with Cheryl Johnson-Odim"; Katherine Elizabeth McAuliff, "Interview with Alice Palmer," Spring 2010, Chicago Anti-Apartheid Collection, Columbia College Chicago, http://digitalcommons.colum.edu/cadc_caam_oralhistories/6.

79. McAuliff, "Interview with Alice Palmer"; Sandra Crockett, "Eight Elated Over Victory in Apartheid Trial," *Chicago Defender*, n.d., PN Madison, Box 7.

80. McAuliff, "Interview with Alice Palmer."

81. Prexy Nesbitt interview with author, October 30, 2020.

82. Heeten Kalan and Jenny Dahlstein interview with author, February 5, 2021.

83. Heeten Kalan and Jenny Dahlstein interview with author, February 5, 2021.

84. Prexy Nesbitt interview with author, September 25, 2020.

85. Prexy Nesbitt interview with author, October 5, 2020.

86. The "momentum created by the state, local and organizational divestment campaigns created an atmosphere in which such sanctions could be enacted" by Congress, Prexy wrote in 1987 upon CIDSA's dissolution. "Final Report of the Illinois Coalition for Divestment from South Africa," December 1987, PN Madison, Box 6.

87. "South Africa to Honor the Late Senator Ted Kennedy," *Boston Globe*, April 25, 2012.

88. Nesbitt, *Race for Sanctions*, 135; Minter and Hill, "Anti-Apartheid Solidarity," 800.

89. Jessica P. Forsee, "Cannot Afford to Publicly Surrender: The Public's Influence on Ronald Reagan's Strategic Relationship with South Africa," MA

thesis (Georgia Southern University, 2021); McCarthy, "Interview with Prexy Nesbitt." After the fall of apartheid, Nomonde returned home to South Africa. Prexy was able to visit her there before she sadly died of AIDS.

90. Nesbitt, *Race for Sanctions*, 142.

91. Minter and Hill, "Anti-Apartheid Solidarity," 802–803.

92. *CIDSA Update*, Winter 1987, PN Madison, Box 6.

93. Prexy Nesbitt, "Expanding the Horizons of the U.S. Anti-Apartheid Movement," *Black Scholar* 16, no. 6 (November/December 1985): 43–46.

4. OUR SOPHISTICATED WEAPON

Epigraph: Committee of Returned Volunteers, New York chapter, *Mozambique Will Be Free*, 1969, Prexy Nesbitt Papers, Box 4, Wisconsin Historical Society, Madison, WI. Hereafter PN Madison.

1. Machel praised Tanzania and Zambia, the OAU, the UN, and internationalist allies for supporting Frelimo and hastening the fall of the fascist regime in Portugal. Samora Machel, "Frelimo's Tasks in the Struggle Ahead," September 20, 1974, in *Mozambique: Revolution or Reaction? Two Speeches by Samora Machel* (LSM Information Center, 1975), 4–19.

2. Elizabeth Banks, "Socialist Internationalism Between the Soviet Union and Mozambique," PhD diss. (New York University, 2019), 37.

3. Allen and Barbara Isaacman, *Mozambique's Samora Machel: A Life Cut Short* (Ohio University Press, 2020), 154

4. Allen Isaacman, "Mozambique: The Struggle for Survival," *Harvard International Review* 12, no. 1 (Fall 1989): 16.

5. R.R., "Teaching a People to Read," *Southern Africa*, March 1980, PN Madison, Box 6.

6. Stephen Gloyd, James Pfeiffer, and Wendy Johnson, "Cooperantes, Solidarity and the Fight for Health in Mozambique," in *Comrades in Health: U.S. Health Internationalists, Abroad and At Home*, ed. Anne Emanuelle-Birn and Theodore M. Brown (Rutgers University Press, 2013), 185.

7. Samora Machel, "The Liberation of Women is a Fundamental Necessity for the Revolution," speech at the First Conference of Mozambican Women, March 4, 1973, in *Mozambique: Sowing the Seeds of Revolution* (1975), 24, 25.

8. Kathleen Sheldon, *Pounders of Grain: A History of Women, Work and Politics in Mozambique* (Heinemann, 2002), 118.

9. Carla Stephens, "The People Mobilized: The Mozambican Liberation Movement and American Activism, 1960–1975," PhD diss. (Temple University, 2011), 257, n.87.

10. Machel, "Frelimo's Tasks in the Struggle Ahead," 8.

11. Machel, 17, 18.

12. Prexy Nesbitt interview with author, October 30, 2020.

13. Malyn Newitt, *A Short History of Mozambique* (Oxford University Press, 2017), 159–161.

14. Isaacman, "Mozambique: The Struggle for Survival."

15. Prexy Nesbitt interview with author, January 8, 2021.

16. Jose Luis Cabaco, "Mozambique: The Right to Survive," *New Internationalist*, February 1989, Nesbitt Papers, Columbia College, Box 7.

17. Samora Machel, speech to the United Nations, October 3, 1977, reprinted in *Samora Machel Speaks/Mozambique Speaks*, ed. Robert Van Lierop (Black Liberation Press, 1977), 24–41.

18. Machel, speech to the United Nations.

19. Prexy Nesbitt interview with author, January 8, 2021.

20. Paul Irish, "Report on Trip to Southern Africa," Africa Fund, September 30, 1980, PN Madison, Box 7.

21. Samora Moises Machel, "A Sophisticated Weapon," n.d., PN Madison, Box 5.

22. Lisa Brock interview with Buffy Satchwell for the Southwest Michigan Black Heritage Society, Kalamazoo, MI, April 29, 2015, https://scholarworks.wmich.edu/engaging-the-wisdom/14/.

23. Oscar Monteiro, "An Unavoidable Leader," in *Samora: Man of the People*, ed. Antonio Sopa (Maguezo Editores, 2001), 62.

24. Prexy Nesbitt interview with author, January 8, 2021; Isaacman and Isaacman, *Mozambique: From Colonialism to Revolution, 1900–1982*; Sheldon, *Pounders of Grain*, 136.

25. Sarah LeFanu, *S is for Samora* (Columbia University Press, 2012), 41. Prexy Nesbitt interview with author, January 8, 2021.

26. Roberta Washington interview with author, February 12, 2021.

27. Roberta Washington interview with author, February 12, 2021.

28. Roberta Washington interview with author, February 12, 2021.

29. Roberta Washington interview with author, February 12, 2021. See the forthcoming memoir: Roberta Washington, "A Mozambican Memoir."

30. Gloyd, Pfeiffer, and Johnson, "Cooperantes, Solidarity and the Fight for Health in Mozambique," 187.

31. William Minter, *Vision and Action over Five Decades: The American Friends Service Committee and Africa* (AFSC, July 2008), 25.

32. Machel, "Frelimo's Tasks in the Struggle Ahead," 9.

33. Isaacman, "Mozambique: The Struggle for Survival," 141–143.

34. Nesbitt interview with author, January 8, 2021; Jose Negrao, "Samora and Development," in *Samora: Man of the People*, ed. Antonio Sopa (Maguezo Editores, 2001), 46.

35. Nesbitt interview with author, January 8, 2021; John Saul, "Development and Counterdevelopment Strategies in Mozambique," in *Afro-Marxist Regimes: Ideology and Public Policy*, ed. Edmond J. Keller and Donald Rothchild (Lynne Rienner Publishers, 1987), 115.

36. Allen Isaacman interview with author, February 28, 2024.

37. Prexy Nesbitt, "An Overview of Southern Africa," *CALC Report*, May 1989, PN Madison, Box 5.

38. Banks, "Socialist Internationalism," 200–201; Isaacman, "Mozambique: The Struggle for Survival."

39. Daniel L. Douek, "New Light on the Samora Machel Assassination: 'I Realized That It Was No Accident,'" *Third World Quarterly* 38, no. 9 (2017), 2045.

40. Allen Isaacman interview with author, February 28, 2024; Prexy Nesbitt interview with author, September 30, 2020.

41. Prexy Nesbitt interview with author, September 30, 2020; LeFanu, *S is for Samora*, 256.

42. Isaacman, "Mozambique: The Struggle for Survival," 18.

43. John Saul, "Development and Counterdevelopment Strategies in Mozambique," in *Afro-Marxist Regimes: Ideology and Public Policy*, ed. Edmond J. Keller and Donald Rothchild (Lynne Rienner Publishers, 1987), 110.

44. Piero Gleijeses, *Visions of Freedom: Havana, Washington, Pretoria, and the Struggle for Southern Africa 1976–1991* (University of North Carolina Press, 2013), 510.

45. Michael Maren, "US Callousness and Mozambique Massacres," *New York Times*, August 22, 1987; William Minter and Sylvia Hill, "Anti-Apartheid

Solidarity in United States–South Africa Relations: From the Margins to the Mainstream," in *The Road to Democracy in South Africa, Volume 3, International Solidarity, Part II*, ed. South African Democracy Education Trust (UNISA Press, 2008), 811–812; E. A. Wayne, "Mozambique Hopes for Warmer U.S. Ties," *Christian Science Monitor*, October 13, 1987; Neil A. Lewis, "US Meets with Mozambique Rebel Figure," *New York Times*, July 13, 1987.

46. Randall Robinson, "Dole and Helms Have It Backward on Mozambique," *Washington Post*, August 10, 1987; *Chicago Defender*, October 10, 1987.

47. Association of Concerned Africa Scholars, *Bulletin* 21 (Southern Africa Resource Project, UCLA, Fall 1987).

48. UN Inter-Agency Task Force, Africa Recovery Programme, "South African Destabilization: The Economic Cost of Frontline Resistance to Apartheid," c. 1989, PN Madison, Box 1.

49. Allen Isaacman interview with author, February 28, 2024. "I was the first person to teach Mozambican history, which is itself a mark of what underdevelopment is when a white guy from the Bronx has to teach Mozambicans their own history because the Portuguese suppressed it."

50. Allen Isaacman interview with author, February 28, 2024. "Prexy played multiple roles and fit into many different communities, always with a sense of purpose and integrity, and like other people, including Samora, Prexy has a good size ego, but he was never driven by his ego, and he made all sorts of personal sacrifices in the name of the struggles."

51. Concerned Africa Scholars, "Announcement: Mozambique Support Network," *Bulletin* 21 (Fall 1987), PN Madison, Box 4.

52. Erin McCarthy, "Interview with Prexy Nesbitt," Spring 2009, Chicago Anti-Apartheid Collection, Columbia College Chicago, http://digitalcommons .colum.edu/cadc_caam_oralhistories/2, 42.

53. MSN, Press Release, October 9, 1987, PN Madison, Box 4.

54. *Mozambique Support Network*, newsletter, October 1987, PN Madison, Box 4.

55. "Mozambique: Turning Sorrow into New Strength," poster, PN Madison, Box 6.

56. "Coalition Asks Omahans to Help Out Mozambique," *Omaha World-Herald* (online), October 24, 1987.

57. "Prexy Nesbitt to Minister Macumbi and Ambassador Ferrao," September 23, 1987, PN Madison, Box 4.

58. "Prexy Nesbitt to Leadership Core of the Mozambique Support Network," December 26, 1987, PN Madison, Box 3.

59. Prexy Nesbitt interview with author, October 30, 2020.

60. Prexy Nesbitt interview with author, October 5, 2020.

61. Allen Isaacman and Roberta Washington to Ambassador Valeriano Ferrao, November 9, 1987, PN Madison, Box 4.

62. Prexy Nesbitt interview with author, January 8, 2021.

63. Committee to Protect Journalists, "Mozambique Report, 2002." https://cpj.org/reports/2002/05/moz-may02/

64. Prexy Nesbitt interview with author, January 8, 2021.

65. McCarthy, "Interview with Prexy Nesbitt," 41.

66. "Positive Fire," *The New Internationalist*, February 1989, Prexy Nesbitt Papers, Columbia College Chicago, Box 7. Hereafter PN CC.

67. Prexy Nesbit interview with author, October 30, 2020.

68. Monica Copeland, "Education Leaders Serves as a Figure of Hope," *Daily Ilini*, March 7, 1989, PN Madison, Box 5.

69. Sylvia Ewing interview with author, February 16, 2024. Eve Ewing has become a major writer/scholar/poet.

70. "Killing Fields of Mozambique," editorial, *New York Times*, April 23, 1988. And yet Kathleen Sheldon, a UCLA historian and former cooperante who lived in Beira for two years, excoriated the *New York Times* for an article soft-pedaling Renamo, written after a right-wing-organized press junket in Mozambique: "Even your correspondent acknowledges that all other available evidence, including a recent State Department investigation, concludes that Renamo is an incredibly vicious and destructive group marauding throughout rural Mozambique. To portray them as genial rebels ignores the reality." Kathleen Sheldon, letter to the editor, *New York Times*, August 15, 1988.

71. William Minter, "Mozambique: Renamo From the Inside," *CLAC Report*, May 1989, PN Box 5.

72. Mackie McLeod, "The Law vs. Covert Action in Mozambique," op-ed rejected by Boston Globe, n.d., c.1987, PN Madison, Box 5.

73. Brian Duffy, "An American Doctor in the Schools of Hell," *U.S. News & World Report*, January 16, 1989, reprinted in the *MSN* newsletter, PN Madison,

Box 4. See also Jane Perlez, "Child Victims of War Tax Mozambique," *New York Times*, March 1, 1989.

74. "Nesbitt Links Apartheid, Racism in the US," *Methodist Reporter*, June 17, 1988, PN Box 5.

75. *South Africa Now*, Episode 303, 1989, Manuscripts and Archives, Yale University Library.

76. Sylvia Ewing interview with author, February 16, 2024.

77. Prexy Nesbitt to MSN Core Members, "Public Speaking on Mozambique," May 10, 1990, PN Madison, Box 4.

78. Isaacman, "Mozambique: The Struggle for Survival"; Loretta J. Williams, "Statement of the Mozambique Support Network," Fifth FRELIMO Congress, July 28, 1989, Maputo, PN Madison, Box 1.

79. Roberta Washington, "Mozambique: Realigning the Course," *CCISSA Briefing*, Fall 1989, PN Madison, Box 5.

80. Jose Luis Cabaco, "Mozambique: The Right to Survive," *New Internationalist*, February 1989, PN CC, Box 7.

81. Joseph Hanlon, "The New Missionaries," *New Internationalism*, February 1989.

82. Toronto Committee for the Liberation of Southern Africa, *Mozambique Update*, 1990, PN Columbia College, Box 7.

83. Prexy Nesbitt, "A Preliminary Examination of U.S. Support to Renamo," c. 1991, in *Mozambique: An Elusive Peace*, a binder of papers prepared by Alice Dinerman for Africa Office and others, 74–81, PN Madison, Box 1. See also, Nesbitt, "Terminators, Crusaders and Gladiators: Western (Private and Public) Support for Renamo & Unita," *Review of African Political Economy*, 42 (1988) 111–124.

84. "Defend Mozambique-Defeat Apartheid," *CCISSA Briefing*, Spring 1990, PN Madison, Box 5.

85. Sessy Nyman, "MUMHCF Established," *Mozambique Support Network* newsletter, February 1991, PN Madison, Box 4.

86. "Delegations Build Solidarity," *Mozambique Support Network* newsletter, Spring/Summer 1991, PN Madison, Box 4.

87. Rachel Rubin interview with author, March 28, 2021.

88. Rachel Rubin interview with author, March 28, 2021.

89. Rachel Rubin interview with author, March 28, 2021.

90. Rachel Rubin interview with author, March 28, 2021.

91. Rachel Rubin interview with author, March 28, 2021.

92. Anne Evens interview with author, December 27, 2023.

93. Anne Evens interview with author, December 27, 2023.

94. Anne Evens interview with author, December 27, 2023.

95. Anne Evens interview with author, December 27, 2023.

96. Anne Evens interview with author, December 27, 2023.

97. Anne Evens interview with author, December 27, 2023.

98. Anne Evens interview with author, December 27, 2023.

99. Anne Evens interview with author, December 27, 2023.

100. Kathi Austin, *Invisible Crimes: US Intervention in Mozambique* (Africa Policy Information Center, 1994), 17.

101. Mozambique Information Office, July 9, 1992, printed in *Baobab Notes*, August 1992, https://africanactivist.msu.edu/recordFiles/210–849–20605 /baobabaug92opt.pdf.

102. Frank J. Murray and Warren Strobel, "Mozambican Leader Vows Direct Talks with Renamo," *Washington Times*, n.d., c.1990, PN Madison, Box 5.

103. Rollie Hudson, "Solidarity Highlights National Conference," *Mozambique Support Network*, newsletter, February 1991, PN Madison, Box 4.

104. Hudson, "Solidarity Highlights National Conference" and Jill Schlueter, "Wisconsin Group Welcomes Mozambique Ambassador," *Mozambique Support Network*, newsletter, February 1991, PN Madison, Box 4.

105. Prexy Nesbitt to MSN members, "The January 1991 Note on Southern Africa," January 11, 1991, PN Madison, Box 3.

106. Nesbitt, "The January 1991 Note on Southern Africa"; Bill Minter voiced a similar view. See Minter to Nesbitt, fax, November 8, 1990, PN Madison, Box 3.

107. Jim Cason, "Organizing Support for Mozambique and Angola," *Africa Today*, 1992.

108. Prexy Nesbitt, "Somehow Song Survives: Dust and Death in Southern Africa," August 1992, PN Madison, Box 6.

109. *Capitol District Coalition Against Apartheid and Racism*, newsletter, 1992, PN Madison, Box 6.

110. *Capitol District Coalition Against Apartheid and Racism*, newsletter, 1992, PN Madison, Box 6; Prexy Nesbitt, "Somehow Song Survives: Dust and Death in Southern Africa," August 1992, PN Madison, Box 6.

111. Prexy Nesbitt, "Somehow Song Survives: Dust and Death in Southern Africa."

112. *Capitol District Coalition Against Apartheid and Racism*, newsletter, 1992, PN Madison, Box 6.

113. "Special Interview with Sister Janice McLaughlin," *Baobab Notes*, September 24, 1992, PN Madison, Box 8.

114. "Conflict and Conflict Resolution in Mozambique," Conference Report, Discussions from Dialogues on Conflict Resolution, Washington, DC, July 1992, (United States Institute of Peace, 1993), PN CC, Box 7, file 2.

115. *Baobab Notes*, October/November 1993, https://africanactivist.msu.edu/recordFiles/210–849–21673/ELCA11–930pt.pdf.

116. Isaacman to Joaquim Chissano, March 12, 1991, PN Madison, Box 2.

117. *Baobab Notes*, January/February 1994, PN Madison, Box 6.

118. *Baobab Notes*, August/September 1993, https://africanactivist.msu.edu/recordFiles/210-849-20965/32-130-147D-84-Baobab8-930pt.pdf; Prexy Nesbitt interview with author, October 30, 2020. Simmons, incidentally, had been president of Hampshire College in 1977 when it became the first US college to divest from South Africa.

5. INTERNATIONALIST CHICAGO AND THE END OF APARTHEID

1. Association of Concerned Scholars of Africa, "Statement On U.S. Companies and South Africa," *Bulletin* 21 (Fall 1987), Nesbitt Papers, Box 6, Wisconsin Historical Society, Madison. Hereafter, PN Madison.

2. Jacob Martin Lingan, "Interview with Helen Shiller," Spring 2010, Chicago Anti-Apartheid Collection, Columbia College Chicago, http://digitalcommons.colum.edu/cadc_caam_oralhistories/1.

3. Francis N. Nesbitt, *Race for Sanctions: African Americans Against Apartheid, 1946–1994* (Indiana University Press, 2004), 153.

4. Basil Clunie interview with Richard Knight, November 17, 2008, https://africanactivist.msu.edu/record/210–849–19616/.

5. "Background of the Illinois Labor Network Against Apartheid," c. 1990, PN Madison, Box 6.

6. "South Africa—Illinois Labor Network Update," May 1988, PN Madison, Box 6.

7. Deseree Zimmerman, "Interview with Kathy Devine," Spring 2009, http://digitalcommons.colum.edu/cadc_caam_oralhistories/20.

8. Press release, Illinois Labor Network Against Apartheid, March 2, 1988, and S. M. Ewing, "Protest Against South African Ambassador," Briefing, Spring 1988, PN Madison, Box 6.

9. Committee to Free Moses Mayekiso, "Free Moses Mayekiso!" pamphlet, March 1988, https://africanactivist.msu.edu/record/210-849-23875/.

10. South Africa Illinois Labor Network Update, May 1988, PN Madison, Box 6. Travis's father was a leader in the Flint sit-down strike of 1937.

11. Sarah Bonkowski, "Interview with Rosetta Daylie," Fall 2009, Chicago Anti-Apartheid Collection, Columbia College Chicago, http://digitalcommons.colum.edu/cadc_caam_oralhistories/27.

12. "South Africa—Illinois Labor Network Update," May 1988, PN Madison, Box 6.

13. Richard Trumka, "Get the sHELL Out of Africa," speech, November 18, 1988, Chicago, https://projects.kora.matrix.msu.edu/files/210–808–6851/trumkaspeech88opt.pdf.

14. Tommie Fry, "Sam Nujoma Visit," CCISSA Briefing, Summer 1988, PN Madison, Box 5.

15. Jeff Schuhrke, Blue Collar Empire: The Untold Story of US Labor's Global Anticommunist Crusade (Verso, 2024).

16. Prexy Nesbitt and Don Will, "AFL-CIO In Africa: A Damning Indictment," Guardian Labor Supplement, Fall 1988.

17. Piero Gleijeses, Visions of Freedom: Havana, Washington, Pretoria, and the Struggle for Southern Africa 1976–1991 (University of North Carolina Press, 2013), 505, 519. Of the 337,033 Cuban soldiers who served in Angola over many years, 2,103 lost their lives. Gleijeses, Visions of Freedom, 521.

18. Terre Rybovich, "Trip Report: Funding Exchange Tour of Southern Africa," January 1989, PN Madison, Box 2.

19. William Minter, "The US and the War in Angola," *Review of African Political Economy*, 50 (1991): 135–144.

20. Jim Cason, "Organizing Support for Mozambique and Angola," *Africa Today*, 1992, PN Madison, Box 5.

21. *South Africa Now*, episode 210, 1989, Manuscripts and Archives, Yale University Library.

22. CCISSA, 1989 Soweto Day Walkathon, part I, https://www.youtube.com/watch?app=desktop&v=e2LqgqK0-ik.

23. CCISSA, 1989 Soweto Day Walkathon, part I, https://www.youtube.com/watch?app=desktop&v=e2LqgqK0-ik.

24. CCISSA, 1989 Soweto Day Walkathon, part II, https://www.youtube.com/watch?v=xQoCNqNPgfY.

25. *CCISSA Briefing*, Fall 1990, PN Madison, Box 5.

26. CCISSA, "Chicago Alexandra Sister Community Project," report, Spring 1990, https://africanactivist.msu.edu/record/210-849-26454/

27. *CCISSA Briefing*, Fall 1991; *CCISSA Briefing*, Summer 1993, PN Madison, Box 5.

28. *CCISSA Briefing*, Fall 1991; Sarah Bonkowski, "Interview with Rosetta Daylie."

29. Nesbitt conversation with author, April 26, 2024; see Cheryl I. Harris, "Whiteness as Property," *Harvard Law Review* 106, no. 8 (June 1993): 1707–1791.

30. Sylvia Ewing interview by author, February 16, 2024.

31. "ILNAA Hosts Ngubo," *CCISSA Briefing*, Winter 1990, PN Madison, Box 5.

32. Basil Clunie interview with Richard Knight, November 17, 2008, https://africanactivist.msu.edu/record/210-849-19616/; Prexy Nesbitt, "An Overview of Southern Africa," *CALC Report*, May 1989, Nesbitt Papers, Box 6. See Ron Nixon, *Selling Apartheid: South Africa's Global Propaganda War* (Pluto Press, 2016).

33. Basil Clunie interview with Richard Knight, November 17, 2008; Claudia Dreifus, "'South Africa Now': A Different Kind of Television," *The Progressive*, February 1991; Sylvia Ewing interview with author, February 16, 2024; William Minter and Sylvia Hill, "Anti-Apartheid Solidarity in United States–South Africa Relations: From the Margins to the Mainstream," in *The Road to Democracy in South Africa, Volume 3, International Solidarity, Part II*, ed. South African Democracy Education Trust (UNISA Press, 2008), 819.

34. "ANC Rep. Tells Chicago, 'This Is Your Victory Too!'" *CCISSA Briefing*, Winter 1990, PN Madison, Box 5.

35. Danny Schecter, *Madiba A to Z: The Many Faces of Nelson Mandela* (Seven Stories Press, 2013), 60–63.

36. Basil Clunie interview with Richard Knight, November 17, 2008; Anne Evens interview with author, December 27, 2023.

37. Erin McCarthy, "Interview with Prexy Nesbitt," Spring 2009, Chicago Anti-Apartheid Collection, Columbia College Chicago, http://digitalcommons.colum.edu/cadc_caam_oralhistories/2.

38. McCarthy, "Interview with Prexy Nesbitt."

39. Prexy Nesbitt interview with author, October 5, 2020.

40. McCarthy, "Interview with Prexy Nesbitt."

41. Cuban-American mayors in and around Miami snubbed him, leading to a major Black boycott of the state for three years.

42. ACOA, press release, June 22, 1990, PN Madison, Box 5; *CCISSA Briefing*, Fall 1990, PN Madison, Box 5; Prexy Nesbitt, "Breakin' the Kneecaps of 'Baaskap': A Brief Discussion of the International Anti-Apartheid Movement and African Solidarity Work, Then, and Now," speech in Durban, South Africa, in author's possession.

43. Lisa January, "June 1990, Notes from the Anti-Apartheid Activist Briefing, Friday, June 22, New York," PN Madison, Box 6.

44. January, "June 1990, Notes from the Anti-Apartheid Activist Briefing."

45. January, "June 1990, Notes from the Anti-Apartheid Activist Briefing."

46. January, "June 1990, Notes from the Anti-Apartheid Activist Briefing"; *CCISSA Briefing*, Fall 1990, PN Madison, Box 5.

47. *Mandela in Chicago*, directed by Ava Thompson Greenwell (The Inquiry Collective, 2021).

48. Heeten Kalan interview with author, February 5, 2021.

49. Nesbitt, *Race for Sanctions*, 159;

50. Danny Schechter, *Madiba A to Z: The Many Faces of Nelson Mandela* (Seven Stories Press, 2013), 144–148.

51. *South Africa Now*, episode N309, March 28, 1990, Manuscripts and Archives, Yale University Library.

52. Schecter, *Madiba A to Z*, 150, 153.

53. Jim Cason, "Organizing Support for Mozambique and Angola"; see also Penny M. Von Eschen, *Paradoxes of Nostalgia: Cold War Triumphalism and Global Disorder Since 1989* (Duke University Press, 2022), 49.

54. Salim Vally and Andy Clarno, "The Context of Struggle: Racial Capitalism and Political Praxis in South Africa," *Ethnic and Racial Studies* 46, no. 16 (2023); Nesbitt conversation with author, May 21, 2024.

55. Nesbitt, *Race for Sanctions*, 165–166.

56. Lisa Brock, "Inkatha: Notions of the 'Primitive' and the 'Tribal' in Reporting on South Africa," in *Africa's Media Image*, ed. Beverly G. Hawk (Praeger, 1992), 151–159.

57. ILNAA, Steering Committee Meeting, January 15, 1991, PN Madison, Box 6.

58. *CCISSA Briefing*, Winter 1992, PN Madison, Box 5.

59. *Mozambique Support Network*, newsletter, February 1991, PN Madison, Box 4.

60. *South Africa Now*, episode N707, March 13, 1991, Manuscripts and Archives, Yale University Library; "Talk by Prexy Nesbitt to Operation PUSH," Chicago, IL, February 9, 1991, http://digitalcommons.colum.edu/nesbittwritings.

61. The Africa Fund, "Stop Apartheid's Violence, Questions and Answers," January 1992, https://africanactivist.msu.edu/recordFiles/210–849–23196/african_activist_archive-a0a8d3-b_12419.pdf.

62. "South Africa Probes Alleged 'Third Force,' Report," *Chicago Tribune*, February 6, 1992; Human Rights Watch, *World Report*, 1994, https://www.hrw.org/reports/1994/WR94/Africa-07.htm.

63. Stuart J. Kaufman, "The End of Apartheid: Rethinking South Africa's Peaceful Transition," presentation, October 2012, University of Delaware, https://www.polisci.upenn.edu/sites/default/files/kaufman.pdf.

64. Jeff Jones, "Into Africa: Two Capital District Activists Report on the Continuing Struggle Against Apartheid," *Metroland*, October 15–21, 1992, reprinted in *Capital District Coalition Against Apartheid and Racism* newsletter, 1992, PN Madison, Box 4.

65. Jeff Jones, "Into Africa," October 15–21, 1992.

66. Jeff Jones, "Into Africa," October 15–21, 1992; Prexy Nesbitt, "'Telling No Lies': The Role of Bernard Magubane in the Struggle for Change in the

United States," talk presented in Pretoria, South Africa, August 26, 2010, in author's possession; Nesbitt phone conversation with author, May 9, 2024.

67. Press release, Illinois Labor Network Against Apartheid, August 4, 1992, PN Madison, Box 6.

68. Basil Clunie, CCISSA, "Dear Friends," January 26, 1993, PN Madison, Box 5.

69. Richard Stengel, "Winnie and Nelson," book review, *The Guardian*, May 14, 2023.

70. J. Daniel O'Flaherty, "Holding Together South Africa," *Foreign Affairs* 72, no. 4 (Sept/Oct 1993).

71. ILNAA presentation to Moses Mayekiso, April 1, 1993, PN Madison, Box 5.

72. CCISSA Proposal to the Funding Exchange, Feb. 1994, PN Madison, Box 2 additions.

73. Nicolas Alexander, "What Ever Happened to the Free South Africa Movement?" *Third Force* 1, no. 1 (April 30, 1993).

74. Alexander, "What Ever Happened to the Free South Africa Movement?"

75. Randall Robinson, *Defending the Spirit: A Black Life in America* (Penguin, 1999), 188–189; Sylvia Hill interview with William Minter, August 12, 2004, http://noeasyvictories.org/interviews/int16_hill.php.

76. Nesbitt interview with author, October 5, 2020.

77. *CCISSA* newsletter, Fall 1993; Spring 1993, PN Madison, Box 5.

78. *CCISSA* newsletter, Fall 1992, PN Madison, Box 5.

79. Lindiwe Mabuza quoted in *Mandela in Chicago*.

80. "Sanctions Lifted!" *Southern Africa*, November-December 1993, PN Madison, Box 5.

81. "Mandela Wins Pledge of $850 Million," *Los Angeles Times*, September 26, 1993; Schecter, *Madiba A to Z*, 151.

82. Naomi Klein, *The Shock Doctrine: The Rise of Disaster Capitalism* (Henry Holt, 2007), 202–204.

83. K. Venda, "Nelson Mandela in DC," *Baobab Notes*, October/November 1993, PN Madison, Box 1.

84. "I'd Go to Prison Again," *Southern Africa*, November-December 1993. In 1989, Chikane was poisoned and almost died. "They had put it in his underwear. The South Africans had done the same thing to SWAPO and ZANU fighters," according to Prexy. A man known as "Dr. Death" admitted his role

to the TRC and was exonerated. Prexy Nesbitt interview with author, September 30, 2020.

85. Prexy Nesbitt, "The Future is Not What it Used to Be," Southern Africa Trip Report, *Baobab Notes*, August-September 1993, PN Madison, Box 1.

86. Dumisani Kumalo, "South African Democracy: Roadblocks on the Way to Elections," *CCISSA* newsletter, Summer 1993, PN Madison, Box 5.

87. *CCISSA* newsletter, Winter 1993, PN Madison, Box 5.

88. Dumisani Kumalo to Dear Friend, March 26, 1994, Africa Fund, PN Madison, Box 8.

89. McCarthy, "Interview with Prexy Nesbitt."

90. Dumisani Kumalo to Dear Friend, March 26, 1994, Africa Fund.

91. *CCISSA* newsletter, Fall 1993, PN Madison, Box 5; "The Crash of Flight 4184," *New York Times*, November 2, 1994.

92. Minter and Hill, "Anti-Apartheid Solidarity," 822; Basil Clunie to Friends, April 15, 1994, PN Madison, Box 5.

93. Sarah Bonkowski, "Interview with Rosetta Daylie," Fall 2009, Chicago Anti-Apartheid Collection, Columbia College Chicago, https://digitalcommons.colum.edu/cadc_caam_oralhistories/27/.

94. Basil Clunie interview with Richard Knight, November 17, 2008, https://africanactivist.msu.edu/record/210–849–19616/.

95. Heeten Kalan, "Observing the Birth of a Nation," *Baobab Notes* 6, May-June/July-August 1994, https://africanactivist.msu.edu/recordFiles/210–849–20970/Baobab5–94opt.pdf.

96. Heeten Kalan, "Observing the Birth of a Nation," *Baobab Notes* 6, May-June/July-August 1994.

97. Hein Marais, "Still No Easy Walk," *Southern Africa Report*, July 1994, https://africanactivist.msu.edu/recordFiles/210–849–24380/sar0905_1001.pdf.

98. Linda Slavin, "An Empangeni Journal," *Southern Africa Report*, July 1994.

99. John S. Saul, "Now for the Hard Part," *Southern Africa Report*, July 1994.

100. Hein Marais, "Still No Easy Walk," *Southern Africa Report*, July 1994.

101. Jonathen Vogel, "Interview with Tim Wright," Fall 2009, Chicago Anti-Apartheid Collection, Columbia College Chicago, http://digitalcommons.colum.edu/cadc_caam_oralhistories/29.

102. Bill Keller, "Mandela Proclaims a Victory," *New York Times*, May 3, 1994.

103. John S. Saul, "Now for the Hard Part," *Southern Africa Report*, July 1994.

104. Heeten Kalan, "Observing the Birth of a Nation," *Baobab Notes* 6, May-June/July-August 1994.

105. Heeten Kalan and Jenny Dahlstein Zoom interview with author, February 5, 2021.

106. "Chicago's Antiapartheid Movement Celebrates and Remembers," *CCISSA* newsletter, Spring/Summer 1994, PN Madison, Box 5.

107. Hein Marais, "Still No Easy Walk," *Southern Africa Report*, July 1994.

108. Hein Marais, "Still No Easy Walk," *Southern Africa Report*, July 1994.

109. Prexy Nesbitt, "South Africa: The Path Ahead," *Baobab Notes* 6, May-June/July-August 1994.

6. A LUTA CONTINUA

1. Salim Vally and Andy Clarno, "The Context of Struggle: Racial Capitalism and Political Praxis in South Africa," *Ethnic and Racial Studies* 16 (2023): 3433–3438.

2. Prexy Nesbitt, "South Africa: The Path Ahead," *Baobab Notes* 6 (May-June/July-August 1994), https://africanactivist.msu.edu/recordFiles/210–849–20970/Baobab5–940pt.pdf.

3. Trevor Noah, *Born a Crime: Stories from a South African Childhood* (One World, 2016).

4. Prexy Nesbitt, "Dreams Deferred: Future Directions of South and Southern Africa," presentation, University of Minnesota, July 15, 1996, https://digitalcommons.colum.edu/nesbittwritings.

5. Prexy Nesbitt interview with author, June 28, 2024.

6. Chris Webb, "John Saul and the Meaning of Solidarity," *Canadian Dimension*, February 4, 2024, https://canadiandimension.com/articles/view/john-saul-and-the-meaning-of-solidarity.

7. Prexy Nesbitt interview with author January 31, 2021.

8. Naiomi Klein, *The Shock Doctrine* (Henry Holt, 2007), 213.

9. Prexy Nesbitt, "Dreams Deferred." Prexy reiterated this point in 2012, after hearing Jacob Zuma's speech at the centenary of the ANC: "Both race and gender relations are 'unfinished business' that should be high on the government's agenda (and in my opinion should have been highlighted as priorities in the President's speech)." Prexy Nesbitt, "Some (Comradely) Reflections on the

Centenary Celebration of the African National Congress," January 23, 2012, unpublished paper in author's possession.

10. William Shoki, "The Story of South Africa No Longer Makes Sense," *New York Times*, May 28, 2024.

11. Prexy Nesbitt interview with author, October 8, 2020.

12. Danny Schecter, *Madiba A to Z: The Many Faces of Nelson Mandela* (Seven Stories Press, 2013), 64.

13. Kasrils quoted in Schecter, *Madiba A-Z*, 151–152.

14. Lisa Brock interview with author, April 25, 2023.

15. Nesbitt interview with author, October 30, 2020.

16. *Mandela in Chicago*, directed by Ava Thompson-Greenwell (The Inquiry Collective, 2021).

17. Jonathen Vogel, "Interview with Tim Wright," Fall 2009, Chicago Anti-Apartheid Collection, Columbia College Chicago, http://digitalcommons .colum.edu/cadc_caam_oralhistories/29.

18. Jim Cason, "Organizing Support for Mozambique and Angola," *Africa Today*, 1992, PN Madison Box 5.

19. Erin McCarthy, "Interview with Prexy Nesbitt," Spring 2009, Chicago Anti-Apartheid Collection, College Archives and Special Collections, Columbia College Chicago, http://digitalcommons.colum.edu/cadc_caam_oralhistories/2

20. *60 Minutes*, "Comrade Capitalist," April 25, 2004, CBS, https://www .cbsnews.com/news/comrade-capitalist/

21. Prexy Nesbitt on "Africa Today," KPFA, November 21, 2016, https://kpfa .org/episode/africa-today-november-21–2016/

22. John Eligon and Lynsey Chutel, "Has South Africa Truly Defeated Apartheid?" *New York Times*, April 26, 2024.

23. Eligon and Chutel, "Has South Africa Truly Defeated Apartheid?" *New York Times*, April 26, 2024.

24. Lydia Polgreen, "South Africa is Not a Metaphor," *New York Times*, June 1, 2024.

25. United Nations Inter-Agency Task Force, Africa Recovery Programme, "South African Destabilization: The Economic Cost of Frontline Resistance to Apartheid," 1989, PN Columbia College Chicago, Box 1.

26. Prexy Nesbitt, "The January 1991 NOTE on SOUTHERN AFRICA," PN Madison, Box 3.

27. McCarthy, "Interview with Prexy Nesbitt."

28. Prexy Nesbitt interview with author, September 30, 2020.

29. Committee to Protect Journalists, "Mozambique Report: The Murder of Carlos Cardoso," c. 2001, available at https://cpj.org/reports/2002/05/moz-may02/.

30. Prexy Nesbitt interview with author, January 8, 2021.

31. Committee to Protect Journalists, "Mozambique Report: The Murder of Carlos Cardoso."

32. Reporters Without Borders, "Mozambique: Journalist's Killer Gets 30-Year Prison Sentence," January 20, 2006, https://www.refworld.org/docid/57bc20012b.html.

33. "Mozambique's Ex-President's Son, 10 Others Jailed Over Corruption," *Aljazeera*, December 7, 2022, https://www.aljazeera.com/news/2022/12/7/mozambique-ex-presidents-son-ten-others-jailed-over-corruption.

34. Allen Isaacman interview with author, February 28, 2024.

35. Heeten Kalan and Jenny Dahlstein interview with author, February 5, 2021.

36. Prexy Nesbitt, Jenny Dahlstein, and Heeten Kalan, "Dear Friends," March 10, 2000, PN Columbia College, Box 7.

37. Andy Epstein and Loretta J. Williams, "Debt Relief for Mozambique," *Boston Globe*, March 10, 2000, PN, Columbia College, Box 7.

38. Sara M. Wiener, "Africa Journal 1989," PN Madison, Box 2.

39. Elizabeth Schmidt email to author, January 4, 2024.

40. Elizabeth Schmidt, "A U.S.-Created Monster in Angola," *Baobab Notes*, March/April 1993, PN Madison, Box 1.

41. Schmidt, "A U.S.-Created Monster in Angola."

42. Piero Gleijeses, *Visions of Freedom* (University of North Carolina Press, 2013), 513.

43. Smith, "Interview with Prexy Nesbitt, Consultant to the Government of Mozambique," n.d., PN Madison, Box 5.

44. Prexy Nesbitt, "The North American Campaign for Southern African Liberation Revisited: Lessons from Struggle," May 31, 2017, Canadian Association for Work and Labour Studies, Toronto, Canada, in author's possession.

45. Prexy Nesbitt conversation with author, April 10, 2024.

46. Prexy Nesbitt, "Breakin' the Kneecaps of 'Baaskap': A Brief Discussion of the International Anti-Apartheid Movement and African Solidarity Work, Then, and Now," speech in Durban, South Africa, in author's possession.

47. Prexy Nesbitt, "Breakin' the Kneecaps of 'Baaskap.'"

48. Heeten Kalan and Jenny Dahlstein interview with author, February 5, 2024.

49. Sylvia Ewing interview with author, February 16, 2024.

50. She served as dean of the School of Liberal Arts and Sciences at Columbia College Chicago and provost and senior vice president for academic affairs at Dominican University. Johnson-Odim interview with author, April 14, 2021.

51. Rachel Rubin interview with author, March 28, 2021.

52. See Damon A. Williams and Daniel Kisslinger, "Help This Garden Grow," Respair Production and Media, 2023, https://www.respairmedia.com/help-this-garden-grow.

53. Prexy Nesbitt interview with author, June 24, 2024.

54. Uhuru Portia Phalafala, "The Light That Does Not Flicker," introduction to *Keorapetse Kgositsile: Collected Poems, 1969–2018* (University of Nebraska Press, 2023), xxxiii.

55. "Remembering Keorapetse Kgositsile 1938–2018," January 5, 2018, https://brandsouthafrica.com/77591/arts-culture/remembering-keorapetse-kgositsile-1938–2018/

56. Nesbitt interview with author, June 28, 2024.

57. Lisa Brock interview with author, April 25, 2023; Lisa Brock interviewed by Buffy Satchwell, Kalamazoo, MI, April 29, 2015, *Engaging the Wisdom: An Oral History Project*, https://scholarworks.wmich.edu/engaging-the-wisdom/14/

58. Prexy Nesbitt interview with author, September 20, 2020.

59. Prexy Nesbitt, "Some (Comradely) Reflections."

60. Prexy Nesbitt, "Some (Comradely) Reflections"; Gleijeses, *Visions of Freedom*, 521, 526.

61. Prexy Nesbitt, "Some (Comradely) Reflections."

62. Prexy Nesbitt interview with author, October 30, 2020.

63. Prexy Nesbitt conversation with author, April 10, 2024.

64. Cheryl Johnson-Odim interview with author, April 14, 2021.

65. Bill Ayers, "The Real Dragon with Stanley Howard," *Under the Tree*, podcast, May 29, 2024, https://news.wttw.com/2023/01/12/reflecting-road-death-penalty-abolition-illinois-20-years-after-sweeping-clemency.

66. Prexy Nesbitt to Friends, "Making the Road in 2017," email, December 28, 2016.

67. David Vine, "Where in the World is the US Military?" July/August 2015, *Politico Magazine*, https://www.politico.com/magazine/story/2015/06/us-military-bases-around-the-world-119321/.

Selected Bibliography

ARCHIVAL COLLECTIONS

African Activist Archive, Michigan State University, https://africanactivist.msu.edu/

> American Committee on Africa Collection
> Africa Fund
> Association of Concerned Africa Scholars
> Campaign to Oppose Bank Loans to South Africa Records
> Jerry Herman Collection
> Chicago Committee for the Liberation of Angola, Mozambique and Guinea-Bissau
> Richard Knight Collection
> Prexy Nesbitt Collection
> Coalition for Illinois Divestment from South Africa
> Chicago Committee in Solidarity with Southern Africa
> Illinois Labor Network Against Apartheid Collection
> *South Africa Now!* Collection

Chicago Anti-Apartheid Collection, Columbia College Chicago
> Prexy Nesbitt Papers

Wisconsin Historical Society, Madison, WI
	Prexy Nesbitt Papers

INTERVIEWS

Conducted by the Author

Lisa Brock, April 25, 2023
Basil Clunie, April 24, 2024
Otis Cunningham, April 13, 2022
Jenny Dahlstein, February 5, 2021
Mimi Edmunds, December 12, 2020
Anne Evens, December 27, 2023
Sylvia Ewing, February 16, 2024
Jimmy Garrett, April 22, 2022.
Allen Isaacman, February 28, 2024
Cheryl Johnson-Odim, April 14, 2021
Heeten Kalan, February 5, 2021
Prexy Nesbitt, numerous dates between 2020 and 2024
Rachel Rubin, March 28, 2021
Walter Turner, December 22, 2020
Roberta Washington, February 12, 2021

Oral Histories

From Columbia College Chicago, Chicago Anti-Apartheid Collection, College Archives and Special Collections, Oral Histories, https://digitalcommons.colum.edu/cadc_caam_oralhistories/

Basil Clunie, 2009
Otis Cunningham, 2009
Rosetta Daylie, 2009
Kathy Devine, 2009
Cheryl Johnson-Odim, 2009
Prexy Nesbitt, 2009
Alice Palmer, 2010

Helen Shiller, 2010
Carol Thompson, 2009
Tim Wright, 2009

NEWSLETTERS AND BULLETINS

African Agenda
Africa Today
Baobab Notes
Black Scholar
CCISSA Briefing
CIDSA Update
MSN Newsletter
Southern Africa
Southern Africa Report

NEWSPAPERS

Chicago Defender
Chicago Tribune
New York Times
Washington Post

DISSERTATIONS

Elizabeth Banks. "Socialist Internationalism between the Soviet Union and Mozambique." PhD diss., New York University, 2019.

Robert Zebulun Larson. "The Transnational and Local Dimensions of the U.S. Antiapartheid Movement." PhD diss., Ohio State University, 2019.

Carla Stephens. "The People Mobilized: The Mozambican Liberation Movement and American Activism, 1960–1975." PhD diss., Temple University, 2011.

Fanon Che Wilkins. "In the Belly of the Beast: Black Power, Anti-Imperialism, and the African Liberation Support Committee, 1968–1975." PhD diss., New York University, 2001.

PUBLICATIONS

African Information Service, ed. *Return to the Source: Selected Speeches of Amilcar Cabral.* Monthly Review Press, 1973.

Alexander, Nicolas. "What Ever Happened to the Free South Africa Movement?" *Third Force* 1, no.1 April 30, 1993.

Biondi, Martha. *The Black Revolution on Campus.* University of California Press, 2012.

Collins, Sheila D. *Ubuntu: George M. Houser and the Struggle for Peace and Freedom on Two Continents.* Ohio University Press, 2020.

Cole, Peter. "No Justice, No Ships Get Loaded: Political Boycotts on the San Francisco Bay and Durban Waterfronts," *International Review of Social History* 58 (2013): 185–217.

Elbaum, Max. *Revolution in the Air: Sixties Radicals Turn to Lenin, Mao and Che.* Verso, 2002.

Emanuelle-Birn, Anne, and Theodore M. Brown. *Comrades in Health: U.S. Health Internationalists, Abroad and At* Home. Rutgers University Press, 2013.

Douek, Daniel L. "New Light on the Samora Machel Assassination: 'I Realized That It Was No Accident,'" *Third World Quarterly* 38, no.9 (2017).

Farmer, Ashley. *Remaking Black Power: How Black Women Transformed an Era.* University of North Carolina Press, 2017.

Frazier, Robeson Taj. *The East is Black: Cold War China in the Black Radical Imagination.* Duke University Press, 2015.

Gaines, Kevin K. *American Africans in Ghana: Black Expatriates and the Civil Rights Era.* University of North Carolina Press, 2006.

Getachew, Adom. *Worldmaking After Empire: The Rise and Fall of Self-Determination.* Princeton University Press, 2019.

Gleijeses, Piero. *Visions of Freedom: Havana, Washington, Pretoria, and the Struggle for Southern Africa, 1976–1991.* University of North Carolina Press, 2013.

Gloyd, Stephen, James Pfeiffer, and Wendy Johnson, "Cooperantes, Solidarity, and the Fight for Health in Mozambique." In *Comrades in Health: U.S. Health Internationalists, Abroad and At Home,* edited by Anne Emanuelle-Birn and Theodore M. Brown. Rutgers University Press, 2013.

Isaacman, Allen and Barbara Isaacman. *Mozambique: From Colonialism to Revolution, 1900–1982.* Westview Press, 1983.

Isaacman, Allen and Barbara Isaacman. *Mozambique's Samora Machel: A Life Cut Short*. Ohio University Press, 2020.

Keller, Edmond J. and Donald Rothchild, eds. *Afro-Marxist Regimes: Ideology and Public Policy*. Lynne Rienner Publishers, 1987.

Klein, Naomi. *The Shock Doctrine: The Rise of Disaster Capitalism*. Henry Holt, 2007.

LeFanu, Sarah. *S is for Samora: A Lexical Biography of Samora Machel and the Mozambican Dream*. Hurst, 2012.

Levy, La TaSha. "Remembering Sixth-PAC: Interviews with Sylvia Hill and Judy Claude, Organizers of the Sixth Pan-African Congress." *The Black Scholar* 37, no. 4 (Winter 2008): 39–47.

Manji, Firoze and Bill Fletcher Jr., eds. *Claim No Easy Victories: The Legacy of Amilcar Cabral*. CODESRIA and Daraja Press, 2013.

Marable, Manning. *Blackwater: Historical Studies in Race, Class Consciousness, and Revolution*. University Press of Colorado, 1993.

Markle, Seth. *A Motorcycle on Hell Run: Tanzania, Black Power and the Uncertain Future of Pan- Africanism*. Michigan State University Press, 2017.

Minter, William and Sylvia Hill. "Anti-Apartheid Solidarity in United States-South Africa Relations: From the Margins to the Mainstream." In *The Road to Democracy in South Africa, Volume 3, International Solidarity, Part II*, edited by South African Democracy Education Trust. UNISA Press, 2008.

Minter, William, Gail Hovey, and Charles Cobb Jr., eds. *No Easy Victories: African Liberation and American Activists Over Half a Century, 1950–2000*. Africa World Press, 2008.

Mondlane, Eduardo. *The Struggle for Mozambique*. Zed Press, 1983.

Nesbitt, Francis N. *Race for Sanctions: African Americans Against Apartheid, 1946–1994*. Indiana University Press, 2004.

Nesbitt, George B. *Being Somebody and Black Besides: An Untold Memoir of Midcentury Black Life*, edited by Prexy Nesbitt and Zeb Larson. University of Chicago Press, 2021.

Nesbitt, Prexy. "Angola Is a Part of All of Us," *The Black Scholar* 11 (1980).

Nesbitt, Prexy. *Apartheid in Our Living Rooms: US Foreign Policy and South Africa*. Political Research Associates, 1987.

Nesbitt, Prexy. "Terminators, Crusaders and Gladiators: Western Support for Renamo & Unita," *Review of African Political Economy* 42 (1988).

Newitt, Malyn. *A Short History of Mozambique*. Oxford University Press, 2017.

Nixon, Ron. *Selling Apartheid: South Africa's Global Propaganda War*. Pluto Press, 2016.

Noah, Trevor. *Born a Crime: Stories from a South African Childhood*. One World, 2016.

Robinson, Randall. *Defending the Spirit: A Black Life in America*. Penguin, 1999.

Rothwell, Matthew. "The Road is Torturous: The Chinese Revolution and the End of the Global Sixties." *Revista Izquierdas* 49 (April 2020).

Saul, John S. *Revolutionary Traveller: Freeze-Frames from a Life*. Arbeiter Ring Publishing, 2009.

Schecter, Danny. *Madiba A to Z: The Many Faces of Nelson Mandela*. Seven Stories Press, 2013.

Schuhrke, Jeff. *Blue Collar Empire: The Untold Story of US Labor's Global Anticommunist Crusade*. Verso, 2024.

Sheldon, Kathleen. *Pounders of Grain: A History of Women, Work and Politics in Mozambique*. Heinemann, 2002.

Sopa, Antonio, ed. *Samora: Man of the People*. Maguezo Editores, 2001.

Stockwell, John. *In Search of Enemies: A CIA Story*. Norton, 1978.

Tate, Florence L. and Jake-Ann Jones. *Sometimes Farmgirls Become Revolutionaries: Notes on Black Power, Politics, Depression and the FBI*. Black Classic Press, 2021.

Vally, Salim and Andy Clarno. "The Context of Struggle: Racial Capitalism and Political Praxis in South Africa," *Ethnic and Racial Studies* 16 (2023).

Von Eschen, Penny. *Race Against Empire: Black Americans and Anticolonialism, 1937–1957*. Cornell University Press, 1997.

Von Eschen, Penny. *Paradoxes of Nostalgia: Cold War Triumphalism and Global Disorder Since 1989*. Duke University Press, 2022.

Walters, Ronald W. *Pan Africanism in the African Diaspora: An Analysis of Modern Afrocentric Political Movements*. Wayne State University Press, 1993.

Zeilig, Leo. *A Revolutionary for Our Time: The Walter Rodney Story*. Haymarket Books, 2022.

Index

communism, 2, 14, 20–21, 30, 51–52, 60, 65–68, 75, 92–94, 99, 102–3, 160, 167, 178, 180, 199, 206, 241. *See also* anticommunism

Conference of Nationalist Organizations of the Portuguese Colonies (CONCP), 39

Congress of South African Trade Unions (COSATU), 119, 179–80, 197, 202–3, 206

constructive engagement, 50, 113, 120, 123, 129–30, 184

cooperantes, 12, 134, 136, 142–45, 154, 162–67, 170

corruption, 110, 145–46, 160, 223, 226–32, 244

Council for Mutual Economic Assistance, 141

Council on African Affairs, 5, 91

coups. *See* military coups

Cuito Cuanavale battle, 184–85

Cunningham, Otis, 67–69, 242

Dahlstein, Jenny, 127, 238–39

Daley, Richard, 44

Danaher, Kevin, 168

Danish, Tommy, 22–23

Dar es Salaam, Tanzania, 3, 29, 37–42

Davidson, Basil, 54

Davis, Angela, 65

Davis, Danny, 120, 186, 188

Davis, Jennifer, 105, 197

Daylie, Rosetta, 180, 182, 186, 215

Decoding Corporate Camouflage (Schmidt), 106

decolonization, 8, 41, 51, 72, 133, 233–34

Dellums, Ron, 130, 177, 186

democracy: anti-apartheid movement and, 81, 121; in Mozambique, 169;

nonracial democracy, 225–26; post-World War I, 20; SCLC and, 44; social democracy, 18–19; in South Africa, 13–14, 176, 180, 186, 190, 194–99, 201–3, 210–19, 223–27, 229–30, 241

Devine, Kathy, 121, 178–79, 186

Dlamini, Chris, 196–97

Dohrn, Bernardine, 247

domestic antiblackness, 4

Donaldson, Ivanhoe, 105

dos Santos, Marcelino, 92, 148, 231, 245

drought conditions in Mozambique, 147, 163, 169, 171–72, 174

Du Bois, W. E. B., 8, 91

Dumba Nengue (Magaia), 156

Dunham, Katherine, 24

Ebony magazine, 79

Edmunds, Mimi, 70

Ellison, Jack, 33

European Campaign Against South African Aggression Against Mozambique and Angola, 169

European colonialism, 8. *See also* colonialism

Evens, Anne, 163–66, 166*fig.*, 194, 240–41

Ewing, Sylvia, 152, 156, 158, 192, 239

fascism, 17, 23, 29, 104, 134, 272n1

Ferrao, Valeriano, 168

Finnegan, William, 158

First, Ruth, 141

Flory, Ishmael, 20, 68

Fredericks, J. Wayne, 208

freedom fighters, 7, 59, 113, 234

freedom struggles, 1–3, 15, 43, 51, 84, 183. *See also* liberation struggles

Freedom Summer, 35

Free South Africa movement (FSM), 10,
    123–29, 131
Frelimo. *See* Front for the Liberation of
    Mozambique (Frelimo)
Front for the Liberation of Mozambique
    (Frelimo): aid from USSR, 141;
    decolonization push, 133–40; foreign
    policy of, 139; formation of, 29–30;
    goals of, 11–12; gradual socialism, 159;
    introduction to, 3–4, 9, 11–12, 26–28;
    Isaacman, Allen and, 150–51; Machel,
    Samora, 52, 58, 134–41, 135*fig.*, 145–48;
    Mondlane, Eduardo Chivambo, 3, 26,
    28, 42, 53–57, 63; Prexy's relationship
    with, 9, 22, 40, 42
Frontline Fellowship, 161
frontline states, 5–6, 51, 132, 185, 192, 195,
    227, 230, 238
Furriers Joint Council, 98

Garrett, Jimmy, 77, 84–85
Garvey, Marcus, 3, 8, 21
Gegner, Lewis, 35–36, 36*fig.*
Gersony, Robert, 157
Gleijeses, Piero, 82
global solidarity movement, 107–8
Gloyd, Stephen, 144–45
gradual socialism, 159
Great Depression, 19
Great Migration, 3, 19
Guebuzo, Armando, 57
Gwenjere, Mateus, 53

Hall, Stuart, 55
Hani, Chris, 141, 206
Hanlon, Joseph, 160
Harris, Cheryl, 122, 241
Hawley, Edward A., 26, 38, 56

Hayden, Robert, 24, 138
Hayes, Charlie, 98–99, 131
Houser, George, 73
Houser, Marty, 46
Huddleston, Trevor, 107
Hunton, Alpheus, 91

Illinois Labor Network Against Apart-
    heid (ILNAA), 178–80, 186, 190–91
Ilonga, Nangolo, 183
imperialism, 8, 79–80, 82–85, 168. *See also*
    anti-imperialism
Independent Electoral Commission,
    217
Inkatha Freedom Party (IFP), 13–14, 131,
    201, 203–4, 217
Innis, Roy, 84
Institute for Policy Studies (IPS), 105–7
International and State Defense Police
    (Portugal) (PIDE), 56
internationalism: of Chicago, 190–93; of
    Frelimo, 49–58, 63–64, 70, 78, 81, 88;
    growth of, 49–89; left-international-
    ism, 9–10, 72, 190–93; roots of, 17–48
International Monetary Fund (IMF), 14,
    155, 163, 167, 211
Isaacman, Allen, 53–54, 150–52, 159,
    174, 232
Isaacman, Barbara, 53–54

Jackson, Jesse, 126, 131, 148, 203
Jackson, Mahalia, 24
James, C. L. R., 55, 77, 79
James, Selma, 55
Jele, Josiah, 245
Jim Crow, 7, 17, 24, 35, 95
Johnson-Odim, Cheryl, 114–16, 119*fig.*, 125,
    227, 239–40, 246–47

Oppenheimer, Harry, 199

Orange, James, 45

Organization of Afro-American Unity, 116

Organization of Angolan Women, 64

Organization of Mozambican Women, 136–37

Palmer, Alice, 124–26

Pan-Africanism, 5–9, 52, 62, 67, 72, 75–83, 184, 195–96, 238

Pan Africanist Congress (PAC), 109–10

Pan-Africanist Youth Organization for Black Unity, 67

Pan African Security Force for Zaire, 104

Party for the Independence of Guinea and Cape Verde (PAIGC), 3, 9, 60

peace talks, 167, 173–75

people-to-people diplomacy, 4, 161

Pinochet, Augusto, 107

Popular Front, 20, 99

Popular Movement for the Liberation of Angola (MPLA), 3, 42–43, 66, 72, 77, 81, 83–87, 86fig.

Portuguese colonialism, 2–3, 17, 26–30, 50, 52, 57–63, 68–72, 85

post-apartheid South Africa, 223–30

Potter, Philip, 108

Powell, Adam Clayton, 22

Prexy. See Nesbitt, Rozell (Prexy), Jr.

Primus, Pearl, 24

Programme to Combat Racism (PCR), 11, 107

Quabi, Joe, 111

racial capitalism, 4, 95, 118, 200, 223

racial discrimination, 20, 36fig.

racialism, 22, 24, 69, 79, 113, 115, 137, 170, 202, 221, 226

racism: in housing market, 31–32; Jim Crow, 7, 17, 24, 35, 95; Prexy's early experiences of, 25; segregation, 2, 7, 17, 20, 22, 24, 26, 33–34, 44, 69, 95, 114, 124, 156; structural, 4, 44; white supremacy, 1, 7, 17–18, 30, 50, 101, 117, 135–37, 153, 221

Radebe, Jeff, 214

Ramaphosa, Cyril, 194, 243

Rangel, Charles, 177

Reagan, Maureen, 148

Reagan, Ronald, 6, 11, 50, 94, 113–14, 130–31, 149

Rebelo, Jorge, 53, 57, 241

Reddy, E. S., 91–92

Redekopp, Orlando, 126

Renamo (Mozambican National Resistance): ceasefire, 12, 169, 171; funding of, 147–48, 171, 176; human rights abuses by, 157–59, 166–68; introduction to, 12, 140–41; Mozambique resistance to, 150–61; peace talks, 167, 173–74; US support for, 145, 149–50

Rhodesia, 2, 6, 12, 29, 40, 45, 50, 81, 89, 102, 134, 139–41, 145, 150, 161

Risquet, Jorge, 244

Roberto, Holden, 72, 74

Robeson, Paul, 91

Robinson, Cleveland, 98–99

Robinson, Leo, 99

Robinson, Randall, 208

Rodney, Walter, 51–52, 82–83, 108

Rogers, Harold, 67–68, 92, 186

Rogers, Ray, 99

Roosevelt, Eleanor, 22

Rubin, Rachel, 162–63, 240

Founded in 1893,
UNIVERSITY OF CALIFORNIA PRESS
publishes bold, progressive books and journals
on topics in the arts, humanities, social sciences,
and natural sciences—with a focus on social
justice issues—that inspire thought and action
among readers worldwide.

The UC PRESS FOUNDATION
raises funds to uphold the press's vital role
as an independent, nonprofit publisher, and
receives philanthropic support from a wide
range of individuals and institutions—and from
committed readers like you. To learn more, visit
ucpress.edu/supportus.